MONTY
He was the tiny ginger kitten who captivated Derek Tangye much against his better judgement, and went on to become the undisputed lord of Minack . . .

LAMA
After Monty's death, Derek Tangye swore that he would never have another cat unless a black kitten without a home came to his door in a storm. That was how Lama arrived . . .

OLIVER
The living image of Lama, he used every wile known to the feline mind to ingratiate himself and leave his wild life to become Minack Cat No. 3 . . .

AMBROSE
Small, fluffy and frightened, he was Oliver's constant companion, and before long he too had made the Tangye's home his own . . .

These are the Cats of Minack – all together for the first time in one captivating volume.

Somewhere
A Cat Is
Waiting

DEREK TANGYE

Drawings by Jean Nicol Tangye

SPHERE BOOKS LIMITED
London and Sydney

This volume is a revised, abridged and edited version of three separate books entitled *A Cat in the Window* (1962), *Lama* (1966) and *A Cat Affair* (1974)

First published in Great Britain by Michael Joseph Ltd, 1977
Copyright © 1962, 1966, 1974, and 1976 by Derek Tangye
First Sphere Books edition 1978
Reprinted 1980, 1982, 1983, 1984, 1985, 1986

Printed and bound in Great Britain by
Cox & Wyman Ltd, Reading

To Jeannie

CONTENTS

Part 1
Monty

first met Monty in Room 205 of the Savoy Hotel. He was six weeks old, and when I came into the room he was tumbling, chasing, biting an old typewriter ribbon that was being dragged temptingly across the carpet by Lois, Jeannie's secretary. He was the size and color of a handful of crushed autumn bracken. At the time I did not notice the distinguishing marks I was later to know so well—the silky white shirt front, the smudge of orange on the left paw, the soft maize color of the fur on his tummy. I did not notice his whiskers, nor his tail with its dark rings against cream, the rings graduating in size to the tip which, in his lifetime, was to flick this way and that, a thousand, thousand times. I saw only a pretty kitten with great big innocent eyes gamboling in the incongruous setting of Jeannie's office, and I wondered why.

"What's this?" I said to Lois, looking down at the two of them. "What on earth is this kitten doing here?" I had seen ambassadors, film stars, famous journalists, politicians of all parties in Jeannie's office, but I had never before met a cat. It made me suspicious.

"Come on," I said, "come on, Lois, tell me what it's all about." But Lois went on playing as if she hadn't heard me. "Lois, you're hiding something from me. Where's Jeannie? What's she been up to? Both of you know I dislike cats and if . . ."

"She'll be back soon." Lois was smiling and refusing to be drawn out. "She had to go over to Claridge's. General Montgomery has just arrived and nobody is allowed to know. She won't be long." It was part of Jeannie's job as public relations officer of the Savoy Group to keep certain news from the press, just as much as it was, on other occasions, to get other news widely publicized.

But on this occasion, on this particular warm summer afternoon, as I awaited her return with Lois and the kitten, her task was especially important.

Monty had arrived to make a progress report to Churchill on the Battle of the Desert.

I came from a dog family. In the walled garden of my rambling Cornish home was a row of wooden crosses with painted cries of Victorian sentiment. "Alas, poor Rosa," "Sweet, gentle Cara," Farewell, Little Gyp." And in my own childhood I remember other crosses going up. My parents had no desire to disclose their emotions so, in their day, only the birth and death and name of the dog appeared on the cross. Rex, Bulger, Bruce, Mary, Lance, Roy, Gay. These sparse tributes to devotion were sometimes countered in my mind by unexpectedly finding my father standing opposite a cross quietly puffing his pipe. Young as I was, it touched me to feel the memories that were passing through him.

My personal friends were first Bruce and then Lance, or Sir Lancelot, by which—until I found the name too much of a mouthful—I first called him. Bruce was a mongrel of indescribable parentage while Lance, an Old English sheep dog, brought with him from the kennels where he was born a list of relations bearing the names of sheep-dog royalty. Bruce was in our family before I was born and by the time I was seven I thought he was immortal. He was to me a brother of my own age, and for hours on end I would tease him or wrestle or play hide-and-seek with him among the gorse and tamarisk-covered land around our home. Bruce was the answer to any doubts my mother may have had as to how I could spend my time.

Then he died and grief being suddenly to me an emotion instead of a word, my father countered by producing Lance.

I matured with Lance. First the same childish games I had with Bruce, then the tearful partings before school terms, wild barking reunions and soon the long walks of doubtful youth, Lance at my side in the winding lanes sharing my puzzlement. I was a man when Lance died.

Dogs, then, had been entities in my life. Cats, as if they were wasps with four legs, had been there to shoo away. They did not belong in my life nor in my family's life. All of us were united that whenever we saw a cat the most important thing to do was to see it out of sight.

But as I moved slowly out of the environment of my family, I found, naturally enough, people and homes who accepted cats as we accepted dogs. Cats were not vulgar as, in some mysterious way, I had been led to believe. I began to note that cats were able to bestow a subtle accolade upon their apparent owners which made these owners rapturous with delight.

I resented this. Dogs, and by this I mean well-mannered, full-of-character, devoted dogs who did not snarl or bark unnecessarily, were to me the true tenants of a home. Cats were vagrants. They did not merit affection.

I sensed, of course, that in a home where there was a cat or cats my attitude was unsatisfactory; so I developed a pose that after a while I made myself believe was genuine. I became "allergic" to cats. The proximity of one produced asthma. I felt dizzy. I behaved so strangely that any owner of a cat who was entertaining me was convinced that if I were not to prove a sickly embarrassment the cat had to be removed.

It was in this mood that I paid my first call on Jeannie's parents in their handsome house on the hill of St. Albans. I sat down in the sitting room and promptly Tim, Jeannie's huge blue Persian cat, jumped on my lap. Unthinkingly I played my customary part. I gave Tim a violent push and, in so doing, knocked over a small table upon which was my untouched cup of tea. From that moment I began to realize it was dangerous to appear to dislike cats.

For Jeannie is a cat lover, not only the slave of an individual, but an all-embracing cat lover. If she sees a cat on the other side of the street she will want to cross over to talk to it. Any pretty little thing, any handsome tom, will receive her caressing and cooing. She fawns on the breed. Little wonder her mother, after my visit had ended, cast a humorous doubt on a successful marriage. Could a cat lover live happily with a cat hater?

My future dealings with Tim were, therefore, cautious. I was careful not to cause offense by throwing any make-believe tantrums, yet I was equally careful not to appear affected by the lofty gaze he sometimes cast on me. I was polite but distant. I was determined to hold fast to my traditional dislike of the species. I was not going to be hypnotized by gentle purrs, soft kneading of paws, an elegant walk across the room and a demand to jump on my knees. I disliked cats. I most certainly would not have one in our home after we were married.

This was still my position as I waited for Jeannie to return from Claridge's. We had been married three months.

Monty chose the moment of Jeannie's return to pounce upon the toe of my shoe, then disappear up my trouser leg, except for a tail. He tickled my leg until I had to stoop and, for the first time, touch him. Jeannie and Lois watched hopefully to see the effect this would have on me. He was very soft, and the wriggle with which he tried to escape me was feeble, like the strength of my little finger. I felt the teeth nibble my hand, and a tiny claw trace a tickle on my skin; and when I picked him up and held him firmly in front of me, the big eyes stared childishly at me with impotent resentment. I had never held a cat in my hands before.

"This is diabolical," I said in pretended fury, addressing Jeannie and Lois, "and don't think I haven't a card up my sleeve. . . . I'm going to chuck this thing over Hammersmith Bridge on the way home." I spoke so vehemently that Lois seemed half to believe me. "Yes, I am," I said, rubbing it in, "I'll stop the car and fling the cat over the side."

"Kitten," murmured Lois.

"Monty," said Jeannie.

There is no defense against women who sense your heart has already surrendered. The head, however astute in presenting its arguments, appears hollow. If Jeannie wanted Monty she had to have him. How could I deny her? The best I could do was to learn to tolerate his existence and make an attempt to impose conditions.

"All right, I won't do *that*," I said, and was immediately irked by the gleam of victory in their eyes, "but I'll tell you what I *will* do . . ." I looked defiantly at both of them. "I'll make quite certain he is a *kitchen* cat. There'll be no question of him wandering about the house as if he owns it."

This display of authority eased me into seeing the situation in a more comforting perspective. Jeannie would be happy, Monty out of sight, and I could continue my aloofness toward the species as before.

"But if he doesn't behave himself," I added, looking at the little ball of fur in my hand, "he'll have to find another home."

The weakness in my attack was that I myself was responsible, though indirectly, for Monty's arrival. We had mice in our cottage at Mortlake. When, at Jeannie's request, I set traps and caught the mice, I was so sickened by the task of releasing the dead mouse from the trap that I preferred to throw both the mouse and the trap into the river.

I complained once again one morning to Jeannie about my trap task. In retrospect I know, of course, I was being ridiculous, but at the time, when I had to perform the task, I felt disgusted.

"Now if we had a cat," replied Jeannie, and she gave no sign that she was trying to influence me unduly, "you wouldn't have to worry about traps at all. . . . You see, the very smell of a cat keeps mice away."

In due course I was to find this statement to be untrue, but at the time, in the frame of mind I was in on that particular morning, it interested me.

"You mean to say that a mouse never comes into a house where there's a cat, and all that catching and squealing takes place outside?"

"Oh, yes," said Jeannie blandly, "mice are very intelligent and they know they haven't a chance if a cat finds them in a house."

"And what about birds?"

"Well," she said, making the answer sound very simple, "all you have to do is to have the cat fixed. Cats only catch birds for their families."

"Anyhow," I said, by way of ending the conversation, "I still don't like them."

On reflection, I believe my dislike was based on their independence. A dog, any dog, will come to you wagging its tail with friendliness if you snap your fingers or call to it. There is no armed neutrality between the dog world and the human race. If a human is in need of affection and there is a dog about, he is sure to receive it. Dogs are prepared to love; cats, I believed, were not.

I had observed too that cat owners (but who, I

wondered, would call himself the owner of a cat?) were likely to fall into two types. Either they ignored the cat, put it out at night whatever the weather, left it to fend for itself when they went away, or else they worshiped the animal like a god. The first category appeared callous, the second devoid of sense.

I had seen, for instance, a person sit rigid and uncomfortable in a chair because a cat had chosen his lap as the whim of its own particular comfort. I had noticed, and been vexed by, the hostess who hastens away at the end of a meal with tidbits for the cat which has stared balefully at her guests throughout dinner. Cats, it seemed to me, aloofly hinted the power of hypnotism, and, as if in an attempt to ward off this uncanniness, their owners pandered to them, anxiously trying to win approval for themselves by flattery, obedience and a curious vocabulary of nonsensical phrases and noises. A cat lover, I had found, was at the mercy of the cat.

I was now to learn for myself whether this was true. My education was about to begin. My morning conversation with Jeannie had made her believe there might be a gap in my armor, and, by the time I had forgotten the conversation, she had already rung up her mother to disclose her hopes. "I think he's weakening," she said, "we must seize the chance."

And so no time was lost. Her mother had an appointment at the hairdressers' and she promised that immediately afterward she would go to the pet shop to see what kittens were available. The visit never took place. At the hairdressers' she confided her mission to the girl who attended her. "But I've got a kitten that nobody wants," the girl said; "it's a ginger, the last of a litter, and if we don't find a home by tomorrow he'll have to be put away."

I would not have agreed if my advice had been sought. One less kitten in the world would not have seemed very important to me. But my advice wasn't sought and Monty was saved.

For the price of my mother-in-law's weekly chocolate ration, he entered our lives.

The cottage, with a roof the shape of a dunce's cap, was within a few yards of the finishing post of the Boat Race, and only the towpath separated the front steps and the river. On the ground floor was the dining room, the kitchen and the spare bedroom; on the second floor, two bedrooms, one overlooking the river, and the other the garden; and on the top floor were the bathroom and the sitting room which stretched the breadth of the cottage. Across this room at door level stretched two massive, old oak beams and from them, dovetailed by wooden pegs, were two triangular spans, ancient as the beams, supporting the inside of the dunce's cap which was the ceiling. In one corner was the fireplace and opposite, along the length of the room, were the windows from which we watched the Thames flowing to the curve at Barnes Bridge, and beyond, the silhouette of London.

The cottage was once upon a time an inn, and one of the innkeepers was a waterman who married a Shakespeare player. I used to dig up broken old clay pipes in the garden, sometimes part of a stem, sometimes a bowl, and when I sent a sample to the British Museum they confirmed they were Elizabethan. From then on I used to hand pieces to visitors, telling them the story of the cottage. "You had better keep this," I would say, "Shakespeare may have used it."

It was a small walled garden about thirty feet long and the width of half a tennis court. At the top end was the concrete shelter in which we crouched during bad air raids.

On the other side of one wall was the garden of the Ship, the pub next door; on the other side of the opposite one was a passageway from the river to Mortlake village; and within a hundred yards of both were Sandy Lane and West Road with the brewery towering in the background. Along the riverbank were three or four houses and beyond them, three minutes from the cottage, was Chiswick Bridge. In time, in the early morning, Monty used to walk with us to the bridge but he would go no farther. He would sit down when we reached the archway and, however much we coaxed him, would not budge. He was never, in fact, to be a wanderer while he lived at Mortlake. His world, for seven years, was to be the small walled garden.

As soon as I picked him out of the wicker basket in which we had brought him home, I explained to our housekeeper that Monty was to be a kitchen cat. "I don't want to see him at all," I said, "he's here to catch mice and although he may be small for that yet, I've been told the very smell of a cat will keep them away."

I looked at Jeannie. She was busily unwrapping a small package "Isn't that true? Didn't you say that?"

"Oh, yes . . . yes."

An object had now appeared from the package. A small *sole bonne femme*. It was freshly cooked and succulent.

"Good heavens, Jeannie." I said, "where did you get that?"

"Latry gave it to me." she said. Latry was the famous maître chef of the Savoy. "He's cooked it especially as a celebration present for Monty." I looked at the fish and then at Monty. Only a few hours before, the girl in the hairdressers' was frightened he would be put away.

"Really, Jeannie," I said crossly, "you can't go cadging food for the cat."

"I wasn't cadging. Latry *gave* it to me, I tell you. He loves cats and felt honored to cook Monty's first meal."

"Honored," I murmured to myself, and shuddered.

Jeannie mashed the fish up in a saucer, put it on the floor and began cooing at Monty who, never having seen a fish before, tottered off in the opposite direction.

"There you are." I said, as if I had achieved a minor triumph, "he doesn't like fish."

Of course he was soon to do so; and during the course of his life he was to eat vast quantities of it, although sole was not his favorite. It was whiting. The cottage, and also in due course our cottage in Cornwall, was often to reek with the stink of it when the water in which it was cooked boiled over from the pan onto the stove.

But on the first morning of his life with us, the morning on which I awoke to a disquieting awareness that the pattern of my life was about to be readjusted, the sole from the Savoy kitchens awaited him. "I wonder whether he has eaten it," Jeannie asked aloud as she dressed.

Oddly enough I found myself wondering too. "I'll go down and see," I said, and was off through the door in my dressing gown.

The stairs were narrow and steep, of polished wood and slippery, and on the third step from the bottom—too frightened to go up or down—was Monty. "How did you get there?" I said, my voice as firm as could be allowed when a child gets caught in a predicament. "Your place is in the kitchen. It's no use trying to learn to climb stairs." The tiny meows did not protest against my firmness; they appealed for my help. And so I picked him up in one hand and took him to the saucer of the night before where it had been placed under the kitchen table. It was empty.

Jeannie was encouraged by my apparent gentleness on this occasion, and I observed, during the days that followed, how she cunningly began to use Monty to help pierce my utilitarian attitude toward him.

The first of these tactics was her good sense in realizing it was unwise to make too much fuss over Monty in my presence. She made up for this apparent coolness in my absence, but this I was not to know, and I was not to know, for instance, that Latry, the chef, continued to supply her with delicacies which she fed to Monty surreptitiously while I was in the pub next door.

Nor when, as he grew older, he began success-fully to climb the stairs, did she encourage him to do so; and on the evening he was found for the first time in a tight ball on the bed, she impressed me with her scolding. Indeed I felt a twinge of sym-pathy for Monty as, on Jeannie's instructions, I carried him back to the kitchen. I found myself wondering against my will whether it was fair to banish him when it was so obvious he was pre-pared to give both of us his affection.

Monty played his own part very well because from the beginning he made it plain he liked me. It was a dangerous moment of flattery when I real-ized this and I believe, had it not been for my en-trenched posture of dislike for the species, I would have fallen for it without more ado. There was, however, a thick enough layer of prejudice inside me for me to hold out.

He would seek to play with me. I would be sitting at dinner and feel a soft cushion gently knocking my foot, and when I put down a hand to stop it my fingers were enclosed by small teeth. In the garden he would perform his most bewitching tricks in front of me, the clumsy chase of a but-terfly, the pounce on an imaginary demon leaving a spread-eagled posterior to face me. And when at the end of the day we returned to the cottage, un-latched the door and went inside, it was strange how often he came to me instead of paying court to Jeannie. Did I perhaps impose an intuition upon him that my prejudice, once defeated, would leave a vacuum that he alone could fill? My prejudice has long ago disappeared, but I am still a one-cat man. I have never developed a taste for a house-hold of cats, each so independent that one of them can disappear for a few days without causing undue worry. I am incapable of spreading my affection so widely. Monty needed only to vanish for a few hours and we both would fill ourselves with imaginary fears.

But the talk of such cat lovers among Jeannie's friends was part of my education. She enlisted their aid. I listened to the language they used, both spoken and unspoken, and became aware there was a streak of connoisseurship in this world of cats. It was the snobbery of an exclusive club; and if the flavor of such conversation was an acquired taste, it was no more so than learning to like jazz or Bach. They perused Monty and unanimously pronounced he would grow into a beautiful member of the fraternity. They admired his head and foretold, quite correctly, it would become like that of a miniature tiger, not snouty and elongated like some ginger cats. They assessed his mother as a tortoiseshell and his father as a tabby. They liked his whiskers, which at that age were wisps of white. They forecast that, as he had been fixed, he would become a huge cat. They discussed him, men and women of distinction in various walks of life, in the tone one associates with relations probing the future of an infant of noble heritage. Would his appearance measure up to his responsibilities? Young as he was, did he show signs of a strong character? Would his movements prove elegant? How thick would his coat become? Monty was fussed over and cooed at as if winning his favor was an ambition of vital importance. I watched amused, comforting myself with the knowledge that Jeannie's friends were not as serious as they appeared. Monty was only a diversion. He was a toy for temporary enjoyment. A cat could never possess a personality which could be remembered except by those with whom he lived.

In any case, during the initial period of this homage bestowed on him, Monty did not appear very attractive. He would not wash. His body was dull and dusty, the white on his left paw a dirty cuff, the crescent of white on his little chest a gray, soiled shirt. "He looks like an alley cat," I taunted Jeannie.

My coolness toward him, my inclination to niggle at any of his failings, naturally increased the sense of protection she had for him, and during this phase of unwash she was afraid I might have the excuse to get rid of him. Yet, to my surprise, I did not feel that way at all. I too felt a sense of protection; and on the evening I returned to find Monty on a chair in the kitchen with his fur shining bright, I was as delighted as Jeannie. I did not know that she, having gone home before me, had damped him all over with plain water; and he had licked himself dry.

It was another homecoming a few weeks later, an unexpected one, which finally witnessed my capitulation. I had spent the day in the cottage and was not thinking of Jeannie's return till the evening. I was in the top room alone when there was a noise at the door as if it were being kicked by a soft boot. I opened it and Monty came scampering in. He rushed to the sofa and jumped up, climbed on the back, walked along it tail up, then down again to the floor and across to where I was standing, arched his back, rubbed his head against my leg and purred. All this in less than a minute, and performed with such élan that it made me wonder whether he was telling me in his particular fashion that I had been making an ass of myself. I bent down and stroked him, and he thereupon carried out a maneuver which he was often to do when he aimed to be especially endearing. He twisted his head as if he were going to fold up in a ball, collapsed on the floor and turned over, and lay with his back on the green carpet, paws in the air, displaying his silky maize underparts while a pair of bright yellow eyes hopefully awaited the pleasure the sight would give me. The reward he expected was a gentle stroke until he decided he had had one too many; then there would be a savage mock attempt to bite my fingers.

But on this first occasion I was holding a pipe cleaner in my hand and I tickled him with that, which led to a game, which led half an hour later to his sitting on my desk, performing ridiculous antics with a pencil.

I was sitting there roaring with laughter when the door opened. In walked Jeannie.

My capitulation was complete, and within a few weeks there was no pretense that Monty was a kitchen cat. Every room in the cottage was his kingdom; and at night, if his fancy was to sleep on the bed, I would lie with legs stiff so as not to disturb him while he curled in a ball at the bottom. I endlessly wanted to play with him, and felt put in my place when, not in the mood, he stalked away from me, tail in the air showing he had something more important to do, like a vigorous—if temporary—wash of the underparts.

Sometimes my games were gently malicious, as if taking a friendly revenge on the way he had captured me. I used to lift him onto the beam in the sitting room where he would glare down at me, then run along the beam to find a place from which to leap to the floor, only to find I had moved along too and was there to stop him. I would put up a hand and receive a slap from a paw.

There was another game with an ulterior purpose but perhaps game is the wrong word for it. Three months had gone by and there was still no evidence that he had caught a mouse; no remains had been found, no victory bellow heard, no sign that there were fewer mice than before. It was disturbing. His presence had brought no fear to the mice and so he seemed as useless as a dog for the purpose required of him. "Perhaps he left his mother too soon," said Jeannie, apologizing, "and she didn't have time to teach him."

I no longer wished to prize Jeannie's defenses; where in the beginning I would have ridiculed such a remark, I now said nothing. Monty was growing fast and his appetite was enormous, so the best thing to do, I decided, was to keep him hungry for a while and let his natural cat's instinct develop out of necessity. After twenty-four hours he was prowling around like a tiger, and Jeannie was yearning to yield to his fury. "You're cruel," she said, "to do this to him." It was often to be like that, Jeannie always ready to surrender to his whims while I, my anticat upbringing still somewhere within me, endeavored to insist on discipline.

But my plan on this occasion was to put him up in the attic, a dark, forbidding world of rafters, cobwebs and, without doubt, mice. Standing on a chair, my arms outstretched above me, I shoved Monty through the trapdoor, and returned to the sitting room to await results. After half an hour Jeannie argued it was time to let him out. After an hour I was restraining her from standing on the chair. She was furious. I was anxious lest my plan had misfired. Another ten minutes and I admitted I was wrong. I stood on the chair to push the trapdoor upward. At that instant there was a wild scramble on the ceiling, followed by squeak, squeak, squeak . . . and a few seconds later, peering down from the opening above me, was Monty with a mouse, like a fat moustache, in his mouth.

As Monty grew larger Jeannie's lap became too small for his comfort, and he transferred to mine. He would approach where I was sitting, arch his back, claw for a brief second at the chair's fabric, leap up and settle down, then turn his head upward to me as if he were saying, "Thank you very much." That was not, however, the moment when I required any thanks because I always felt flattered he had chosen me, above all other comfortable spots in the house, to rest on awhile. It was later I deserved the thanks, when my feet had gone to sleep, my legs had gotten cramped, and I had refrained from doing any job I had intended to do. I never dared move him. I would watch him comfortably dozing, occasionally adjusting his posture while I sat stiff as a ramrod. Such a gesture as selecting my lap was an accolade I could not refuse. I was to spend hours, days, weeks of my life like that, while Jeannie sat opposite watching the two of us.

There were times, however, when first he paid me this attention, that circumstances forced me to move him. It was the period of the little blitz, the bitter late winter of 1944 when Hitler again attacked London. The sirens would wail while we sat upstairs in the sitting room and we would wait, pretending we were not tense, until the guns began firing. "They're not very busy tonight," I would sometimes say, which only meant I had not heard any bombs fall in the neighborhood. But there were other times when a stick would fall uncomfortably close, and then I would tuck Monty under my arm and we would all hasten to the shelter at the top of the garden. We would crouch there, the dark being flashed into brilliance while Jeannie, a hand clutching Monty, would declare she was more afraid of the spiders than she was of the bombs.

On the night a near miss blew the roof off, leaving our sitting room facing the stars, we were not in the shelter. It was the evening of our first wedding anniversary and a number of friends were celebrating with us when we heard the stick coming . . . one, two, three, four and wham! The brewery had a direct hit and the fire that followed lit the night into daylight, and we knew that this tempting sight might lead to another attack. None of us was hurt, only covered with plaster, but the room we loved so much was a terrible sight; and Jeannie and I were standing at the door looking at it, thinking how only an hour or two before we had spent such care getting it ready, when suddenly she said, "Where's Monty?"

We ran down the stairs asking as we went whether anyone had seen him. We ran into the kitchen shouting his name, then in the dining room, then into the spare bedroom that led from the kitchen. No one had seen him. I ran into the garden calling his name, the guns still firing, the flames in the brewery leaping into the sky; and I remembered how even in that moment of distress I found myself marveling at the silhouette of a fireman's ladder that was already poised high against the fire, a pinpoint of a man at the top of it. "Monty," I yelled, "Monty!" No sign of him there so I went back to the house asking everyone to look, then out onto the riverbank where I knew Jeannie had gone. I found her, but no Monty; and after searching for a while we felt our task hopeless, nothing to do except go home and wait. "He'll turn up," I said, trying to encourage her.

And half an hour later into the kitchen came one of our guests, a burly Australian war correspondent, with Monty held in his arms like a child.

His fur was powdered with plaster, as white as if he had spent the night in a bakery.

"He'd got in his foxhole," the Australian said with a grin on his face. "I found him upstairs in the linen closet!"

He was unharmed except for the temporary mess of his fur; and later, when dawn was breaking and the raiders had gone, he decided to sit on the kitchen table and receive the homage of the firemen for whom Jeannie was pouring cups of tea. The powdery plaster had been licked away and he sat, tail gently flicking, eyes blinking, dozing like a miniature tiger in the midday sun, utterly sure of himself amidst the hubbub of chatter. He was calmer than any of the humans around him.

And when, to commemorate this end of our first year of marriage, we asked the firemen to sign their names in our visitors' book, one of them scrawled alongside his signature:

"Monty, the handsomest cat I ever saw."

We left Mortlake two days later to become evacuees with Jeannie's father and mother at St. Albans, and within an hour of arrival at his temporary home there was an incident which had an effect on Monty for the rest of his life. He had always been suspicious of dogs, but until St. Albans, he had never come face to face with one in the same room.

The house, Bryher Lodge, stood on the hill facing east toward London; and on nights when duties did not keep us in the city we would stand on the terrace above the garden and watch the inferno in the distance. First the little blitz, then, a few weeks later and shortly before we returned to the cottage, the beginning of the flying bombs. We would watch for a few minutes this insanity of the human race, then return indoors to the private war between Judy, the Scottie of the house, and Monty.

With Judy, when we came, was Tim the Persian. Tim was the placid old cat, with blue-gray fur so thick that it made him look as if he was wearing a muff, whose unwelcome attention on my first visit resulted in me knocking over the table. I was friends with him now, of course, and he was so placid that even Monty's sudden appearance could not annoy him. Tim and Monty tolerated each other from the beginning but Judy, after one look at the evacuee, decided she would not give him a moment's peace. Monty was an interloper, and Judy was never to allow him to forget it.

My own opinion is that Jeannie and her mother were partly to blame because of the method of introduction they chose to arrange. I myself favored a gradual acclimatization—an interchange of leftover sniffs after one or the other had left the room, a sight of each other in the garden with one of them safely behind a window. I was cautious; I had an instinct of inevitable trouble if suddenly they were placed nose to nose.

I expect trouble was inevitable in any case, but it certainly exploded with the least delay. I unloaded our luggage, lugged it up to the bedroom and then heard Jeannie cry out: "Come on downstairs, we're going to introduce Monty to Judy." Their theory, and I suppose there was some sense in it, was that as Judy and Monty were going to live in the closest proximity, they might as well learn to be friends as quickly as possible. I arrived in the room just as the introduction was made.

It was over within thirty seconds. Judy leaped at Monty and snapped at his paw. Monty then jumped on a table, crashing a vase, remained there for an instant with fur like an upturned brush, then onto the floor, dashing between the legs of Jeannie's mother who grabbed him, holding him until he freed himself, whereupon he raced across to the blue velvet curtains, up them like a monkey and remained on the valance, snarling like a mad thing at Judy yapping hysterically below.

We ourselves, for a moment, were quite silent. Each of us was wondering how such enmity could possibly be handled during the weeks to come. Monty and I, and Jeannie—despite it being her old home—were guests in the house and we could not be expected to be popular if we brought chaos along with us. Jeannie's mother was saying to herself that at all costs the welcome of our arrival must be brought back to normal. She did so by never disclosing that Monty had gashed her so sharply with his claws that the following day she had four stitches in her arm.

Monty and Judy never came face to face again, yet the atmosphere of their hate remained. If one was allowed free in the house, the other was shut in a room; and the one which was free would be aware of the door behind which was the other. Judy would scratch, Monty would sniff and his fur rise up. It was an unhappy period for both of them, and the immediate effect on Monty was to lessen the affection he had for Jeannie and me. He became remote from us. There were no purrs. It was as if he had lost his personality and was just an animal on four legs which had no thoughts in its head except to eat and sleep. He would not play. He would not sleep on the bed. His behavior, in fact, made me lose interest in him. He was a silly, characterless cat.

This zombie attitude continued for four months until, the cottage repaired, we returned home; and within a few minutes of our arrival Monty's old self returned too. He proved it by jumping out of the kitchen window. The window had been his own private entrance. We had always kept it half open for him, day and night, and he would leap to its frame, pause a moment and disappear outside. Or at night we would be in the kitchen and become suddenly aware that Monty had silently appeared from the darkness outside and was poised up there, watching us. On this occasion he had not been in the kitchen a minute before he jumped up to this window, then down to the garden; and without waiting he was up again to the window and into the kitchen. We watched him repeat this act, as if it were a celebration dance, four or five times; and as we watched we could sense the dull attitude disappearing, and the old relationship becoming real again. "He's actually glad to be home," I said to Jeannie, as if I were surprised such a feeling could exist within him. "He really *knows* he's home."

Later that night when I was lying awake, I found myself thinking that as I had learned to get on perfectly well without considering Monty while at St. Albans, I had better do the same now at home. I was fast becoming as cooing as the cat lovers I used to despise, submerging my own personality for Monty's benefit, becoming a slave to his wayward habits, and it was time for me to stop.

St. Albans had taught me that one could give a roof to a cat without losing one's own identity; and although Monty had been plainly uncomfortable he did not run away, he remained clean, he had a good appetite. He could, therefore, lead a useful life with us at the cottage, have his meals and his freedom to wander about, but, as at St. Albans, there was no need for him to enter the stream of our life.

I would not, for instance, become excited just because he jumped in and out of the kitchen window. I would not consider myself favored when he sat on my lap; I would push him off if it suited me. Lying there in the dark I realized I had been showing all the faults of the convert. all the undisciplined enthusiasm the novice displays. I had been behaving, before the change at St. Albans, like a fawning servant before its master. It was ridiculous, and tomorrow I must set out to regain my independence whatever tricks Monty might produce. Of course Jeannie was going to be difficult; but if I were cunning, if I did not take any positive action against Monty, if I were polite but distant, she would have no need to suspect the great change that had suddenly taken place inside me.

She was sound asleep, and Monty was also on the bed, down at the bottom alongside my feet. I suddenly thought, Why not set the pace of my new attitude toward him immediately? My legs were cramped and had he not been occupying so much room, I could have stretched them and been comfortable, and I might even have fallen asleep. Here goes, I said to myself, and gave him a shove. A second later there was a thud on the floor; then, a few seconds later he was on the bed again. Another shove. Another thud.

And at that moment Jeannie woke up, shouting excitely as one does when alarmed from a dream: "What's wrong? What's wrong?"

"Nothing at all," I said soothingly; "only Monty fell off."

ad he been human, Monty's memory of Judy might have been eradicated on a psychiatrist's couch; but as it was, the rage he felt against her simmered inside him, erupting in explosions at intervals during the rest of his life. He was determined to fight a ceaseless battle of revenge.

His first victory, soon after our return, was over a bulldog pup belonging to a friend who lived close by. Outside our front door was a tiny garden, enclosed by a three-foot wall to help keep out the high tides of the Thames; and we went over this wall from the garden to the towpath by a ladder of stone steps. These steps were never a particular favorite of Monty's, indeed he usually avoided the tiny front garden as if he disliked the bustle of the towpath on the other side of the wall. But on occasion, he liked to sun himself there, and one pleasant morning he was lying on the top step when along came the bulldog pup.

The pup was a bandy-legged brindle and he came jauntily down the alleyway from his home with a sniff here and a sniff there, up to the mailbox and across to the lamppost. I was standing by the open front door and I watched him amusedly; he looked like a schoolboy on vacation without a care in the world.

But Monty was watching as well. He watched until the pup was within five yards of the steps, then, crouching as if to spring at a mouse, he waited for it to come another yard nearer . . . and pounced. I was so surprised that I just stared. But the pup, thank goodness, had been attracted the same instant by the railings on the other side of the towpath, and he moved away as Monty sprang, so his stumpy stern met the onslaught instead of his back. A yell of fright from the pup and it set off at a gallop for Chiswick Bridge. It was still galloping along after Monty had stopped the chase; for Monty, as if to put fear into a bulldog was victory enough, returned nonchalantly to the steps after a chase of a few yards and unconcernedly began an elaborate wash. He never attacked the pup again; it never came near enough to let him.

Monty did not seek out his battles with dogs, creating a quarrel because he had nothing else to do. I often, for instance, saw him sitting in contemplation while a dog passed by without his ever making a move. It was when we were about that he became enraged. He either considered himself our protector or, more likely, the mémory of Judy ground such jealousy in his mind that for a few moments he reverted to the wild cat of the jungle. No dog was safe, whatever the size or breed, and, for that matter, no human was safe who tried to stop the attack.

The first human to suffer was an elderly lady who arrived at the cottage with a small terrier on a leash. We did not fully appreciate Monty's temper at the time, and we had taken no steps to shut him in a room when the lady and the terrier entered the downstairs hall. Bang! Monty was hurtling out of the kitchen straight at the terrier and in the shambles that followed the poor lady was gashed in the leg. I had to take her to the hospital.

This incident, of course, put us on our guard.

We had, so to speak, to put a notice outside the front door: "Beware of the Cat." We had to meet anyone who arrived with a dog and shout, "Wait out there a minute while we put Monty away." And if Monty could not be found, the visitor and the dog had to be sneaked in, then rushed upstairs to the sitting room, and the door firmly shut. Then, when the visit was over, I would act as a scout and see whether Monty was lurking anywhere on the stairs. I had to act like a conspirator, and I used to be thankful when the visitor and his dog were safely waved away.

Yet I never met a dog owner who did not at first believe we were playing a joke. The snag lay in the fact that unless the dog owner had visited us before, the reaction was not what we intended. The answer to our alarm was a display of supreme confidence.

"Oh, don't worry," would come the lofty reply, "our dog *never* chases cats!" We would try to explain how it would be Monty who did the chasing. "Don't you understand?" we would plead, "Monty will chase *your* dog!" Meanwhile the dog would be running around and, in the distance, we would see a menacing Monty approaching.

At Mortlake we had the front door as the barrier, and so a clash was comparatively easy to avert. But when we came to live at remote Minack, our cottage in Cornwall, Monty could be lying in wait anywhere, so the attacks at Minack were more frequent. Monty was only making certain he would never again share his life with a dog.

It was also at the time of his return from St. Albans that he developed a growl. Most cats growl at some time or other but it is a sound that is a close cousin to a purr. Monty's growl was a deep-

39

throated challenge of such resonance that he might have acquired it from one of the larger dogs he hated. Yet it was not a weapon of war, a threat to frighten an opponent. It was a means of self-reassurance, a method of bolstering himself when he found himself in a situation not to his liking. Any odd noise he did not understand would bring forth the growl and, for that matter, any big noise too. He growled at the guns which fired at the flying bombs, and at thunder, and when rockets took the place of flying bombs he growled at them. The first rocket which ever landed in Britain landed within a mile of Mortlake; and it is Monty's growl I remember, not the explosion.

Sometimes the growl made us laugh because he uttered it when caught in a predicament. There was an elm tree close to the cottage at Mortlake and up it he went one day, leaping from branch to branch, higher and higher, showing no sign that he was soon to lose his nerve. I have never understood this particular blind spot of cats, how time and again they will climb to inaccessible places with the greatest of ease, then become transfixed by the height they have reached. I hate heights myself. I have an occasional nightmare which has me racing to the top of Everest; nothing hinders my climb, no hint of fear, until there I am looking out above the world . . . and quite incapable of descending. Monty too was incapable of descending and I had to fetch a ladder, and when the ladder did not reach him I had to climb up to him branch by branch. He was obviously terrified but he was not meowing. He was growling.

At one time we had chickens at the top of the garden, a dozen Rhode Island Reds penned in a small compound by wire netting on the side that faced the garden. On the other sides were high walls and on some point on these walls Monty would sit looking down on them while they clucked in troubled excitement. He was fascinated by their antics. Hour after hour he would crouch like a Buddha, eyeing them, trying to make up his mind what could be the purpose of their presence. At last he decided to make a closer investigation and he descended from the wall to the compound. I did not see him make his descent but I was in the garden reading a book when I heard the cacophony that hens make when a fox is among them. It was only Monty, an embarrassed Monty, surrounded by twelve furious ladies whom he was keeping at bay with his growl.

My midnight revolt, my show of independence when I kicked Monty off the bed, was in retreat by the next morning. It takes two to sustain a revolt. You cannot keep up a revolt if the opposition insists on showing affection. Monty ignored my offhand behavior, forcing himself on my lap whenever he wished to do so, kneading my knees with his claws, letting me watch his back bulge like a bellows with his purrs. For my part I could not refrain from stroking his silky fur, gently massaging his backbone and tracing a finger around his beautiful markings. I would have been of stone if I hadn't. His presence was therapeutic, and he brought a calm to the hectic life we led.

In the years which followed the end of the war we were seldom home in the evenings except on weekends. The nature of our work rushed us from party to party and we used to return home increasingly exhausted as the week developed. One becomes casual in such circumstances. One is so absorbed in fulfilling the basic responsibilities that one is inclined to be blind to the subtleties that enrich life. Monty was a subtlety, and although we were always sure to give him a rapturous greeting whatever hour of the night we got back, he was, I think, treated by us more as a toy than an animal. It was a period that I look back upon as distressing, and yet it had its value. It helped us in due course to form our decision to pack up our jobs and leave London. It helped us, for instance, to realize it is more important to be true to oneself than to accept unthinkingly the standards of others.

Monty, in this period, was like a toy because the haste in our life only spared us the time to bestow affection on our own terms. He was like a child in a Victorian family who was shoved into the drawing room by a nurse only at times when the parents were in a mood to see him. He would be used as a receptacle of our emotions, hugged and kissed in times of distress, expected to play games if we demanded them, shown off like an exhibit to appropriate friends. I have seen many cats, and dogs, treated in this way and have disliked the sight of it. When human beings use their pet animals as agents of their own exhibitionism it means humiliation both for the human being and

the animal; except that the human being concerned is too dumb to feel it. Often, of course, there
are people who are frightened to show affection, or
think it a curious kind of bad form either in themselves or in others; they think pets should be
treated as if behind bars in a zoo. These are the
people who bury a cat or a dog one day, and buy a
substitute the next, preferably of the same color or
breed so that the sequence of outward appearance
remains undisturbed. Sometimes, of course, this is
done not because of callousness but of fear, a fear
of being unable to live awhile with a memory. Either case provides an attitude which is unfair to
the pet, for the first suggests it was no more important than an old kitchen chair while the second
proposes that the death of a friendship can be
swapped for a physical resemblance. I do not advo-
cate a mourning, but I suggest that as a pet is a
giver during its life and a human is usually a
taker, a human should not accept an animal in his
home unless he is prepared to make sacrifices
which deserve affection.

One can also go to the other extreme and behave to an animal like a neurosis-ridden parent to
his child. Pampered animals can be observed any
day of the week. Yet this other extreme need not be
a form of neurosis or, for that matter, of exhibitionism. One can love an animal overmuch because of
its vulnerability, because it makes one feel secure
in an insecure world, because as it grows older it
reflects the years of one's life. In due course we
loved Monty overmuch but at this time, at this
brittle period of our life, he was a toy; but a toy
which had the merits of an anchor in our restless
existence.

He would glare at us from inside the dining

room window as we arrived home, the sweep of the headlights shining on his fierce face. "We're in trouble again," I would say as I put the key in the door. It was perfectly true that he had the knack of making us feel we had misbehaved, that two o'clock in the morning was a disgraceful hour to return home. We would switch on the light and hurry into the dining room ready to gush a greeting, only to find he had not moved, that he was still staring out of the window pretending to be unaware of our arrival except for the sharp flicks of his tail.

Jeannie used to come ready to bribe on these occasions and after she had purposely clattered plates in the kitchen and unwrapped some small paper package that had been donated by the Savoy restaurant, Monty would enter with the air of a cat who was ready to let bygones be bygones. He would devour the delicacy, lick the pattern off the plate but, unfortunately, would not pay the price expected of him. Jeannie's caresses were spurned and he would struggle free from her arms, jump first on the sink then up through his private entrance above the kitchen window, and disappear into the night. He was an opportunist, not a weak character open to a bribe.

But there were other times when there was no doubt about our welcome. I knew the sign when we stood at the front door and heard him come thumping down the bare wood stairs, wakened by the sound of the car as we drew up. He did not bellicosely clean the plate, then away into the night. He would eat a little then look up at us watching him; and I defy the person who does not believe he was saying thank you. And afterward he would not refuse to pay the price of his meal.

Jeannie was permitted to hug him, as many hugs as she wanted, and carry him upstairs and deposit him on the bed where he lay curled through the night. There was now no fear of my kicking him off.

He was not on his own all the time. We did not leave him at nine in the morning and let him fend for himself until our return at any old hour. He had his friends. There was our cleaning woman, Mrs. Hales, who had to stand in line for his whiting before she arrived at the cottage. Mrs. Hales was ill one day but as she lay in her bed she realized that the whiting, bought and cooked two days before, must have been consumed. "Oh, dear," she said, explaining the situation to us later, "oh, dear, there I lay thinking of poor Monty. Whatever will he do, I said. All by 'imself and nothing to eat. It mustn't be, I said. So I got up and called a neighbor through the window. 'Our Monty,' I said, "asn't got 'is whiting. Do me a favor, will you?' I said, 'Go to the fish shop and get three nice whiting. I can manage to cook 'em . . . then I'll send me 'usband up to Monty when 'e comes 'ome from work.' "

And there were Mr. and Mrs. Foster, who lived next door at the Ship. The Fosters had been pub-keepers since 1912, through the times when the Ship, as the pub at the finish line of the Boat Race, was a pivot of the great day. Maharajas, cabinet ministers, famous actors and actresses, as Gus and Olivette Foster never ceased telling us, used to be their customers then, shouting the crews to victory between glasses of champagne. There was none of that now; the bars were crowded on the big day, the steps of the pub and the towpath in front were jammed with people, but for the Fosters it

45

was a poor imitation of what they remembered.

A high wall divided our small garden from theirs and this wall was Monty's favorite. He would reach it by way of the kitchen window and the flat roof of our spare room which ran along a short way beside it. Thus Monty, as he patrolled the top of this wall, could be observed not only from our side, but also from the back windows of the Ship and by anyone—such as the Fosters' son with the nickname of Whiskers—who might be at work in the garden.

Both Whiskers and his sister Doris had a particular interest in Monty, but as Doris worked in London during the day, it was Whiskers, the barman in the pub, who mostly kept a watch on his outside activities. He was in his garden one day digging a patch of ground when he heard a terrific hullabaloo on the other side of the wall as if it came through an open window from inside the house. Quite obviously the noise was of two fighting cats and one of them, presumably, was Monty.

Now the Fosters kept the key of our front door for just this kind of emergency, and we always considered Whiskers as a guardian of Monty in our absence. He was about to rush in for the key when the noise suddenly rose to a crescendo, followed a few seconds later by a huge tabby racing along the top of the wall with Monty at his tail. Whiskers said afterward he was so delighted to see such a victory that he shouted, "Well done, Monty!" at the top of his voice. But Monty, left alone on the wall after the tabby had fled over another, was obviously hurt. He lifted up a paw, looked down at Whiskers and meowed loudly.

So Whiskers fetched the key and went inside

our cottage and into the garden, and coaxed Monty down from the wall and into his arms. It was a nasty bite and we had the vet for him that evening, for Whiskers had immediately phoned Jeannie to tell her of the battle.

And what was the battle about? Instead of the stink of fish in the kitchen there was the stink of a tomcat. The tabby had stolen Monty's whiting.

Not only the Fosters but others along the riverbank kept a watch on Monty. He was a talisman to the passersby as he sat in the dining room window, hour after hour, waiting for our return. One autumn we spent a month in Paris and when we got back we were looked at reproachfully by those who had seen him day after day in the window. "You should have seen him late at night when the street lamp lit up his face," said a neighbor; "he looked so mournful." We hated to hear such remarks because we felt we were in the wrong. Of course he had been well looked after by his guardians but he had been very lonely. And yet what does one do if ever one wishes to go away for a vacation with an easy conscience? Deposit a cat at the vet and you may think it is safe but you cannot possibly persuade yourself that the cat in such strange surroundings does not believe it has been deserted and has been left in a prison. There seems to be no answer except never to go away.

Monty's big day in the dining room window was the day of the annual Oxford-Cambridge Varsity Boat Race. Our preparations, of course, began at the crack of dawn and as it was always a marathon day of festivity, large quantities of food were prepared to cope with late breakfasts, lunch, tea and those who still had the stamina to stay for supper. For Monty these preparations were a nuisance and this might be considered surprising because, with so much food about, one might have expected him to be the official taster. But he was never a greedy cat. He ate his requirements and no more, although like all of us he had certain favorite dishes, chopped pigs' liver, for instance, which he gobbled faster than others. He considered these preparations a nuisance, I think, because he wanted to get on with the party. He had a role to play, and it was a role which he enjoyed.

He would keep out of sight, the linen closet being the ideal hiding place, until he had the good sense to realize the towpath was waking up; shouts of small boys who without reason for loyalty to either university were violently partisan on behalf of one or the other of the crews, odd couples finding places on the railings, then the appearance of vendors with dark and light blue favors. There was a pleasant atmosphere of impending excitement, and it was now that Monty appeared and expected attention.

Both Jeannie and I were Cambridge supporters and before our first Boat Race party Jeannie had bought Monty a large light blue ribbon which she tied in a bow around his neck. I did not approve. I thought such a gesture was ostentatious and silly and I anticipated confidently that Monty would wriggle free from the encumbrance as soon as he had the chance. He did not do so. True, the ribbon became more and more askew as the day wore on, with the bow finishing up under his tummy, but this had nothing to do with any action on his part. It was the attention he received which caused that.

So the light blue ribbon became an annual ritual and invariably, after the bow had been tied, he would sit in the dining room window staring with a lordly air at the crowds; and the crowds, looking for a diversion until the race began, would call to him and shout to their friends about him. He adored this period of glory. So much on his own but now at last receiving his due. And when our guests arrived, a hundred or more packing the cottage, a cacophony of laughter and talk, cigarette smoke clouding the rooms, people sitting on the floor and the stairs, glasses everywhere, Jeannie and I rushing around with bottles and plates of cold food, Monty was as cool as a cucumber. He would stroll from room to room, pausing beside a guest when the praise was high, even deigning to jump on a lap, ignoring the cat haters, refusing with wellbred disgust any morsel dangled before him by some well-meaning admirer. He was unobtrusively sure of himself; and when the rackety day was over, when Jeannie and I had gone to bed feeling too tired to sleep and we put out a hand and touched him at the bottom of the bed, we both felt safe. Safe, I mean, from the tensions among which we lived.

Sometimes I wonder if we would ever have come to Cornwall had it not been for Monty. Decisions are often based on motives which are not obviously apparent, and cool intellects certainly would not believe that two people could change the direction of their life because of a cat. Such intellects, however, are free from turbulent emotions. They are the human version of the computer, to be envied, perhaps, because they are spared the distractions of light and shade. They can barge through life indifferent to the sensibilities of others because they have none themselves. Materialism, in their view, is the only virtue.

Monty became a factor in our decision because he reflected, in his own fashion, stability. It did not matter how tired we were when we reached home, how irritated we might be by the day's conflict of personalities, how worried by inflated anxieties, how upset by apparent failures—Monty was solidly there to greet us. His presence, you might say, knocked sense back into us. He gave a clue to the kind of reward we might have if we exchanged our existing way of life for one that had a more enduring standard of values. We did not say this self-consciously at the time, too many other factors were involved; but on reflection I realize his example helped us to take the plunge.

When we first came to the cottage at Minack the floor was of earth covered by thin, rat-eaten boarding; and the first night we slept in it we lay on a mattress listening to the rain dripping from the roof, and in the morning there was a puddle in the middle of the room. It was a contrast to the night before, when Jeannie had entertained the American ambassador, Mr. Lewis Douglas, and A. P. Herbert in her offices at the Savoy; and yet the cottage, in her mind, was like Aladdin's cave. She had sensed it from the first moment that she saw it during a holiday we had spent at Lamorna. We had walked westward along a tortuous cliff path from Lamorna Cove, then in a steep climb to a point called Carn Barges; and when we had reached the top we looked inland and saw the cottage half hiding in the trees a mile away. "There it is!" cried Jeannie, pointing toward it. There was never any doubt in either of our minds that however difficult the task might prove to be, the little cottage was going to be our home; and that its security, once gained, would make us, in our personal view, the luckiest, happiest couple in the world.

The process of changing over from a city to a country life was spread over a year and more. We made several sorties to the cottage near Land's End during that time, and Monty was usually a companion. He appeared to be quite unconcerned by the long car journey except once, and that was my fault. I was naturally on guard against him jumping out of the car in a panic whenever I had to slow down or stop; but there came a time when I exchanged my ordinary car for a Land Rover. A sedan you could shut tight, but a Land Rover, with its canvas top, had potential gaps through which a determined cat might escape. I therefore bought him a basket and at the instant of leaving Mortlake I pushed him in it, banged down the lid and tied it. It was an appalling miscalculation. Instead of appreciating my action as a gesture toward his own safety, he took it as an insult. He was enraged. He clawed and spat and cried and growled. I had gone twenty miles when the noise of his temper forced me to stop, and I gingerly lifted the lid up an inch. A pair of eyes of such fury blazed through the slit that I hastily banged down the lid again.

Jeannie was with me on this occasion and inevitably this incident developed an argument. She wanted to take him out of the basket. I was too scared that once allowed to be free there would be no holding him. My imagination saw him gashing us with his claws as he fought to escape, then away like a madman into the countryside. She, however, insisted that only the basket angered him and he would be his old gentle self as soon as he was let out. So the argument went on, past Staines, past Camberley, past Basingstoke; it was not until we reached the outskirts of Andover, two hours after we had set out, that I gave in. Monty was released and, with a look of disgust in my direction, the purrs began.

On another occasion he traveled as a stowaway on the night train from Paddington. Jeannie was always very proud of this exploit as she was the architect of its success. She was due to join me for the weekend and was dining at the Savoy before catching her sleeper when she suddenly decided she would like Monty to accompany her. She dashed back to Mortlake, found him, after a five-minute desperate search, crouched on the wall at the end of the garden, and arrived at Paddington with three minutes to spare. Monty was an admirable conspirator. He remained perfectly still as she rushed him along the platform wrapped in a rug. Not a meow. Not a growl. And nobody would ever have known that the night train had carried a cat, had Jeannie been able to curb her vociferous enthusiasm when she arrived at Penzance.

But she behaved as if the crown jewels were in her compartment. She was in such a high state of excitement when I met her that she did not notice the porter was directly behind me as she slid open the door to disclose her secret.

Monty's aplomb was superb. With regal indifference, he stared at the man from the bunk. And as I recovered from my surprise and Jeannie muttered feeble excuses, all the porter found himself able to say was, "Good heavens, what a beautiful cat!"

Five minutes later we were in the car on the road to Minack.

Monty was wary in the beginning at Minack. He did not relax on those initial short visits, seldom put his nose outside the cottage, making even a walk of a few yards in our company a notable occasion. He was seven years old and needed time for readjustment.

Minack is a cottage a few hundred yards from the cliff and cupped in a shallow valley with a wood behind it. The walls grow up from great rocks which some farmer a few centuries ago decided would make the ideal foundation; the stones of the walls are bound together with clay. There are two rooms; one, which is the length of the cottage, is our living room and kitchen. The other, a tiny one, is our bedroom, and there is a third room, which we added as an extension along with a bathroom, that became known in his lifetime as Monty's room. On one side of the cottage the windows stare out undisturbed, except for the old barn buildings, across rocky moorland to the sea and the distant coastline rimming Mount's Bay; on the other, two small windows on either side of the door face a pocket of a garden. The old farmer, the architect of Minack, wished to defend the cottage against the southwesterlies; and so this little garden, and the cottage, were set in a hill that rose away to the west. Thus, if we walk up the hill fifty yards and look back, the eye is level with the massive granite chimney, the chimney which to fishermen sailing back to Mousehole and Newlyn in a stormy sea gives the comfortable feeling they are near home.

There is no house or eyesore in sight, and this freedom amid such untamed country provides a sense of immortality—as if here is a life that belongs to any century, that there is no harsh division in time, that the value of true happiness lies in the enduring qualities of nature. The wind blows as it did when the old farmer lived at Minack, so too the robin's song, and the flight of the curlew, and the woodpecker's knock on an elm. This sense of continuity may be unimportant in a world with the knowledge to reach the stars; but to us it provided the antidote to the life we had led, Jeannie in the hectic public relations world, myself as a member of MI-5, the British secret service. It was a positive reminder that generations had been able to find contentment without becoming slaves of the machine. Here around us were the ghosts of men and animals, long-forgotten storms and hot summer days, gathered harvests and the hopes of spring. They were all one, and our future was part of them.

Our plan was to earn a living by growing flowers, and—the specialty of the district—early potatoes, in pocket meadows on the cliff. We were, however, more influenced by the beauty of the environment than by its practical value, and so we presented ourselves with difficulties which had to be borne as a sacrifice to our whim. There was, for instance, no lane to the cottage. A lane ran a half mile from the main road to a group of farm buildings at the top of the valley, but once past these buildings it became rougher and rougher until it stuttered to a stop amid brambles and gorse. In due course we cut a way through and made a road, but in the beginning the nearest we could take the car to Minack was the distance of two fields, and across these two fields we used to carry our luggage . . . and Monty.

Jeannie put butter on his paws on the first visit. There had been a sad, remarkable case in a newspaper of a cat that had been taken away from his home near Truro to another near Chester from which he had immediately disappeared. Several weeks later he arrived back at his old Truro home so exhausted and close to starvation that he died a day or two later. I do not pretend I believed this story, documented in detail as it was, but Jeannie did, and she had a vision of Monty dashing from Minack and making for Mortlake. So she used the old wives' recipe for keeping a cat at home by buttering his paws, the theory being, of course, that the cat licks off the butter and says to himself that such a nice taste is worth staying for. A slender theory, I think, though comforting.

But it was soon made clear on that first visit, and repeated on succeeding ones, that Monty had no intention of running away. It was the opposite that provided us with problems. He never had the slightest wish to leave.

During this period he distrusted the outside around the cottage, made nervous perhaps by the unaccustomed silence and the unknown mysterious scents, and when we urged him to come out with us, he would usually turn tail and rush back indoors as soon as we dropped him to the ground. He was, in fact, sometimes so timid that he annoyed me, and I would pick him up again, deliberately deposit him a hundred yards from the cottage, then, impotently, crossly, watch him race back again.

Why, then, did he always disappear when we were due to start back for Mortlake? The bags would be packed, one load perhaps already lugged across the fields to the car, and there would be no sign of Monty. Obstinately remaining inside the cottage when we wanted him to be out, he was now out when we wanted him to be in. But where? The first disappearance delayed our departure for two hours, for we had no clue where to look. He had no haunts to which he might have sneaked, because he had never been long enough out of the cottage on his own to find one—no haunts, that is, that we knew of. Yet apparently on one of his brief excursions he had made a note of the barn, and how at the bottom of the barn door was a hole big enough for him to wriggle through. As the barn at the time was not ours and the door was kept locked, and the key kept by a farmer ten minutes away, it was a wonderful place to hide in. It became a ritual for him to hide there at the end of each visit. The key fetched, the key returned, and in between I would have had to climb to a beam near the ceiling where Monty glared balefully down at me. Or was he saying, "I like it here. Hurry up and make it my home?"

It became his home one April evening when the moon was high. We had now cleared a way through the brush of the lane and, though the surface was too rough for ordinary cars, it was suitable enough for a Land Rover. On this particular evening we bumped our way along it, the canvas top bulging with our belongings, Monty alert on Jeannie's lap, both of us ecstatically happy that at last the time-wasting preliminaries had been completed. We drew up with a jerk and I switched off the engine. It was a beautiful moment. No sound but that of the surf in the distance, the moon shimmering on the cottage as if it were a ghost cottage. Here was journey's end and adventure's beginning. All we had worked for had materialized.

"Good heavens, we're lucky," I said, then added briskly as if to foreshadow the practical instead of the romantic side of our life to come, "I'll get the luggage out. . . . You go ahead with Monty and light the candles."

But it was Monty who went ahead. He jumped from Jeannie's lap, paused for a moment to see she was ready to follow, then sedately led the way up the path. A confident cat. A happy cat who knew he was home.

Some enjoy the hallucination that if you tear up one part of your life and substitute another, congenial to your imagination, that you become immune to trouble. There is the gay, hopeful belief that if you can steel yourself to surrender the tedious, or tense, routine of life to which you have reluctantly become accustomed, problems inward and outward will dissolve. They do not. There is no such act as escapism. Wherever you go, whatever you do—emigrate, change jobs, find the dream cottage, pursue your true ambition—you have yourself as a companion; you have the same grim fight to earn a living. What you do gain, if you have the luck of Jeannie and me, is the chance to embrace an environment which you love, and which softens the blows when they come; for the expanse of sky helps to free us; so also does the sense that the wild animals, the foxes, the badgers have been going their mysterious ways for centuries, and that the sea is as it always was. The reward, if you have the luck, is to become aware again that values have never changed, that true pleasure is as it has been since the beginning, that man is nobler than the bee. The aim to be free does not lie in association with the herd, for the herd has not the patience to probe. One has to delve into one's secret self. No one else can help. But if one lives in the environment of one's choice, the task is made easier, the mind is more willing to explore.

Monty's transition into a country cat was a gradual affair. An urban gentleman does not become a country gentleman simply by changing his clothes. He must learn to adopt a new code of manners and a new approach to the outdoors, to be less suave and to show more bluster, to accept the countryside as a jungle which has to be mastered by skill and experience. Monty, as an urban cat, had a lot to learn.

He first had to get used to having us always around and he showed his delight in various ways. There was, for instance, the in-and-out window game, a game which was designed not only to display his affection, but also to confirm his wonderment that we were now always present to obey his orders. Thus he would jump on a windowsill and ask to be let out, only to be outside another window asking to be let in a few minutes later. This performance would continue for an hour until one of us lost patience, saying crossly, "For goodness sake, Monty, make up your mind what you want to do." He would then have the good sense to stop the game, replacing it probably by a short, though vigorous, wash.

There were the unsolicited purrs. A cat has to be in a very bad mood if a human cannot coax him to purr. There is little honor in this achievement, only the satisfaction that a minute or two is being soothed by such a pleasant sound. But the unsolicited purrs belong to quite another category. These are the jewels of the cat fraternity, distributed sparingly, like high honors in a kingdom. They are brought about by great general content-. ment. No special incident induces them. No memory of past or prospect of future banquets. Just a whole series of happy thoughts suddenly combine together and whoever is near enough is lucky enough to hear the result. Thus did Monty from time to time reward us.

My own preference was for the midnight unsolicited purr. For the first years, until we found a fox waiting for Monty to jump out, he had the freedom of the window at night. He used to go in and out and we were never disturbed if he chose to spend the night outside, perhaps in the barn. But when he did choose to remain indoors, and instead of settling on the sofa, preferred a corner of our bed, we felt flattered. It was then that I have relished, when sometimes I lay awake, the rich, rolling tones of an unsolicited purr.

In those early days the unsolicited purr was bestowed on us frequently. Later, when country life became to him a continuously happy routine, it became rarer. But in the beginning the new pattern of his life was so ebulliently wonderful that he could not restrain himself. There he would be on the carpet in the posture of a Trafalgar Square lion and suddenly the music would begin. For no reason that we could see. Just his personal ecstasy.

There were other times when his show of affection was awkward. How do you summon up courage to dismiss a cat who is paying you the compliment of sitting on your lap?

If you have a train to catch, if your life is governed by rules not of your own making, the excuse for removal is ready made. But in my case time was my own, the work to be done was the product of my own self-discipline, I could not blame anyone else if I shoved off Monty when he was comfortably enjoying a rest on my lap. I would gingerly start to lift him up, my hands softly encircling his middle, with the intention of placing him gently on the spot I was about to vacate, and he would hiss, growl and very likely bite my hand. True, this was a momentary flash of temper with more noise than harm in it. But the prospect of its display, the certainty that I was offending him, were enough time and again for me to postpone any action.

My subservience was made to look even more foolish when Jeannie, as she often did, served a meal on a tray. My seat was always the corner one of the sofa and so I used to try to balance the plate-filled tray partly on the sofa arm and partly on Monty's back, taking, of course, great care, not to put any weight on Monty. If, however, he showed signs of annoyance, if he woke up from his sleep and turned his head crossly around at me, I would edge the tray farther over the arm so that it balanced like a seesaw. I enjoyed many meals this way in the greatest discomfort.

Rational people would not behave like that. I can imagine my own sneers if, a few years before, I had seen into the future and found I was going to behave in such a fashion. But there it was, I enjoyed it. I was glad to be of some service, and I used to be tinged with jealousy if he chose on occasion to honor Jeannie instead. Such occasions were rare because her lap was not up to his measurements. He overfilled it like a large man on a small stool. She would sit, transfixed into immobility, and if at the time anything was being cooked in the oven it was sure to be burned.

These incidents may suggest that, now that the three of us were always together, Monty was spoiled. But is not a cat's nature, any cat's, impervious to being spoiled? You can spoil a child and it can become a nuisance. You can spoil a dog and everyone except its owner is certain to suffer. A cat, on the other hand, however luscious the bribes may be, remains cool and collected. Indulgence never goes to its head. It observes flattery instead of accepting it. Monty, for instance, did not consider himself an inferior member of the household, a pet, in fact. Thus he loathed it when condescension was shown to him, and many a misguided stranger trying to lure him with snapping fingers and "kitty-kitty talk" has seen his haughty back. He was cotenant of the cottage. He was not to be treated in that imbecile fashion so many people reserve for animals. The compliments he wished for were of the kind we gave him; we set out to implement any decision he made on his own by helping to make the result as successful as possible. We played the role of the ideal servants and we won our reward by watching his enjoyment. And there was another reward which Jeannie called "paying his rent."

His rent was making him do what he did not want to do. This was the reward we forced him to give us when we felt in the mood to assert our authority. Jeannie might suddenly pick him up, hold him in her arms and hug him when it was perfectly obvious that he wished to be left by himself. He would lie in her arms, a pained expression on his face, as she talked sweet nothings to him; and then, the rent paid, he would rush across the room to a windowsill and sit there, tail slashing like a scythe, demanding to be let out.

I always maintained that Jeannie demanded more rent than I did. I think she had good reason to do so because she was responsible for his feeding. She was always filling plates or picking up empty ones or asking him to make up his mind what he wanted. "Oh, really, Monty," she would say in mock fierceness, with Monty looking up at her as she stood by the sink, "I've just thrown one saucer of milk away, you can't want another!" Or it might

62

be one more morsel of fish required, and out would come the pan and down would go the plate.

His menu, now that we lived near a fishing port, was splendidly varied, and twice a week Jeannie would collect from Newlyn a supply of fresh fish. None of that shop-soiled whiting he used to have but sea-fresh whiting, boned megram sole or a little halibut, or what became his most favorite of all—John Dorey, the fish which fishermen themselves take home for their suppers. He would gobble John Dorey until he bulged; it was one of the few things which lured him to greed, and to satisfy this greed he would try to show his most endearing self to Jeannie. The spot where his saucers were placed was opposite the front door on the carpet at the foot of a bookcase which hid one corner of the sink. When he was hungry, a normal hunger not too demanding, he would sit on this spot, upright with front paws neatly together and the tip of his tail gently flicking them. His eyes would be half closed and he would sway imperceptibly to and fro. A meal was due but he was in no hurry.

Yet if John Dorey was on the menu, and was simmering in a pan on the stove, he could never restrain his impatience. He would walk excitedly up and down the room roaring with anticipated pleasure, rubbing himself against Jeannie's legs, looking up at her as if he were saying, "I love you, I love you." Here was a cat who was no longer retaining his dignity. Nothing could hide the fact that at this particular moment Monty was thinking that Jeannie was the most wonderful cook in the world.

He would then have been ready to promise her, I am sure, all the rent she required.

Monty's hunting at Mortlake has been limited to indoor mice, or indoor mice which happened to be outside. He soon began to find at Minack a variety of potential victims the like of which he had never seen before, and in some cases he was at a loss as to the technique of attack required. I found him once, for instance, staring at a patch of ground under which a mole was digging.

My own first experience of a mole digging was on the morning after a night out. It upset me. I was walking across a field, my head down, when I was suddenly aware that a patch of soil the size of a hat was moving. I stopped, stared and pinched myself. The soil circled like a slow spinning top, rising upward. The first time Monty saw this he was as startled as I had been. He put out a paw as if he were thinking of touching a red-hot coal, then leaped backward with a growl. "It's only a mole, old chap," I said knowledgeably, "only a mole digging a molehill." He was reassured enough to advance again. He touched the soil with his paw, then, meeting with no reaction, in fact finding there was no danger or excitement for him at all, he walked away with nonchalant composure, as cats do when they suspect they have made fools of themselves.

Another puzzle for him was what to do when he found an adder. A lizard, a slow worm or an ordinary grass snake was an easy excuse for a few minutes of play, but an adder he sensed was a danger; and he was certainly right. We have too many of them about. We are always on guard during the summer, wearing rubber boots whenever we walk through the undergrowth; although it is in a warm spring when they are at their most viperish. I have been happily picking daffodils on the cliff when I have suddenly seen the poised head of one within a few inches of my hand, hissing like escaped steam. In the summer they will wriggle away as you advance toward them and will whip up their heads and strike only if you step on them or tease them. In the spring they will attack at the slightest provocation, and, as they have been hibernating through the winter, the venom injected into the wounds made by the fangs is a dose built up over the months. I learned my lesson after the daffodils episode, but Monty never learned his lesson not to tease.

I have seen him touching the tail of an adder with his paw as if he were playing a dare game. It might have been a form of Russian roulette because an adder can kill a cat, though this is very rare. As an adder is thirty inches long, perhaps he was deceived into thinking that the head was too far away to catch him, or perhaps I was worrying unnecessarily. He certainly never was bitten by an adder, nor for that matter did he ever kill one. He flirted with the danger. It was a game . . . and yet, I wonder. There is a tradition in Cornwall that the capture and killing of an adder is the peak of a cat's hunting career; and when the rare victory is achieved the trophy is ceremoniously dragged whatever distance to the home and deposited on the floor of the kitchen for all to admire. Perhaps this was Monty's secret ambition. Perhaps above all he longed for the plaudits awarded to an adder killer. If so, the fates were against him.

I will not, fortunately, ever know the differences in flavor of mice—indoor mice, harvest mice, long-tailed mice, short-eared mice and so on. Shrews must be unpleasant because Monty, although he would catch them for fun, never ate them. But it seems obvious to me, after watching Monty, that outdoor mice have a far better flavor than the ordinary household mice. At Mortlake he became, without being flamboyantly successful, a sound indoor mouse catcher. At Minack he spent so much time outside on the alert that often he lost the desire to fulfill his inside duties; and since the excitement of the chase should be the same both in and out, it occurred to me sometimes that the cause of his extraordinary behavior may have been a bored palate.

I would be quite wrong to suggest that we were riddled with mice at Minack. For months we would be totally free of any sign of a mouse, but at intervals one or two would arrive and cause us annoyance. They would make an unwelcome noise on the boards which provided our ceiling, and on occasion would descend to the sitting room where Monty was often sleeping on the sofa. "Monty!" I would say sharply, "there's a mouse in the cupboard." And Monty would go on sleeping.

The cupboard concerned was the shape of a large wardrobe with shelves climbing two sides while the back was the wall of the cottage. Apart from the china on the shelves with cups on hooks, there was a table in the cupboard on which stood a gas refrigerator. Under the table was the gas cylinder, pots and pans, a bread bin and various other household paraphernalia. Thus the cupboard was crowded and a mouse had a wonderful place to hide unless we set about clearing a space by removing everything into the sitting room. We would perform this tedious task, then wake up Monty, carry him to the cupboard and deposit him there. Except for the gas cylinder, which was too much trouble to move, he was alone with the mouse.

Here, then, was a situation that was often repeated: Monty on one side of the gas cylinder and the mouse on the other, and Monty had only to race once around the cylinder to catch it. Yet he would not budge. He would sit looking at me as if he were trying to tell me the mouse was his dearest friend. "Go on, Monty!" my voice rising to a crescendo, "go on, you ass. Catch it!" The mouse would move its position and I would push Monty toward it so that they met nose to nose. Still not a whisker of interest. Nor any sign of fear from the mouse. I would push and exhort and be angry and in the end give up in despair. Monty had a pact with the mouse and nothing I could do would make him break it.

But why? He was swift as a panther when outside. He would be across the land and into the hedge and back again with his capture inside a few seconds; and when necessary he had infinite patience. I always found it an endearing sight to look through the window and see him in the distance perched on a rock, staring intently at the grass a yard away, then begin to gather himself for the pounce, shifting the stance of his paws, swaying gently forward and backward, until he gauged the great moment had come. And when he missed, when by some miscalculation he ended up in the grass with his back legs spread-eagled and a waving tail denoting his failure, I sensed with him his disappointment. His successes, of course, were loudly trumpeted. He consumed his victims not at the place of execution but on a square yard of ground on the edge of the path leading up to the cottage. No matter how distant the capture he would return with it to this spot. I would see him coming jauntily up the lane, a mouthful of grass along with the mouse. A few minutes later when nothing was left he would let out the bellow of victory. "Well done, Monty," we would say, "well done!"

Monty never touched birds, except once when I saw him catch a wren which annoyed him. Wrens can be foolish and this one was foolish. They are so small that if they kept to themselves no one need know their whereabouts. Instead they proclaim their presence by the cross rattle of warning and, in spring, enjoy baiting any objects they dislike. There was Monty lying somnolent in the garden while a pair of wrens rattled around him until he lost his temper and snatched one. I dashed forward, caught him and put a hand to his mouth, and as I did so, he let the wren go and it flew safely

68

away to a bush where it began its rattle again. And Monty went back to doze.

Monty's docile attitude to birds met its response from them. They showed no fear of him. It was I who felt fear; I was always waiting for the incident that never happened.

become vague when I try to isolate the years. I would like to have them arrayed in my mind in neat compartments but I find instead they merge into each other, and incidents connect themselves by haphazard association rather than by dates. Thus the flower seasons here at Minack, each of which has a slow-moving yet mounting dramatic entity of its own, become dissolved in my mind into all flower seasons. The hours I have crouched weeding anemones or picking violets, lugging baskets of daffodils to the packing shed, rushing the flower boxes in the morning to Penzance Station, these hours do not belong to one year but to all years. So also appear the storms that have battered Minack, and the lazy pleasure of hot summer days, the first scent of the may, the arrival of the chiffchaffs, the wonder of an angry sea with a fishing boat fighting for home. I have grown older not by passing each incident as if it were a milestone, but by being absorbed by them.

As Monty grew older his contentment was so obvious for all to see that we felt part of it. If something had gone wrong, if we had suffered some defeat which left us despondent, the sight of his magnificent person poised perhaps on some wall with the sun glinting his red bracken coat, his head alertly surveying the scene around him would be enough to quell our momentary fears. His example was a positive contribution to the life we had chosen for ourselves.

I suppose it was this contentment that produced in him his calm attitude to birds. There was no need for him to kill for the sake of killing because he had so much else to do and, for that matter, so much else to think about. He was a great thinker. We saw him so many, many times blinking away in the sun, not asleep, not awake, sitting upright with paws bunched, a shining white shirt front, tail around his haunches, the tip flicking delicately. "Look at Monty," Jeannie would say, "he's having his million and one thought."

And while he was contemplating, the birds would be hopping around him. We had a bird feeder in the pocket garden opposite the front door and inevitably the crumbs we put on it used to be blown off onto the ground; neither Monty nor the birds were perturbed as they collected them. Of course if you live in the country you are certain to make friends with individual birds which respond to your approach with more trust than others. In our case we had two particular friends who hopped around Monty collecting the crumbs. We called them Charlie and Tim.

Charlie was a chaffinch and Tim a robin, and they both treated Monty as if a cat was the most harmless thing in the world. Charlie was a bossy character who, in the spring and summer, used to follow us around cheeping all day. Even a bird's voice can sometimes sound too persistent and we used to scold Charlie for the monotony of his cry. A gentleman chaffinch, if you look at it closely, is a beautiful bird. There is a touch of the Tropics about its plumage of slate-blue, pink, chestnut, black and white wings and tail; only its voice is humdrum. Charlie's voice, as he perched on certain favorite places, was a high-pitched note repeated over and over again, until I marveled sometimes that Monty was not irritated into action.

Charlie would hop, for instance, at the entrance of the flower house while Monty was dozing on a bench and we were bunching the daffodils, piping away on and on until in exasperation I would say, "For goodness sake, Charlie, think up another song." Or he would perch on a certain stunted old apple tree under which Monty used to like to slumber in the lush grass. There would lie Monty curled in a ball while above him, with the monotony of a pneumatic drill, sang Charlie.

In winter Charlie was a more silent individual, as if the summer had consumed his song. His feathers would lose their sheen, he would crouch rather than perch on a branch as if days were made to be borne instead of enjoyed. Sometimes he would disappear for weeks on end, and there was one winter when he was so long away that we made up our minds that he was dead. We missed his perky presence. We regretted our rudeness about his voice. We yearned to see his busy little nature once again. And we did. In the spring he suddenly appeared one day in the wood while Jeannie was feeding the chickens, the same old song, the same old Charlie, bossy as ever.

Tim was a gentle robin, if you can think of a robin as gentle. At least we ourselves never saw him attacking another or trying to assert his personality at the expense of other birds. Charlie would drive him off the bird feeder at any time. Tim simply did not fancy a battle. He preferred to wait cunningly until Charlie had had his fill, then he would return and stay there until perhaps a tomtit would harshly tell him to go. Tim, in fact, believed in appeasement. This possibly was the reason why he liked so much to be indoors with us, or in the flower-packing shed when we were there. He found life less troublesome, felt safer, if he sat on a corner of my desk, despite the fact Monty might be wandering about the room. It was a remarkable sight seeing Tim on the back of a chair while Monty was on the chair itself. Or looking for crumbs on the carpet while Monty lay stretched by the stove. Or just flying around the room while Monty appeared not to take the slightest notice. Of course, Monty knew he was there. He observed Tim out of the corner of his eye, but it was an eye that never had the suspicion of a glint.

Yet Tim at times became so overconfident that he seemed to be going out of his way to court attack from Monty. I remember him once in the flower-packing shed standing delicately on one leg on the cup of a daffodil that rose from a galvanized pail. The pail was with others on the floor and there was Monty threading his way between them until he reached the spot where Tim was on the daffodil looking down on him, while a paw-stretch away he was looking up at Tim; but neither bothered to show any interest.

The height of Tim's foolishness was when he urged his lady of the year to build a nest at ground level among a bed of polyanthus. Heaven knows what caused him to choose such a place because it was in an area fifty yards from the cottage, which Monty had found a particularly fruitful hunting ground. Perhaps Tim had done so because it was so near to the packing shed, which meant he could have an idle time indoors without being too far from his mate. Anyhow I found the nest while I was picking the polyanthus, flushing the mate away as I did so.

At that moment, I saw Monty coming toward me, walking earnestly between two rows of plants, tail erect, a benign expression on his face which suggested that for some reason I was particularly popular. This was a moment to enjoy not to spurn, but I hastened toward him, swept him up in my arms and carried him, now cross, away to the cottage. Then I returned with bamboo sticks and a coil of wire netting and proceeded to encircle the nest in a cage. It looked safe when I had finished, but my activities had upset even Tim. The nest was never used again.

A third friend was Hubert the gull. He was far too superior, of course, ever to use the bird feeder, and he would stand on the rim of the roof waiting for us to throw food to him. Quite often Charlie would be there too, hoping to pinch a bite from under Hubert's beak; and Charlie would look ridiculous, so tiny beside Hubert yet so importantly awaiting us, that I used to call out, "Charlie sea gull is up on the roof!"

Hubert behaved toward Monty in his large

way as Charlie and Tim did in their small way.
Monty himself at first was not sure of him. Hubert
would sweep down from the roof, land on the path
and advance toward Monty who retreated nervously, looking around every few seconds and curling his mouth in a soundless snarl. I feel sure Hubert had no intention of attack. He was curious
perhaps. He succeeded, however, in those first
weeks after his arrival at Minack, in establishing a
moral superiority for a while over Monty.

Yet if a cat and a gull can like each other these
two did, or at least they learned to tolerate each
other. I have seen them both on the flat rock that
stretches out from one side of the cottage like a
sacrificial stone, Monty at one end, Hubert at the
other, and neither of them appeared to be perturbed.

Hubert never behaved so calmly when another
gull arrived on the roof. The roof was his personal
kingdom and if a gull swooped down and settled at
one end, Hubert exploded in fury, half ran, half
flew toward it, lunged out with his beak, then
sailed into the sky in a storm of squawks, chasing
the offender this way and that until both disappeared over the fields toward the sea. A few minutes later he would return, fluff out his feathers
and be at peace again as king of the roof.

There were times when Monty was certainly
jealous of him. During those meals outside when
Charlie and his squeak were ignored, Monty would
watch Hubert suspiciously as he stood with the
presence of an eagle a little way off. As soon as he
began to come too close, Monty would advance
timidly but surely until Hubert decided it was wise
to retreat. But it was when Hubert accompanied
us on our walks that Monty became most annoyed,

for he liked to have us to himself on these occasions and Hubert spoiled his pleasure.

Hubert would leave the roof as we set off down the lane, come swooping low over our heads, then up again into the sky, wheeling with the grace of a swallow; and when he came low again, his wings hissing the air with their speed, Monty would crouch and look up and glare. At other times we would be wandering around our meadows and fields with Monty trotting along with us when Hubert would dive from the sky, land on the ground twenty yards away, then strut on a parallel course; or if we had paused he would remain stationary, looking at us as if he were saying to himself, "I wonder what they are up to?" These moments particularly infuriated Monty. He would begin to creep along the ground, stalking Hubert as he would a mouse, getting nearer and nearer, making a weird noise which was neither a growl nor a meow. It was a comical sight. Both knew there would be no attack. Both knew the parts they had to play. It was a question of split-second timing. As soon as Monty had arrived within a few feet, Hubert, to save him the embarrassment of coming any nearer, flew off.

In spring, Monty's thick coat began to molt and we used to give him a daily combing. He would lie on my lap as I traced the comb up and down his back, on his sides and up around the jowls of his neck. He loved it. He purred happily until I turned him over and began the same task on his underparts. There would now be silence except for a series of little grunts. He found it awkward to purr on his back.

And when it was all over I would collect the silky fur in my hand, go outside and throw it into the wind. It floated into the air soaring and billowing, eddying in the end to some thorn bush or tussock of grass or entangling itself in the sea pinks on the wall. It did not stay in any of these places for long. The fur was much sought after. Most nests around Minack were lined with it.

As the years went by we became increasingly sensitive to the hazards that faced Monty. In the beginning we were so content with our new way of life that we foresaw the possibility of trouble neither for ourselves nor for him. Then, as the nature of our struggle became clear, we realized that we were going to have anxiety as well as contentment. The defeats and shocks we suffered, the lost harvest of daffodils, a field of beautiful anemones destroyed in a night by a southerly gale, a drought at a time when moisture for cliff potatoes was vital, brought home to us the extent of the battle in which we were engaged. So there were times when nervousness was substituted for calm and the foolish mood of anticipating trouble created unnecessary fears.

This foolish mood developed one evening at dusk when I saw an owl chasing Monty, diving at his upturned startled face as if it were aiming to peck out his eyes. I rushed forward, shooing it away, only to have it come back ten minutes later, and again the following evening, and the evening after that. I treated it as Monty's enemy, obsessed with the idea that it might blind him. "That damn owl is there again," I would say, and hasten to frighten it away.

Jeannie's attitude toward it was quite different. She viewed my actions as utterly stupid and whenever I hurried to perform them she would crossly say, "Leave it alone. It's perfectly harmless . . . it's *fond* of Monty."

Nothing would shake her conviction that the owl pursued Monty out of a curious kind of affection; and when several weeks had passed and no unpleasant incident had occurred, I had to admit that my fears were probably groundless. I refused to accept, however, that the owl *liked* Monty, and yet there were certain features of the relationship which were a puzzle. The tawny owls at Minack, and this was a magnificent tawny owl, nest at the top of the elms which surround a meadow close to the cottage. Very few cats could climb the specially favorite elm, and Monty was certainly not one of them. But the annual nest in this elm, just a cleft in the tree trunk, was a very foolish one and, usually, one or other of the nestlings would fall out. I would find one on the ground, a bundle of white feathers and two large unhappy eyes, and then laboriously climb up the tree and replace it beside its fellow. During this particular spring, however, I found no bewildered baby owl and as, later in the summer, I frequently saw the two owls sitting together like identical twins on various trees in the wood, it was clear no casualties had occurred. Hence Monty, against his nature and in a fit of madness, could not have climbed the elm and attacked the nest or killed a fallen nestling. He had, in fact, done nothing to incur the ire of the parent.

Yet there it was, the owl haunted him. It pursued him like a large dog with wings, swooping up and down as he walked innocently down the lane, cracking the evening air with its harsh cries of *kewick*, *kewick*. Nor would it leave him alone if he were happily curled on a chair indoors. It wanted Monty to be out with him. It would demand his presence by perching on the wall outside the front door harshly repeating again and again *kewick*, *kewick*. "Didn't I tell you?" Jeannie would smile and say. And I would reply abruptly, "For goodness sake don't be so whimsical."

In the end I learned to take the relationship for granted. It went on throughout the summer and, as I never saw the owl make a direct attack on Monty, I lost my concern that it might do him harm.

I had other fears for Monty which were to prove more tangible. He was too like a fox, for instance. I did not appreciate this until a farmer one day came hurrying up the lane to warn me he had seen a fox in the field close to where we kept the chickens. It was Monty, of course, a Monty with a burnished bracken-colored coat which, I thereafter realized, certainly did make him look like a fox. The same mistake was made at another time by a man with a gun whom I saw stalking beside

78

the hedge which ran up from the wood. I charged across the field shouting at the top of my voice and when I reached the fellow, flustered and out of breath, he looked at me with disdain. He was about to shoot a fox. Up there in the corner where the winter gorse was in bloom. Can't you see it? Look, it's moving . . . and Monty, alert at seeing me, came quickly through the grass toward us. These alarms put us on guard about the hunt. The hounds might mistake Monty for their quarry, and so when the meet was at St. Buryan or Lamorna Turn or anywhere else nearby, we used to keep him in all day.

But the hounds only once rushed through Minack and Monty was curled up on the bed at the time, and the reason we were so lucky is that it is obviously dangerous for the hounds when they run for the cliff. Thus when a fox makes for our area the hounds are called off and the fox, sidling along the hedges of our fields to the impenetrable brambles and thorn trees which slope steeply to the sea, is safe. My instinct is always to be on the side of the fox. I suppose I have found that when one lives as we live, our daily existence posted like that of the ancient gray rocks which heave out of the untamed countryside everywhere around us, one is incapable of killing for sport. We share our life with the wild. We are part of it. So I will kill should an animal become an enemy, but never for fun.

Yet a fox, as everyone knows, can become an enemy; and one summer when Monty was growing old, a neighbor found a fox's lair outside of which were the skeletons of four cats. The discovery thus explained why cats over a period of time had been disappearing from the homes of our neighbors, disappearances which hitherto had been blamed hopefully on the wandering instincts of farm cats. Then, two or three weeks later, a friend of mine saw a fox catch a cat. He saw the cat, three fields away, intently looking at a point in the hedge, then poising for a jump, so full of concentration that it was deaf to the fox that was stalking through the grass behind it. My friend yelled at the top of his voice but the sound disappeared in the wind. He could do nothing but watch the fox pounce, then hurry away.

I do not believe that all foxes are cat killers. You get a rogue which develops the taste for them, just as you get a rogue badger which brings calumny on his race by developing a taste for chickens; but whatever the case, whether one fox or two were guilty, a cat killer was at large around Minack and Monty was in danger. We kept watch on him within the limit of ever being able to keep watch on the peregrinations of a cat; and although he did not usually wander far, he obstinately chose this period to do so. "Have you seen Monty?" I would ask Jeannie, and when the answer was no, we would forget the importance of what we were doing and set out to search. We used to hasten around his known hideouts, a dozen or so of which found favor in rotation, and when he was in none of these we were inclined to develop a panic.

On one such occasion I ran one way toward the sea and Jeannie another up the field toward the farm buildings at the top of the hill. When I rejoined her she had Monty in her arms, holding him tight and telling him what a fool he'd been. This is what had happened. She had reached the entrance to the field that faced our lane and was looking across the field to the far side when to her horror she saw a red object chasing another red object. She instantly guessed a fox was chasing Monty, and she began to run across the field calling his name. She had run only a few yards when the second red object stopped and looked back at her. It was Monty. He was chasing a cub. Of course he did not know that it was running back to the lair where the cats had been killed.

Soon after this we realized the killer was after Monty. We had proof of this one evening when we heard a fox barking as if on the doorstep, followed by Monty flying in through the window. He plummeted at my feet and then turned glaring at the open window, growling. I ran to the door and out to the corner of the cottage which looks down the lane. I saw nothing and all I could do was to make a noise, the human version of an angry animal, which I thought would frighten the fox away. But Jeannie and I were now to behave extraordinarily foolishly.

We accepted the fact we had been stupid enough to allow him out at night without keeping him company, and so we decided from then onward he would be kept indoors after dusk. Monty was furious. He had lived at Minack for six years and was over thirteen, and for the first time in his life he was forbidden the freedom of the night. He made such a hullabaloo, woke us up so often with his meowing demands to be let out that three days later—and this was our foolishness—we gave in. "All right, you go out," I said: "I'm not going to be kept awake by your fuss. I'm tired. I want to sleep. But you look out for that killer. He was after you last week. He'll be after you again."

Our bed lay alongside the window so that if Monty was lying on it, then decided he wished to investigate what adventure awaited him outside, he had only to creep from the bedclothes to the sill and jump down onto the flower bed below. On the very next night after his freedom had been foolishly granted, he woke me up with the noisiest growl I have ever heard. I put out my hand and felt him creeping for the window. And then, from the daze of my sleep, I suddenly sensed there was danger. I grabbed Monty with one hand, and with the other found my flashlight, and when I shone it out of the window I saw a magnificent sight.

A fox, the size of an Alsatian. At first directly beneath the windowsill. Then gliding away down the lane, so silently, so superbly a thoroughbred that for a moment I forgot he was a killer and I called out to Jeannie:

"Quick! Wake up! You'll never see such a beautiful fox!"

After that thrilling but frightening night, we contrived a cunning device to prevent a recurrence. The contraption was like a window frame, except that wire mesh acted as a substitute for glass. Just before we went to bed we used to fix it in the window, and so Monty was stopped from making dangerous nocturnal adventures while Jeannie and I continued to sleep with the window open.

here were other hazards beside foxes; and there are two episodes in Monty's life at Minack that I would like to forget, but which remain painfully in my mind. Yet, and this is the paradox, I like also to remember them because of the happiness which followed, that magical sense of happiness when someone you love is reprieved.

The first took place the year before myxamatosis swept the rabbits away from our area, and when the gin trap was still the method used for their elimination. Such was our isolation at Minack that the fields where the traps were set were in a ring around us; and we were so far from other habitations that we alone suffered the hell of the traps' successes. We heard the momentary screams and the silence which followed. We lay in bed awaiting the next anguished cry, as we once awaited the next stick of bombs. A long way away those who were responsible for setting the traps would be pursuing their evening enjoyment while Jeannie and I, as if in the midst of a battle, listened.

A chill went through us whenever we heard the signal of traps being laid, the metallic sound of the trapper's hammer; and if Jeannie heard it first she would run looking for me, and we would both then go looking for Monty. I admit that rabbits had to be controlled in some way, but it was the manner in which gin traps were used which was so barbarous. It was seldom that any steps were taken to cut short the pain of the trapped. The traps, set perhaps an hour before dusk, reaped most of their harvest in the first half of the night as the rabbits came out of their burrows. The screams then followed each other as if they were an endless series of echoes and we would have little time to remain tense, waiting for the next; but after midnight we had to wait, ten minutes, half an hour, or suddenly two or three, one after the other, then silence. It was not often that anyone considered it humane to come at midnight and kill those animals caught during the evening flush. We had to lie there thinking of them.

It was late one lovely May afternoon that Monty got caught in a trap. We knew that traps had been laid in the field adjoining the cottage but traps were not supposed to be actually set until dusk; and thus Monty should still have had an hour or two in which he could have wandered around in safety. Nevertheless we were nervous for him. We were in the mood to anticipate trouble and I said to Jeannie, "I don't think we ought to let Monty out of our sight for an instant this evening." There seemed to be no reason why we should. Our day's work was ended and we were both pottering about the garden and the cottage while Monty was in one of his benign moods. He was lying half-hidden among the wallflowers outside the front door, blinking sleepily, as if he were relaxing after a large meal. He was the epitome of contentment, a much-loved magnificent ginger cat who was at peace with his private world, and heaven knows what prompted him suddenly to go somewhere he had never been before.

Unseen by us, he left his nest under the wallflowers, entered the field where the traps were laid and walked the length of it, miraculously threading his way through the traps until he was caught by one at the far end, close to a gap in the field which led down to the cliff.

I do not think five minutes had elapsed before I noticed his absence from the garden; and instinctively I knew what had happened. I shouted to Jeannie to follow me, then ran the few yards to a bank which rose above the field. I saw nothing but young green corn until suddenly in the far distance I saw an object at ground level languidly flopping up and down. It was Monty's tail.

The next twenty minutes are a jumble in my memory. We raced across the field, enraged that our care for him had cheated us; and when we reached him and saw his yellow eyes looking trustingly up at us while his little front paw with the white smudge on it was squeezed in the trap we broke out with curses against those responsible for setting it.

"I'm going to throw it away!" Jeannie cried, "right away in the sea." But this outburst did not help us release Monty. He began to struggle so I put my hands firmly around his body while Jeannie tried to open the trap. As only a few weeks before she had released a trapped dog she could not understand why, on this occasion, the fangs had stuck fast. Poor Monty; sweat began to moisten his fur and his mouth frothed, and then panic seized him and for an instant he freed himself from my hold.

"Look out!" I shouted. He lashed out with his

three free legs, claws like spikes, too quick for Jeannie to move away in time and I saw a line of blood on her arm. A second later he was quiet again, lying panting on his side, tongue lolling, uttering little cries, and his paw still trapped.

I do not wish to remember again the ten minutes which followed. A hideous time against the background of a sea-scented evening, larks exultant in the sky, early swallows skimming in from the south, the pilchard fleet chugging out into Mount's Bay. I do not wish to remember the anguish of those ten minutes, only the sweet relief we had when at last we had him safe. He lay exhausted for a while on the sofa while Jeannie tried to tempt him with warm, sugared milk and we angrily discussed what we should do.

The trap would go into the sea. I would make a complaint. We both, in fact, blistered with fury; and yet, maddeningly enough, there was nothing we could righteously be furious about. We did not own the field concerned, and so Monty, in the legal sense of the word, was trespassing. Thus the whole incident revolved around the question of standards. The countryman had grown up to expect a layer of cruelty in his life. We had not. Thus when Jeannie threw the trap away and I made my angry complaint, it was inevitable that a feud should begin. We did not mind of course. We at least had proclaimed our indignation against cruelty. And in any case the vet had seen Monty. No permanent harm had come to his paw.

The other episode took place when he was fourteen years old. We now had a splendid greenhouse a hundred feet long and twenty feet wide, and during this particular winter we were growing sweet peas for early spring flowering. We spent hours of our time pinching them out and layering them and it was only natural that Monty should be with us during these sessions. He amused us while we pursued the monotonous task. For no reason at all he would race up and down the rows or ridiculously treat a sweet pea tendril as an enemy, or interrupt the flow of our work by turning upside down at our feet requesting his tummy to be tickled. There were no signs that he was an old cat. He looked in magnificent condition and when one day we put him in a basket which hung on the potato scales, he weighed eighteen and a half pounds net.

Yet there were a couple of incidents during the daffodil season—it begins with us late in January and ends according to the warmth of the spring in the latter part of March—that made us puzzle about him. On each occasion he appeared momentarily to stagger and yet so briefly that it could have been an accidental lack of balance and not a signpost to coming illness. In between times he was completely normal, with the usual large appetite and as agile as ever.

Then one day at the end of March we went out and did not return till after dark; and, as so often happened, as we came up the lane to the cottage the headlights lit up his fierce face as he glared at us from the bedroom window. He had the gift of making us feel we had neglected him. It was an echo of those late Mortlake nights. "Where have you been?" he seemed to be crossly saying.

On this occasion we performed the inevitable rites of apology, picking him up and hugging him, and hastening to bribe him to return our affection by the obvious method of filling his plate with fish. Jeannie had turned to the sink to collect the fish pan when I suddenly saw Monty begin to stagger and half stumble across the carpet to a spot under my desk, where he collapsed.

"Look at Monty!" I shouted, and rushed over and knelt beside him, stroking him; and because I met with no response, his eyes seemed to be glazed and unseeing, I picked him up and carried him to our bedroom. He was desperately ill.

"You stay here," I said to Jeannie, not certain whether I was asking her to carry out the best or the worst of the two tasks, "while I race up to the farm and telephone the vet. If he's in he'll be here within half an hour." And miraculously he was in and, within half an hour, he was at Minack. We both looked at his face as he carried out his examination, seeking to read the signs we hoped to see. "Is it a heart attack or a stroke?" I murmured, fearing his answer.

He was a quiet Scot with a comforting assurance, and goodness knows why but I always prefer it when advice comes in a Scot's accent. "I don't think so," he said slowly, "you see his eyes are rolling, and look how he's struggling." He paused for a moment. "You haven't been putting any poison down, have you?" I hadn't, but I suddenly remembered the sweet peas and the dust we had been using on them to check disease, and I rushed out into the night to find the can. I brought it back and the vet slowly read the instructions and list of chemical ingredients.

"That's the trouble all right," he said; "he's been poisoned though there's no mention here the dust is dangerous. The fact is he's absorbed the dust in his fur and body over the months and now he's got enough inside to hit him."

He was in a coma for two days and nights. He lay on the pink bedspread in the spare bedroom while one of us sat always with him. The treatment was bicarbonate of soda every four hours and as it required both of us to pour the dose down his throat the one who was on night duty woke up the other when the fourth hour came around. About six o'clock on the second morning we had carried out our duty and we were standing together watching him . . . and suddenly there was a purr.

"Oh Monty, Monty!" cried Jeannie. "You're safe. You're safe!"

For us the remaining year of his life had the delicate pleasure of borrowed time.

In previous years we had occasionally to go away, never for more than three or four days, and elaborate arrangements of course were made for Monty's welfare. A traveling fish salesman supplied fish from his van, and whoever it was we had helping us at Minack at the time would cook it, and keep a saucer filled with milk from the farm. Monty was allowed to wander about as he liked during the day but in the evening he would be locked indoors; and when we were going to bed three hundred miles away in London, there was comfort in the thought he was safely ensconced within the cottage. We hated leaving him and he in his turn thoroughly disapproved of our absence; and on one occasion he nearly made us miss our train.

We were going by night, and while Jeannie was packing in the afternoon, he sniffed around the suitcases in that apprehensive fashion that both dogs and cats are likely to show when travel is scheduled. He then quite suddenly began to limp. I had never seen him limp before but there he was, hobbling about as if he had only three legs. This continued for an hour, and so theatrical were his gestures that Jeannie declared she would not catch the train unless he was seen by the vet. The vet was fetched and he pronounced Monty a malingerer. There was nothing wrong with him at all; and Monty, admitting his bluff had been called, promptly began walking normally again.

Our returns usually had a chilly reception. He liked at first to pretend that he could get on perfectly well without us and it was immaterial whether we lived at Minack or not. The pretense lasted until we went out for a stroll to see how things had been growing while we had been away. As we walked we would suddenly hear a bellow of a meow, then see Monty running toward us. We would continue our stroll with him at our heels, while at intervals the bellow was repeated. It was a touching experience, for in the sound was the agony of loneliness. We knew then how much he had missed us.

But in the last year of his life there was no need to go away, and although sometimes we were absent during the day we were always with him at night. He recovered splendidly from the dust poison, and by the early summer he was his usual beautiful self. "Oh, what a beautiful cat!" some hiker would say as he passed through Minack, seeing Monty perched aloofly on a stone. "How old is he?"

No one believed he was nearly fifteen. Nor did I for that matter. Time deceives in its pace, luring years into yesterdays, garlanding memories without intervals, seeping the knowledge of age into one's mind. I did not want to say how old he was. I did not want to remember that for so long he had been the recipient of our secret thoughts. Each of us had talked to him in that mood of abandon which is safe within friendship. Maybe it was only a cat's friendship, but secure, never to be tarnished, easing problems because the aftermath of confession did not breed the fears of disclosure.

He was an integral part of our failures and successes at Minack, and a hulky miner from St. Just whom we once had helping us called him the foreman. "Look out, the foreman's coming," he would shout as he lunged away with his shovel in a potato meadow; "we'll be fired if we don't do our job properly." Monty would appear and walk leisurely down the row where he had been digging, sniffing the discarded potato tops which spread-eagled on the side as if he were checking that all the potatoes had been collected from the plants. It was always a solemn inspection. There were no games. And when he had completed it, and had left the meadow, disappearing out of sight, the hulky miner would stab his shovel into the ground, rub his hands together and call out, "All clear, boys. We can have a smoke now."

He was sometimes an inconvenience when we

were picking flowers. At daffodil time the pace of picking has to be so fast that there is no time for distractions; and yet Monty would often insist on accompanying us, walking ahead between the daffodil beds at a very slow pace of his own choosing so that our feet tumbled over him. "Hurry up, Monty," I would say, but at the same time I did not want to sound too brusque. I was glad that he wished to be with us, and so I would stop the rhythm of my picking and bend down and stroke him. Then, if he did not move, I would step over him.

He had a passion for violet plants and, in his time, we used to grow three or four thousand every year. The variety was called Bournemouth Gem and each plant bushed dark green leaves that perfumed the meadow in which they were grown even before the violets themselves appeared. Monty liked rolling among them. The rich orange of his fur against the dark green was a pretty sight, and although you would have expected him to harm the plants, little damage was done; the plants were such fat cushions that the few broken leaves had plenty waiting to replace them. So we let him roll and only became alarmed when he jumped on a plant, gathered as much of it as he could with his four paws, turned on his side and proceeded furiously to disembowel it. The fact is he liked the smell of violets. I often saw him walking on his own down a row, his tail pointing like a periscope above the leaves, smelling the plants on either side of him. "Monty's picking violets," I would say to Jeannie as a joke.

He enjoyed sitting on the bench in the packing shed hemmed in by galvanized cans of wallflowers or jars of violets or anemones. He would sandwich himself in a space and if you looked in from the outside you would see through the window a splendid array of early spring and in the midst of it all the dozing face of Monty. I remember a flower salesman coming to see us one day who was so amazed by what he saw in the packing shed that he nearly forgot to discuss his business, for there was Monty among the daffodils, and Tim the robin up on a shelf warbling a song from a jar of anemones, while Charlie the chaffinch was looking up at us, calling his monotonous note from the floor. These three had three flower seasons together and this particular occasion was the last.

Monty was always tempted by boxes. If a package arrived and Monty was in the room when we unpacked it, he was certain to fill the vacant space. He certainly loved flower boxes and the tissue paper we put in them, and many a time we used to relieve the intensity of our work by pretending Monty, lying in a flower box, was indeed a flower. "Shall we send him to Covent Garden?" one of us would say. "They'd certainly call him a prize bloom," the other would reply. When we were working at great pressure, it was a relish to have Monty to distract us, in so kind and pleasant and trivial a way.

One of Monty's lovable characteristics was the way he enjoyed going for walks with us, trotting along like a dog at our heels. Sometimes when we wanted to go on a proper walk, a walk far longer than he could manage, we would sneak down the path planning to get out of sight before he realized we had gone; but from some hideout in which he was spying upon us, he would suddenly appear, all smiles as if he were saying, "Going for a walk? Good idea, I'll come too." Then, of course, we had

93

to cancel our plans and go on a limited walk instead.

He played games on these walks, some of which were vexing, some charming. He had the usual whim of a cat to tear up trees as if the wind were in his tail, but as many of the trees were elders he never climbed high. It was at night that these climbs were annoying.

We would be taking a late-night stroll and wishing to return to go to bed when he would race up the elder which is opposite the old barn and obstinately stay there. My voice would at first sound coaxing, then commanding, and then frankly I would lose my temper. "Come on, Monty, come down!" I would shout at him. He would not budge, so in the end, with Jeannie standing beside me holding the flashlight, I would climb the tree toward the pair of phosphorescent eyes which stared down from above. I would be up there among the branches trying to grab him, while Jeannie was laughing at both of us in the darkness below.

He had an endearing game he played when he thought a walk required livening up, or perhaps because he decided we were not giving him enough attention. He would wait until we had gone several yards ahead of him, crouching meanwhile on the path and shifting his paws as if he were about to spring . . . and then race at terrific speed up to and past us, coming to a full stop a couple of yards away. Thereupon we inevitably bent down and made a fuss over him. Then we would go on, and soon the game would be repeated.

The longest walk he used to take was to the Carn, the large rock-pile we can see from our windows at Minack and which stands above a cascade

94

of rocks that falls to the sea below. It is a rough walk most of the way, a track through gorse and brambles and bracken while on either side of a long stretch of it there is a whole series of badger sets. In springtime the land around is sprayed with bluebells while may trees plume white from among them; and ahead is the Carn and the panorama of Mount's Bay.

We used to make it an early-morning walk when the dew was still wet on the grass. It was a peaceful one if Monty was in a docile mood, but there were times when we would pass the badger sets thinking he was behind us, and suddenly find he had disappeared down one of the cavernous holes. It would take us a few minutes before we found which hole he had chosen, then we would see him looking up from the dark, just out of reach. I found myself thinking on these occasions he was taking a mischievous revenge on the only time I ever had power over him—when he wanted me to open a door or a window—for there he would be holding up the walk, and there was nothing we could do except await his decision to rejoin us.

His favorite walk, or stroll I should call it, was fifty yards down the lane to the stream, a stream which rushed water from November to June, then dried up and became a dip in the roadway. It was a stroll that now has a significance for Jeannie and myself because it represents in our memories the joy of his first stroll and the sadness of the last.

The first night on which we came to live at Minack the moon was high, and after I had transported our luggage to the cottage, we celebrated the freedom we had captured by taking this stroll. The moon was shining, except for the murmur of the sea and the hoot of owls, on silence.

Monty, who in the first week or two was going to be shy in daylight, came with us, nosing his way down the lane which to him was full of imaginary dangers, sniffing, hesitating, taking no action except to advance steadily toward the sparkling water that ribboned ahead of him. And when at last he reached it and put out a paw in puzzlement, I felt this was an occasion when I must not allow him to have any further apprehension so I bent down to pick him up and carry him over. He was quick to expose my foolishness. He slipped from my hold, and with the grace of a gazelle he leaped the stream. From that moment, this miniature valley across the lane became Monty's Leap.

It was in daffodil time that his illness began to threaten the normality of his days. Nothing sudden, no pain, just a gradual ebbing of strength, so that first the bluebell walk to the Carn had to be abandoned, then the one we used to take along the top of the cliff, and then even the strolls to the leap became less frequent. I would watch him from the corner of the cottage wending his way down the lane, and my heart would yearn to see a spring in his movements I knew I would never see again. He would reach the stream, drink a little, then turn and come slowly back. This stroll was the yardstick of our hopes, and sometimes Jeannie would come running to me: "He's been twice to the leap this morning!" . . . and her voice would have the tone that the inevitable was going to be defeated.

But I knew sooner than Jeannie that there was nothing we could do, nothing that her loving care and nursing ever could achieve. Each time I saw him set off for the leap I was on guard; and there was one evening, the last evening, when on seeing him start down the lane we ran to follow him only

(*top*) Monty   (*middle*) Lama   (*above*) Ambrose and Oliver

to find that after a few yards he had lain down. Then on a few yards and down again; and yet he was such an old warrior that when I picked him up he tried weakly to struggle free . . . as if he were saying, "Let me be, I can make it!" I gently gave him to Jeannie to take home to the cottage, and as I watched her I realized that she too now knew that our life with him was over.

Jeannie wanted to paint him. She knew he had only a few hours to live, and she believed she would be happier if she remembered these moments on canvas. Just as she was finishing the picture, a picture which now hangs on the wall of the sitting room, she ran out of paint. There were still three faint orange stripes to do on his forehead, and she was at a loss how to manage them. Then she suddenly had a bright idea. We were growing that year a meadow of orange marigolds, and Jeannie ran out to the meadow and picked a handful. She came back to the cottage, plucked some petals from the cup of a marigold, then rubbed them on the canvas. They produced exactly the right color.

He died on a lovely May morning in his sixteenth year. I had hurried to fetch the vet and on my return I found Jeannie had taken him out into the warm sun and he was breathing gently on a bed of lush green grass. Up above on the roof was Hubert, quite still, his feathers bunched, as if he were waiting for something; and within a yard or two of Monty were his other two friends, Charlie and Tim. No sound from either of them. Tim on a rosebush, Charlie on a gray rock. They were strange mourners for a cat.

The next day, soon after the sun had risen above Lizard peninsula far away across Mount's

Bay, we carried him down the lane to the stream and buried him beside it. Between his paws we placed a card:

Here lies our beloved friend Monty who, beside the stream that crosses the lane and is known as Monty's Leap, is forever the guardian of Minack.

Part 2
Lama

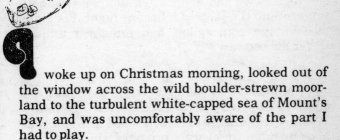

I woke up on Christmas morning, looked out of the window across the wild boulder-strewn moorland to the turbulent white-capped sea of Mount's Bay, and was uncomfortably aware of the part I had to play.

"Merry Christmas!" I said cheerfully. Too cheerfully.

There was a second's silence.

"Merry Christmas!" said Jeannie, murmuring her greeting into the pillow.

Some people have no feeling for anniversaries. They consider a happy anniversary as a duty occasion when it is remembered in time, or an annoying one when it is remembered too late. They are unperturbed by sentimental anniversaries. They do not get bothered as some of us do by the thought: "This time last year . . ."

Our bedroom at Minack is very small. If you stand in the middle, holding the handle of a mop, you can touch each wall. There are two windows, each the size of a dinner plate when we arrived, but now enlarged so that they are casement windows; one of them faces the moorland and the sea, and the other looks out on the square of grass which I call a lawn.

There is a William and Mary chest of drawers wedged between the foot of the bed and one of the rough-faced, white-painted stone walls; and there is a small dressing table for Jeannie, and a little walnut desk like a school desk where she keeps her papers. There was also, under the bed, the antifox contraption we had made after Monty had almost jumped into the jaws of a fox one night. For eight months the contraption had remained unused under the bed.

"I'll get the tea!"

I proposed this easy way out to gain favor because I wanted to postpone the moment of present-giving. I was unsure of myself. I had had Monty as a companion at every Christmas since Jeannie and I had married; and there had been a ritual, one of those foolish family rituals, in which Monty and I took Jeannie's presents to her together. And those that I gave her, and those that I provided Monty to give her, were accompanied by badly rhymed, well-meant verses possessing some immediately topical personal aspect. Occasionally such verses gained greater applause than the presents themselves.

I poured a little of the milk which we collect from the farm at the top of the hill into the cup, filled the rest of it from the teapot, then took it to her.

"What," I asked in mock seriousness as I did so, "would you like as a Christmas present?"

I expected the reply. I knew exactly what she wanted, but she was not going to get it.

"I want a kitten," she replied, laughing at me, aware that my question was a game.

Monty had not converted me into a cat worshiper. Of course I had learned to notice other cats, just as one notices the makes of cars on long journeys, but in all the years with Monty I never became a cat worshiper like Jeannie, for in her eyes any old cat merited a coo and the wordy rigmarole associated with cat worshipers.

At this stage, in view of what happened, I think I should say that there was a chink in my armor as far as one type of cat was concerned: the black cat. Somewhere in my childhood an incident of much good fortune must have occurred involving the presence of a black cat. I have no recollection as to what it might have been. All I can say is that all my life I have had a lilt in my heart when a black cat has crossed my path. It never appeared to me as an animal in that I said to myself, "Look, there's a black cat!" It was just a shadow wishing me good luck, a dart which struck my superstitious Cornish nature. Time and again, at moments of unsureness, the fleeting sight of a black cat in front of me had been the source of unreasonable comfort.

But my cat devotion was for Monty himself. He was my companion at Minack as a dog might have been, and the emotion that came to me when he died was the same as anyone feels for someone who has shared many adventures. I had no desire to replace him. I had no intention of doing so. A substitute could not be found for Monty, as one might find a replacement for a broken chair. My only wish was to have comfortable memories of him. A period of my life was over, and I would be forever grateful for the happiness he had given me, and for the sympathy I had gained by his presence in troubled times. Monty, as far as I was concerned, was irreplaceable; and that was that. No well-meaning person was going to be made welcome who came to us saying, "I hear you've lost your cat. I am very sorry, so would you like this kitten?" None of that. I was going to remain loyal to Monty. I was going to cherish the years he had given us.

I was going to prove it was true that I was a one-cat man.

But in the evening of the day he died, I said something to Jeannie which was not prompted by sense. The words came out of me as if I were wanting them to be a pillar against which I could lean. A wild hope hidden in a conundrum. An impulse from my subconscious. I am quite sure there was not a flicker of reason behind them.

"On one condition only will I ever have a cat again," I said boldly to Jeannie that night, "and that is if a black cat comes to the cottage in a storm . . . and we never can find where it came from."

"I want a kitten!" Jeannie said that Christmas morning.

Not a chance.

of course did not know I was being watched. I had met people on occasion, those who possessed a special dottiness for cats, who claimed that as soon as a cat vacancy occurred it was broadcast cat fashion to all members of the local fraternity. Soon after Monty had died, for instance, I had met a sweet old lady in Penzance who said to me in a tone of irritating certainty, a charming, knowing smile pressing the point home: "Don't you be upset about your Monty, Mr. Tangye. Next on the list will soon be with you!"

"Rubbish," I replied under my breath.

As the months passed after Monty died it was arguable whether I was justified in maintaining my sense of loyalty toward him. Jeannie's devotion to him had been no less than mine, in fact more so; and yet she was prepared to introduce another cat to Minack. Why not me? I had no reasonable answer but I continued to say a sharp no whenever Jeannie mentioned the prospect. There was no Christmas spirit about me as far as this matter was concerned.

We now had Jane and Shelagh working on the flower farm. Each of them had started with us when they were fourteen, and they belonged to the wild cliffs on which we lived as the crying gulls belonged. Jane with fair, shoulder-length hair, who padded barefoot about her work at Minack during the summer months, Shelagh, so introspective, a gentle cup of a face, a waif. These two, I look back upon and know, were part of the truest period of our life at Minack. I see them now lugging the baskets of flowers up from the meadows, or at the packing bench bunching daffodils as fast as they could, or on hot summer days patiently, yet always enthusiastically, planting drooping wallflower plants, hundred upon hundred of them, into a parched field. I laugh also when I think of them. They were always allies of Jeannie's in any matter concerning me, those mock, joking occasions which spice a working day.

"Let's hide the shovel and see him getting cross!"

"I'm going to tell him the violets were killed in the frost last night . . . then watch his face when we show him the baskets!"

They were Jeannie's allies too about gaining a successor to Monty. In the weeks which followed Christmas, as the flower harvest gathered speed, these two would share with Jeannie a nudging, persistent, humorous campaign to make me change my mind. Almost every day one of them would announce, "I know of a kitten you can have!" And if it were Shelagh, she would add, because she was always careful, "It's free!"

And while we were laughing we were being watched.

The first news of this came one afternoon while Jeannie's mother was staying with us. It was the last week in February, the period when the flower harvest is rushing toward its climax, and the meadows are massed with bed upon bed of daffodil buds; and when we are not interested in anything except picking, bunching, packing and rushing to catch the flower train at Penzance. I scarcely listened when Jeannie's mother recounted her story. It certainly had no significance as far as I was concerned. It was just an incident on a walk.

For the first time she had brought Angus, her Scottie, with her. Angus had always been banned from Minack while Monty was alive, for Monty would never have allowed him into the cottage. He was a cheerful little dog, successor to Judy, who had chased Monty up the curtains at St. Albans; and because his home was an apartment in London, Angus treated his walks around Minack as those in paradise. On this occasion he and his mistress had taken a walk to Pentewan meadows, which we rented from our neighbor and in which we grew potatoes as well as daffodils.

Jeannie's mother returned from this walk, and as always when she was excited her slight Scottish accent became delightfully pronounced.

"Did you know you have a little black cat on your land? Angus chased it, he did. Right through the daffodils at the top of the big field, and the wee thing disappeared over the hedge into the moor."

My only reaction, an instinctive annoyance, was that such a chase should not have been allowed to happen in the daffodil beds.

We were earning a living, we couldn't risk damage. Why wasn't Angus called off the chase?

But as had happened once before, when Monty came into my life, Jeannie's mother knew better. A damaged daffodil did not compare in value to a little black cat.

"Such a pretty wee thing it was," she said, and looked at me.

Angus on this, his first visit, slept on a rug draped in a small armchair. He had no wish to sleep for long; the gorgeous extent of his holiday was so wonderful that every second had to be experienced, and as we were always up as the pale sun stretched from the Lizard peninsula through the window of our bedroom, we used to open the door and let him out. Jeannie's mother was also usually awake, and she would say in the manner of someone glad to be the witness of pleasure. "Go on, Angus, go for a walk, have a good time!"

On this particular morning Jeannie went straight into the packing shed to begin packing the flowers we had picked and bunched the day before; and I took Angus for a quick run down the path to the big field, then right, toward the Pentewan meadows. I was on my way back, Angus ahead of me, when he suddenly barked; then, ears back, stumpy tail upright, he set off in a fussy gallop. I saw him disappear around the bend into the big field, and I knew he was making for the daffodil beds again. I ran after him, uselessly shouting, and when I reached the gap that led to the field he had already reached the far hedge, and with legs too short to give him a chance to jump up it, he was revenging his impotence by barking furiously. I had seen no sign of his quarry.

"What was Angus barking about?" asked Jeannie when I got back to the packing shed. "Did he see the little black cat again?"

"*He* may have," I said, showing no enthusiasm, "I didn't."

Angus and his mistress went back to London a day or two later, and there were no more chases before he left. But in the afternoon of the day they had gone, Shelagh, who had been picking wallflowers in a meadow overlooking the sea, arrived back in the packing shed in high excitement.

"I've just seen the little black cat!" she said breathlessly. "I surprised it asleep in the wall-flowers, and it ran away and dashed down the badger hole in the corner!"

"The badger hole?" I murmured. There was a notorious set at one end of that meadow. Then I added, meaning to annoy, "A nice meal for a badger anyhow."

"How heartless he is, Mrs. Tangye," said Jane, busily bunching, with a mock heavy sigh.

Jeannie, of course, behaved predictably. She was standing alongside Jane bunching flowers.

"I'm going to look for it," she said, hurriedly finishing a bunch. And off she went.

She found nothing, but the incident had introduced a new zest into the flower season. And while I remained humorless, enmeshed in the mechanics of prices, making fanciful calculations of what we might earn the following week and the week after, worrying whether or not we would have enough in the bank when it was all over to keep us going, the little black cat began to imprint its personality on Minack. It was no longer a black dash. It began discreetly to remain in sight of us.

Thus, as March advanced, the chatter tended to concentrate on its activities. Jane and Shelagh would bring in their flowers to the shed, unload them from the baskets, put them in galvanized pails or glass jars according to their varieties, and then start bunching those that had already been in water for twenty-four hours.

"I saw it this morning."

"So did I."

"Where?"

"As I was bicycling down the lane," said Shelagh, "just this side of the well."

"Joe," announced Jane one day, "says he's seen it in the quarry."

Joe, who worked for the same farmer as her mother, was known as a keen observer of small incidents.

"Did he say anything about it?" I asked, the first occasion I had shown interest.

"Only that he's seen it a number of times, but never further from Minack than the quarry."

The quarry was extinct. Once upon a time it provided the blue elvin stone which served as a base for many of the lanes around St. Buryan. It was small, and above the lower Pentewan meadows. It also marked our farthest boundary.

"You see," said Jane, smiling at me, "the cat never goes farther west than the quarry, nor farther east than the well. Never strays from your land."

he cat quite clearly was closing in on me. At the same time, I was so absorbed with mundane matters that I was not truly conscious of what was happening. Then, as I went about my business, I began to notice saucers left in odd places; sometimes they were brimming with milk, sometimes they were empty. I also realized that the cat was now being regularly seen and it was no longer a sensational piece of news to announce. I saw it myself, several times, at the far end of the stable meadow through the packing shed window. What was more significant, I began to sense that there was a conspiracy against me, and that the cat had these powerful allies of Jeannie, Jane and Shelagh. There was developing an uncomfortable atmosphere that once again I was the odd man out.

"Stop courting the cat," I said one day crossly, after the mail had brought details of bad prices and I was about to take another load of flowers to the station, "it's never going to live here and it's selfish of you to deceive it." I started the Land Rover and drove off, but disquietingly I noticed that the three of them said nothing. Heads down, they continued with their work.

They were plotting. As soon as they saw the back

of the Land Rover disappearing up the lane, they would laugh and make their plans.

The cat, however, was not cooperating. I was quite sure of this. Had they been able to approach it, had it shown any sign of yielding to their blandishments, they would have trumpeted news of their victory. Instead there was a scheming silence. Saucers continued to be left halfway up the lane. Others were placed on the path down to the big field. And all this seemed to add up to the fact that the cat was not ready to accept them.

The first person who touched it was me.

We kept a few chickens in those days, and their home was a house in the wood. They had a good run and it was surrounded by wire mesh netting to protect them from marauding foxes and badgers. One early morning when I went there to open up their door, I found the cat outside awaiting me. But not for long. It had one terrified look at me, then bolted across the run to the far side.

One's life is littered with actions not governed by the intellect, and much is gained thereby. Time and again in my own life I would have been left standing in a backwater had I allowed my mind coolly to appraise a situation, and the same thing would have happened now had I permitted logic to decide. Up to now I had crossly condemned the antics of Jane, Shelagh and Jeannie to court the cat. Yet here I was rushing across the run in pursuit of it.

When I reached the other side, the cat was battering itself frantically against the wire netting, plunging its little head into one of the holes as if by so doing it could squeeze its body through to safety. My presence only made it plunge more frantically.

I instinctively put out my hand to stop it, and momentarily my fingers clasped the bony, thin little body. Then terror really seized it. It raced away from me, leaped onto the top of the chicken house, from there to a branch, then another leap over the top of the wire and away into the depths of the wood.

I was, nevertheless, one up on the others. With all their talk they had not been even within a few feet, let alone touch it. The situation titillated me. My ego was flattered. I now had a story to tell them which would compel envy. Lighthearted envy, of course.

"How is your dear little cat?" I said innocently, when they were all gathered together in the packing shed.

"Why do you ask?" said Shelagh suspiciously.

"Just wondered."

"He's up to something," Jane said, looking across to Jeannie. "I feel it. There's a look in his eye which means trouble. Has he told you anything, Mrs. Tangye?"

"Nothing," said Jeannie.

"I certainly don't mean trouble," I said, "but I've got something to boast about. I've *touched* your little black cat."

A few days earlier another event had occurred which had startled me. I was walking along the path toward Pentewan when I saw, out of the corner of my eye, that I was being observed. A tiny black head, two little ears, and a pair of slit amber eyes, almost hidden in the blaze of marigolds, followed my person as I passed. It was a weird experience because under this scrutiny I felt almost self-conscious, as if I had discovered I was being secretly assessed for a job. It was not until later that I remembered about Jeannie using the marigold petals to finish Monty's portrait.

There was soon to be a most bizarre coincidence. It is, of course, convenient to call anything a coincidence which cannot be rationally explained. It is comforting, in this age when men like to think their plans can control the future, to dismiss the unexplainable as a coincidence. It is a reassurance that man, in his time on earth, is still the omnipotent force his ego needs to imagine himself to be. So, for want of a rational explanation, I call the final entrance into my life of the little black cat a coincidence.

A few hours after Monty had died I had made that strange remark to Jeannie. I had said that I myself would never have another cat because my cat loyalty was only to Monty, the sort of remark people often make when an animal dies with whom they have shared the experiences of years. But I had added, you remember, that I would make an exception if a black cat whose home we never could trace came to the door of Minack in a storm.

On Easter Sunday, a week or so after the incident of the marigold meadow and that of the chicken run, a tremendous storm blew up from the south. The rain and the gale swept in from the sea, roaring against the cottage, so that inside we had to raise our voices in order to hear each other.

There was a pause in our conversation. Jeannie was sitting in the armchair in front of the stove, and she was a little upset because she was reading her diary of the year before. Quite unreasonably she was feeling that she could have done more for Monty in his illness than she had done—a common belief of those who have loved.

Suddenly I said, "Did you hear that?"

Quite distinctly I had heard a sound which was strange to the wild noises of the storm. It was a meow.

"I heard *something*," said Jeannie.

I got up from the sofa where I had been sitting and went over to the door. When I opened it part of the storm came into the room. And so did the little black cat.

We put it on the bed that first night and left the window open. We thought that after sleeping off the huge meal Jeannie had given it, it might regret its decision to enter the cottage; and so we left it free to escape if it wished. But it never moved. Instead a friend came through the window to visit it. I was lying awake when it arrived, and saw the shadow on the sill.

"Jeannie!" I shouted as I switched on the flash-light, "our black cat is a girl. Sammy from the farm has just jumped in through the window!"

We had never investigated. We were so affected by the magic which had brought it to Minack that we had taken it for granted that it was male. I had never thought in terms of a female cat. My mind only associated itself with the gorgeous male which was Monty.

"You're right!" cried Jeannie.

The light shone on a crouching figure a foot away from the bottom of the bed—Sammy, an active sandy tom, notorious for his wanderings in the neighborhood.

"Psst!" I hissed as fiercely as I could. Not a move.

"Get out!" I shouted.

But Sammy, either too frightened to budge or too influenced by the charms of the black cat, remained still. I then picked up a glass of water from beside the bed and cruelly flung its contents at him. He disappeared through the window.

"Well," I said as I got up and shut the window after him, "this is awful. Supposing the cat is going to have kittens?"

"Let's go to sleep."

"It's all very well," I said, "but this puts a very different complexion on the situation. We don't want kittens all over the place."

"*You* don't!"

"All right, I don't. I never visualized having more than one cat. You see . . ."

"Stop arguing. Talk about it in the morning."

The little black cat, meanwhile, had remained quite undisturbed throughout this activity. She was dead to the world. She had consumed, prior to being carried to bed by Jeannie, a large saucer of bread and milk, a liberal portion of the chicken we were having for dinner and a slice of the liver from the morrow's dinner. She lay in a tight ball at the bottom of the bed, dreaming perhaps that her feast was a dream.

And as she dreamed I roamed my selfish thoughts over the merits of having another cat. Of being tied again. We had nothing dependent upon us at Minack at this time except the few chickens, the wild birds and Hubert the gull; and Jane and Shelagh could look after them. We were free to go away without tedious and elaborate plans to cover our absence, or more accurately, perhaps I should say I *felt* free to go away.

I was facing the old challenge of having to decide the degree of worthwhileness in giving up a part of one's independence. One is flotsam if there is no sacrifice. The belief that personal freedom is obtained by cutting the shackles is an illusion. The pure happiness exists when the mainstream represents the base one has struggled for, but the edge is provided by the giving. Even to a cat.

In the morning Jeannie said she would take the Land Rover and telephone the vet. We do not have a telephone. When people want us urgently they send us a telegram, asking us to phone them; and that means we are protected from those who would phone us on the spur of the moment. When we ourselves want to telephone, we drive a couple of miles to a phone booth, or to the Queens Hotel in Penzance.

The vet, the quiet Scotsman, in due course arrived. When he entered the cottage the little black cat, like a snarling tigress, shot away to a corner of the room. She had gone wild again.

"Come now," he said in his soft accent, "nothing to worry about. Let me have a look at you."

She was under a bookcase behind my desk.

117

"Look at this liver," coaxed Jeannie, proffering the saucer, "delicious . . . you loved it last night!"

The shadow, merging with the old, feet-thick stone walls of the cottage, was not to be bribed.

"Come on, come on," said the vet very softly as if he were caressing her, "you're safe with me, you know."

She did not agree. Each time one of us approached her she dashed to another part of the room, then crouched there, fur upright, spitting at us, blazing with rage.

The vet smiled. "I don't see you keeping her for long," he said; "she's so wild that only a zoo could keep her."

In the end it was Jeannie who cornered her and picked her up. Savagely squeaking, struggling, she was ready to scratch her way free again.

"Shut up!" Jeannie said firmly. And miraculously she shut up.

"That's certainly a victory for you," said the vet. "Now come on, see if she can't be the same with me."

She sullenly let it be so. I watched the smoldering yellow eyes as the vet prodded her.

"I don't think she's more than three months old," he said, "and if I were you I'd let me take her back to my office. In a week you can collect her, and there won't be any toms to go after her again."

A week later we did collect her. She was in a basket, the same basket we bought for Monty when he first came to Minack. We reached the top of Boleigh Hill, then turned left into the lane which leads to Minack.

And as we did so, from out of the basket there came a great volume of purrs.

We called her Lama. The Dalai Lama was escaping from Tibet at the time of her arrival at Minack. "DALAI LAMA SAFE" we read in a headline one day, and cut it out of the paper and stuck it on a beam in the stables. A suitable name we therefore thought, since they had something in common in the sense they had both escaped from danger.

The night that she came back from the vet, she had jumped on the bed, put her head on Jeannie's shoulder and stayed there the night through, periodically bursting into purrs.

"I've got a cramp."

"Turn over, then."

"I can't."

"Why?"

"Lama's so comfortable."

"Oh, heavens," I said, "so this game has started all over again."

I don't mind admitting that I had greatly enjoyed the interval during which I had slept in comfort. Night hours and night hours during Monty's lifetime I had spent with limbs numbed while Monty lay against a leg or a foot, blissfully asleep at my expense. And now the performance was scheduled to start again.

"Don't you think," I said gently, "that it might be a good idea to have a new regime with Lama? After all she's been accustomed to sleep in any old place."

"I can't wait to see *you* pushing her off the bed."

Jeannie's knowledge of me was, of course, quite correct. The discomfort, the readiness for self-sacrifice, had always received its compensation when I stretched out my hand and touched a paw or traced a finger on a forehead, for Monty all his life had provided me with reassurance during dismal wakes in early mornings, and now Lama could do the same. I was, therefore, defeating myself if I were so selfish as to try to ban her from a portion of the bed.

"Well," I said, "you're probably right."

There was a pause.

"Lama," murmured Jeannie, "you've won."

On reflection I find the strangest feature of Lama's advent was our certainty that she would stay. We never had any qualms that she was only using us as a hotel, having a rest and feeding herself up before moving on to somewhere else or going back to where she came from. And we were silently cross with those who prophesied that we would soon be alone again.

"I know all about these wandering cats," a friend who had three cats said importantly, "they simply live with you for a while, take all your attention and just when you have become fond of them, off they go."

"I had a cat," said another, "which came to our door in a starving condition just like yours and stayed three months. We were quite sure it had made its home with us, then one day it disappeared. We found it later at a farm two miles away, but it wouldn't come back. It had become tired of us, just as it would become tired of the next farm."

"Vet-treated she cats," said a third gloomily, "never live for long in the country. All the farm cats in the neighborhood will descend upon her, corner her and kill her."

Heaven knows why some people sadistically enjoy giving advice when it is too late for the advice to be accepted. We could do nothing now about Lama, and yet our informant continued to describe in detail the fate of one of his she cats. "Farm cats are real killers," he added, "when it comes to treated she cats."

"I don't believe a word of it," I said, while Jeannie got up and went out of the room, "and what a damn stupid thing to say. It can only worry us."

There was meanwhile the question to be answered: where had Lama come from? We had to find out whether there was somebody unhappily looking for her . . . but where *could* she have come from?

There were two farms at the top of the lane on the way to the main road. Farm cats galore inhabited them. Lama ought to have come from there, but she hadn't. No one knew of a little black cat being lost. There was a farm a quarter of a mile farther on toward Lamorna, and another the same distance in the other direction. No help from either of them. There were other farms within a radius of three miles or so, and here also we drew a blank. None of them had any cats which were lost, nor could they help us with information about mother cats who had disappeared at the moment of confinement. And in any case, why should a mother cat disappear from the comfort of a house or a barn to have her kittens outside, in the midst of a hard winter? For if the vet was correct in his calculations, Lama was born in December.

My investigations had, of course, been pursued before Lama had been taken away to be treated. I had to admit, however, that they had been done in a hurry. A lip-service investigation so to speak, and each time I had asked, "Have you lost a little black cat?" I had prayed for the answer to be no. The source of my anxiety was romantic rather than practical. I might have found Lama's original home, and then been kindly told by the owner that we could keep her. But this would not have suited me at all. I wanted to combine the act of keeping her with the maintenance of an illusion, and because she had arrived so mysteriously, I hoped that her past would also remain mysterious. An indulgence on my part. A desire to see the remark I had made after Monty had died come true. I was indeed like someone who was wanting to bend the facts to suit his wishful thinking.

Having failed to find any clues through my personal inquiries, I was for a short time content to believe that I could do no more.

"She's ours, Jeannie," I said after I had come back from the last farm; "nobody knows anything about her."

"She's a magical cat."

"It's not as if we were in a town where she could have come from a hundred different homes in the neighborhood. There's only a choice of nine or ten."

"She may have traveled a long distance, I suppose."

"How could she have survived the bitter weather?"

"She's such a *little* cat."

"And why should she have traveled toward Minack, passing the farms on the way, then stayed around here?"

"She'd heard of the vacancy."

"She took long enough to make up her mind once she got here. After all she hardly rushed to introduce herself."

"That was feminine intuition," said Jeannie;

"you'd have thrown her out if she'd forced herself on you."

"Oh, yes, I understand all that fanciful nonsense," I said, laughing, "but she must have come from somewhere. I feel sure logically minded people would have a clear answer."

"You don't *want* a clear answer," replied Jeannie, "so I wouldn't worry anymore."

I remained, however, uneasy. I am prepared to fool myself temporarily, prepared to make any situation coincide with my preconceived hopes, but fortunately I have a belated toughness which erodes my momentary satisfaction as soon as I am freed from the emotion which the situation has created. Overenthusiasm soon cools into reappraisal or, conversely, indignation simmers into proper perspective. In this particular case the aftermath of my investigations was this unease. Somebody, somewhere, must have known her when she was a kitten. It wasn't as if she was any old tabby. She was a beautiful little black cat which anyone would clearly remember. Even a farmer, with a horde of cats lodging among his farm buildings, would have noticed Lama.

Then suddenly I remembered the traveling fish salesman from Newlyn, and I wondered why I had not thought of him before. Here was a man who was ideally placed to solve the problem once and for all, a man who was known to every cat on the Land's End peninsula. He once told me that when his van drew up at a farmhouse he used to see cats racing across fields to join the group around him as he showed his wares to the farmer's wife. He was the cats' friend. Each day of the week he visited a different area, loading up at Newlyn market in the morning not only with fresh fish to sell but also with less favored fish to give away. No wonder cats recognized his gray van. No wonder they remembered the day of the week on which he called. He was the Pied Piper of fish salesmen. He knew the cats who lived twenty miles and more away from Minack. He took a personal interest in them, and if he observed a regular was absent from the group around the open back door of his van, he would ask the farmer's wife for news. He was part of the stream of feline life in West Cornwall. Kittens were introduced to him by their mothers. Old cats, past hunting days, relied on him. No one was in a better position to tell us where Lama had come from.

I asked him to call, and we showed him Lama. He had never seen her before. A week went by, and as he traveled his daily rounds he made inquiries at every stop. Then I saw him again.

He had met no one who had lost a little black cat.

Where, then, had she come from? It was a long time before we learned her secret.

We now began to become acquainted with Lama. She was, as I have said, very small. She remained very small. In Monty's heyday when I put him on the potato-weighing machine, the scales read eighteen and a half pounds. The same scales, when I weighed Lama, read seven and a half pounds.

She was the epitome of a calendar or Christmas card cat. The allure of a cat is at its perfection when its head is in perfect proportion to its body, and when its tail has a character of its own. Lama's tail was like the handle of a cup, a firm curve demanding to be clasped and lifted. I developed, in fact, the trick which Lama permitted, whereby I clasped this handle of a tail so that in one movement I lifted posterior and back paws.

The paws were tiny, with black pigments. They were like little black powder puffs and yet, when she was on the attack, they stabbed with the viciousness of needles.

She was black from the tip of her nose to the tip of her tail, except for a wisp of a white shirt. Monty had a white shirt which was so bold that you could see it in the dark before you caught sight of his figure. You had to look hard to see Lama's even in daylight, just a vague hint of white, a shadow against black. She also had a single white whisker. It was on the left as she stared at you, and

Jeannie alleged it came and went according to the long-distance prospects of the weather. If the weather was going to be cold and wet and stormy, the whisker flourished; if a heat wave lay ahead, it wilted and dropped off. I do not vouch for this fanciful interpretation of the life of the whisker. I had intended to take notes, plot a weather chart and draw a graph displaying the growth of the whisker week by week, but somehow the project was never realized. In the meantime the whisker blossomed for a month or two, looking incongruous against its lush black neighbors, then suddenly disappeared.

"White whisker has gone," one of us would say, as if we were mentioning the end of a cherry tree's blossom time. And we would also remark a little later, when we had been observant enough to notice it, "White whisker is growing again."

Lama was very soft to touch. She was, of course, so light when you held her in your arms that you felt there was no weight to carry, or if there was a weight you could describe it as being a parcel of swan's feathers. This gossamer quality was deceptive. Hold Lama against her will and you felt her muscles stiffen into a ramrod; as your hands clasped her you were uneasily aware that you held a small stick of dynamite. All claws and hisses. A pivot of intense fury in a small body. And if you were wise you would immediately disengage from this cat who had momentarily gone wild. And you would do it promptly.

Cat lovers, I have found, those all-embracing lovers of every kind of cat, show great irritation when their love receives little response. A battle of wills ensues and it sometimes appears to me that the cat lover, the alleged cat lover, is a bit heartless. Vanity is wounded when purrs are not immediately forthcoming. Tempers are even frayed if the cat concerned remains obstinately aloof. Cats, it seems, are expected to throw their arms around their human lovers with the same enthusiasm as the latter throw their arms around cats. And if they don't, the lovers' knot is often cut. One day, for instance, after many people had visited us, Lama had gone to bed first and settled comfortably, as far as she was concerned, a few inches below my pillow. I tried, like a contortionist, to get in between the sheets without disturbing her; and while I was twisting my way past her, Lama watching me with a baleful eye, I suddenly caught sight of a gap in her fur, just at one side of her spinal column. I looked at it in astonishment. One of the visitors had cut away a tuft about an inch square.

We never did find out how it happened.

Lama's eyes were Oriental to look at, amber slits slanting upward, and when strangers looked at her closely, they would say, nine times out of ten, "There's something strange about her. I can't quite place what it is." Of course with her black eyelashes and the black background of her fur, the slanting amber eyes were accentuated. Yet there *was* something strange about her. She didn't look like any of the cats in the district.

When she was first with us, she had the most terrible nightmares. She would be curled up somewhere asleep when suddenly her whole little body would start shuddering, accompanied by gasping, whimpering cries, until the fear in the dream became so real that she woke up.

Nor did she know how to play, or how to knead. She did not, therefore, have the attributes of a normal kitten, and we had to help her to develop them. I am inclined to believe that kneading is a more subtle expression of pleasure than a purr. A purr is a boisterous acclamation in comparison. The knead, that gentle in-and-out movement of paws and claws, is a private demonstration of serene ecstasy; and it is, I feel, the surest sign of all that a cat is content. The conventional knead requires, of course, a cushion, or something soft and inviting like the counterpane of a bed; but the happiest knead of all to watch is a cat lying with lazy abandon on its side or its back, with nothing for it to clasp, no object being used as a victim, just kneading. You see then the wonderful secret thoughts finding their way to expression. A cat in a private heaven.

The first game I tried to play with Lama was with a piece of string, dragging it temptingly in front of her. The gesture to her was incomprehensible. I tickled her with a pipe cleaner, I pretended my hand was a mouse by rustling it in a tuft of grass, I played all sorts of silly games without receiving the smallest reaction. She was above games. She was a Ninotchka. Life was deadly serious, and there was no time for humor. It was pathetic to watch her ignore any effort to entertain her, and depressing too.

"Isn't she *ever* going to play?" I said almost in despair after one particularly patient attempt on my part.

"She will," said Jeannie.

We had to wait a long time. The summer and autumn passed by, and it was not until a week before Christmas that the breakthrough took place. It was Shelagh's doing. Jane used to go back across the fields to her cottage for lunch but Shelagh, living farther away, brought sandwiches.

She used to sit eating them in the flower house, and she had two companions who often shared them with her, and who fortunately never met. One was a mouse who sat on her knee, the other was Lama.

We were particularly rushed at that time bunching freesia for the Christmas market, and we used raffia to tie the stems of the bunches. The raffia comes to us tied together at one end, but the other end is a bush of dried grasses. These grasses are cut off at the length required for the bunches.

The raffia was hanging from a nail above the packing bench, and Lama was on this bench. Shelagh pushed a pencil through the bush so that the tip appeared mysteriously a few inches from Lama's face. A paw was doubtfully raised. Then the paw tried to attack the tip, treating it as if it were a red-hot poker. Violent interest was aroused. Inhibitions disappeared. And by the time Shelagh's sandwiches had been consumed, the truth had dawned on Lama.

They were playing a game.

It was a pleasant curtain for Christmas.

erry Christmas!"

I was holding Lama in my arms and between her paws was a package for Jeannie.

"Merry Christmas!"

The package was deceptively large. There was a great amount of unnecessary wrapping. An elaborate intention to prolong the discovery of Lama's first Christmas present. A small brooch. And attached to it was a verse I had made up.

"*What* a lovely brooch!" said Jeannie. And I gave her Lama, and Lama then fell on the wrapping paper spread on the bed; and she obviously wondered what all the fuss was about.

Her first Christmas at Minack was Angus's second. In Monty's time, when Jeannie's mother was joining us, Angus spent the period of festivities in kennels. But this Christmas, against my better judgment, Angus was invited, and I had depressingly awaited the outcome of the first confrontation between him and Lama. Still vivid in my mind was that terrible encounter between Monty and Judy, and the explosion seemed ready to be repeated. Lama had had nine months on her own. No dog had visited us. How would she cope with a dog sharing the three rooms of the cottage? I was ready for the worst.

It is my nature to prepare for the worst. I feel that by so doing I leave a large margin of potential happiness in any problem in which I am involved, since the result can never be quite as bad as I expected. Hence, to whatever extent I am rebuffed, I am also relieved.

Jeannie had met them at Penzance station. They had traveled on the Cornish Riviera and Angus had spent the journey in the compartment. I have myself in the past felt resentful when a dog has been brought into my compartment. I have rustled my newspaper in an exaggerated fashion in order to display my annoyance. I have glared at the innocent creature. I have even changed to another compartment. But I always noticed that the dog's owner was quite unperturbed. Angus was Jeannie's mother's only companion in London and she too was unperturbed. "Everybody loved him on the train," she thus said as she walked with Jeannie down the platform; "he's such a good little dog."

And this was true. He did not have the pugnacity of Judy, or of some Scotties. He was friendly without being obsequious. He did not yap unnecessarily. True he pulled hard when on his leash, and so Jeannie was sometimes concerned that he was too strong for her mother. Yet who can blame a dog for a small vice like that when he lives his life in a London apartment, his regular walks are on pavements, and even in a park he cannot run at random? No wonder he reveled in his visits to Minack.

I watched the Land Rover splash through Monty's Leap and come up the last stretch of the lane past the stables, then around the steep piece to the right, and pull up in front of the window through which I was watching. Then Jeannie's mother appeared. The new coat, the new hat. I saw in the instant of watching that here again I was witnessing the wish to please. Not to be thought casual. An effort made, much thought before the choice was finally decided upon. Another Christmas, and yet seemingly no gap since the last one. Gaily wrapped parcels in the two suitcases in the well of the Land Rover. Just the same as it always has been. Only the wink of an eyelid to note the passing of time.

I have never looked upon time as a hill, hiding the past on its other side. Time to me is a plain, so that if the circumstances are right, if the associations are in union, the past can be seen like a fire; and the feelings repeated, recognized again after being forgotten, the old story of Citizen Kane remembering his beginning, of Marcel Proust's *madeleine*, of all our minds when we are not controlled by doctrine. You touch the past as if it were the present. You meet yourself again as a ten-year-old at a moment of anguish or great joy, you are there again at first love; nothing has changed, you are as you always have been.

And so it was when Angus came into the room and Lama was lying beneath my desk. Sixteen years ago when Monty was introduced to Judy. A heaving of time and yet to me I was living again the same moment. I had the same tenseness, the same belief that a decision had been made at the expense of sanity. An explosion was about to detonate, either the cat or the dog would be hurt, the Christmas would be spoiled before it had begun, an armed camp would be set up as at St. Albans those years ago; and, as then, I was aware that I was impotently watching.

It was at this point the similarity ended. My role of "I told you so" never matured. There I was, the figure of doom, being forced to smile. I am resilient in such matters and when I am proved wrong, I do not sulk. I appear gay, a gaiety which is genuine enough though others might take it as a pretense. Here I stood then, in the middle of the room, welcoming my mother-in-law in peace, instead of amid the cat and dog fight I had foretold. I was beaming with relief. I was thankful that the spirit of Christmas was apparently assured.

Angus came rollicking into the room, stumpy tail wagging, rushed up to me putting his nose to my shoes, nibbling the toe caps, grinning, making a gurgling noise and showing such total signs of delight that he was back in the country again that it was crystal clear that he was in no mood for argument. Thus it all depended on Lama.

There she was beneath my desk. And while I was being flattered by the attentions of Angus, out of the corner of my eye I was observing her. It was as if I were looking at a child who was assessing a child visitor. The aloof stare hiding intense interest. The mysterious process at work to judge the extent of competition. An apparent nonchalance which deceived no one who knew her. And yet pervading her manner there was the suggestion she was prepared to be friends on reasonable conditions. Such conditions, I guessed, revolved around Jeannie and me. During Angus's stay we had to make a quite exceptional fuss over her. There must not be a shadow of suspicion that she had been supplanted as queen of the household. With no difficulty we accepted these conditions. Angus could flounder in happiness while Lama was caressed. It was a satisfactory compromise.

The following day was Christmas Eve, and in the evening there had been the customary busy gathering of presents, names scribbled on holly-edged cards, separate little groups of packages placed side by side under the Christmas tree. All day Angus and Lama had tolerated each other. Angus fussed in and out of the cottage, rushing up and down the path outside, and when we took him for a walk he skedaddled across the fields, stumpy tail wagging, a joyous little dog on holiday. Lama, on the other hand, maintained a distant air. *She* did not have to behave with vulgar abandon. *She* was the chatelaine of the cøttage; this dog, however amiable he might be, was an interloper. She wouldn't be rude, but there was no need to behave as if she *liked* his presence. You could see he was pampered and that he knew all about Christmases. This was her first. The first in the company of human beings who were so clearly anxious to pay court to her. It was advisable for her to remain distant in any case. It was a defense. How could she know how to behave?

Jeannie and her mother, as part of the game of Christmas, filled a gauze stocking each for Angus and Lama. A packet of dog biscuits and a can of meat for Angus and little presents of only sentimental importance; and a packet of cat food and a toy mouse for Lama and one or two other things which Jeannie put in and were really meant for me. But, as a special gesture toward the occasion, Jeannie had cooked in advance the turkey giblets and, wrapped in waxed paper, she had shared them between the two stockings. Each stocking was hung by a thumbtack at one end of the bookcase.

Early on Christmas morning Jeannie and I

were awakened by a crackling, crunching sound. Not noisy. Just a reminder as to what happens when a mouse is consumed.

Our fault, of course. Lama had found the giblets.

TWO YEARS LATER

Lama's at the window."

"I saw."

"Let her in. I'm peeling the potatoes."

"I've just let her out."

"Mrs. In and Out . . ."

I got up and opened the door. Lama had been sitting on the window ledge so that she had only to jump down on the stone paving outside the cottage and then come in through the porch. She hesitated, peering below her.

"Boris is waiting to pinch her tail," I said to Jeannie.

Boris had come to Minack after a boyfriend of Jane's had offered him to her for dinner. He was a magnificent Muscovy drake, a large white bird the size of a goose, with dark green feathers on his back, a pink beak with a red bobble, huge yellow webbed feet, intelligent eyes and the habit of raising the crest of feathers on his head when annoyed. The boyfriend had arrived at Jane's cottage with Boris in a sack. He was, so Jane told me later, very proud of his gift, confident that it was an imaginative way of wooing her. But he could not have known Jane very well. She burst into angry tears, accused the young man of great cruelty, rescued Boris from the sack and carried him upstairs. And when Jane came to work across the fields next day she was carrying Boris in her arms. She also brought a message from her mother: Boris, her mother thought reasonably enough, was too much of a handful to be kept in a bedroom. Would we give him a home? And of course we did.

Boris had arrived three months after Lama, and so they had grown acclimatized to Minack together, and while doing so had watched each other closely. Their relationship for a long time was warfare without battle, and I sometimes interpreted their behavior toward each other as being an example of old-fashioned class consciousness. Boris considered himself as good as Lama, and he preened himself and strutted about sure he was a noble bird. But why should he live in an old chicken house, have to wait in the morning for the door to be opened, while *she* enjoyed a pampered life indoors? The trouble was that Lama encouraged him to think in this way. She would walk past him with a nonchalant, provocative lilt, a young lady sure of her elegance and financial security; and this air of subtle superiority provoked Boris with his splendid though heavy appearance into floundering, into being enraged like a blindfolded giant, into clumsily weaving his head of raised feathers to and fro and vulgarly hissing toward Lama as she passed him, and leaving the impression after Lama had serenely gone by, that he was cursing himself for having fallen into her trap, and had attacked instead of remaining loftily silent.

Boris, therefore, was sometimes a little distressed. He believed himself placed at a disadvantage. He was basically farmyard, Lama was a creature of soft cushions. Why should birth be so unfair? His revenge was to harry her, to make her beware of his presence, to keep her always in doubt whether his fierce appearance was genuine or show; and Lama countered with an upturned nose as she passed him. Indeed she was never seriously concerned by his behavior, for instinct told her he was feigning. And in any case Lama, since her arrival from the wild, had clearly developed the belief that harm would never threaten her. She was a cat in heaven, and the world was always kind. Thus her mood toward Boris, appearing sometimes to be haughty, was that of indifference. His hisses, to her way of thinking, were as empty in content as the last gasp of a soda water siphon.

Nevertheless her confidence occasionally resulted in overconfidence, and for a while afterward she would treat him with greater respect. There was a period, for instance, when they each took the same liking to a small empty greenhouse we have near the cottage. A pleasant sun parlor for them both.

"Lama and Boris are having coffee together," Jeannie would say. It was there that I witnessed one of Boris's rare victories.

Boris near the open door, Lama on a sack in the center. Lama, dozy in the warmth, lulled into off-guard contentment, had turned on her back, four tiny paws at different angles in the air, an inviting black silk tummy, eyes shut, blissful thoughts; and suddenly into this sweet oblivion Boris decided to advance.

Boris was heavy enough to make a sound on gravel like a person walking on the path. I have often heard the noise of his webbed feet, and been deceived and cried out to Jeannie, "Somebody's coming!" But it was only Boris plodding up the path, wanting a piece of Jeannie's homemade bread or just needing our company. But on this occasion he walked with stealth. A Muscovy drake's tiptoe. His beak had a target.

I arrived by chance at the greenhouse at the instant of strike. The supple softness of Lama was hopelessly vulnerable. There she lay lost in her dreams, the careless abandon of a happy cat, a nymph at the mercy of the hypnotic powers of the sun; and I suddenly saw Boris a split second away from making his dab.

It was only a dab. I saw for myself there was nothing vicious in its intent. His head, feathers tufted, moved toward her center, backward and forward, nearer and nearer, like the uncertain movements of an old-fashioned movie; and it only needed one dab from his beak which hit the middle of her tummy for Lama to leap to her feet like a cornered cowboy drawing pistols in a flash and firing them at the sudden enemy. Only in her case the weapons were fur flushed upright, arched back, a growl and claws like daggers.

Boris gloried in his triumph. He wagged his tail feathers fussily in delight. He had made a fool of her. He stood a few feet away, opened up his huge wings and flapped them noisily and with such vigor that the draft put up a little eddy of dust and scurried a leaf across the ground of the greenhouse. His was a demonstration of how to say boo to the boss. Or to an acquaintance with superior airs. A little cunning, a little finesse, a second of impetuous courage, and the moral victory is won. No question of pursuing the joke any further. Let her simmer in vanity-wounded fury. He would stump off. He had no wish for a brawl. He would leave her to ruminate upon her indignity. And I watched him plod away through the doorway, a cumbersome, happy drake . . . pad, pad, pad, until he reached the camellia bush opposite the packing shed which, for the time being, was his favorite resting place. He fluffed his feathers and settled down to wait. How would she behave when next she saw him?

I observed, after the attack, how Lama concurred with Paul Gallico's cat comment: "When in doubt, wash!" Lama washed in an exaggerated, busy fashion as if panic had seized her because the Queen was paying a visit, and her only dress was suddenly dirty. Lick, lick, lick; the vigorous action was aimed to cover up her enormous embarrassment. She had been caught napping. The ponderous yokel had nipped her. And her confusion, her reaction to the insult, the flash of fear in being so suddenly awakened, had been witnessed. No one, certainly not a cat, likes to be seen to be foolish. She was suffering the penalty of accepting civilization. In the old days she could react to danger, real or apparent, with all the flamboyance of someone on the lone trail and no one would know if sometimes the panic was misplaced. But this role she had chosen, this acceptance of the lush life, demanded that she could be laughed at if the situation deserved it.

Lama washed. And when she realized that her deceptive effort was making me smile, she got up and went over to one of the wooden trestles we had in the greenhouse, and elaborately began using it as a scratching board. All she was doing was giving herself time to think, to recover her composure and to work out her next move.

And as it happens her next move was predictable. She stopped her clawing, sauntered apparently unconcernedly out of the greenhouse, then suddenly went on the alert.

She was pretending she had heard a mouse in the grass.

One early afternoon that winter, not long before Christmas, we lost Lama down a badger hole. She had gone down badger holes before, indeed she was fascinated by badger holes, and so we ought to have learned our lesson. We hadn't, and there came a moment when we thought we would never see her again.

Jeannie and I had gone on a stroll around our daffodil meadows, and Lama had chosen to accompany us. I never found taking Lama for a walk a particularly peaceful experience. There are so many delays. There I am walking happily along, and suddenly I am told by piercing jungle meows that I am going too fast. I am not. I am deliberately dawdling so as not to rush her, and yet for some reason of her own, just to assert her authority perhaps, she bellows her protest and I have to stop. She then trots fast toward me, takes no notice when she reaches me, and scampers quickly ahead. Then she waits for me to catch up with her, waits behind after I have done so and performs the same rigmarole all over again. Sick humor on her part, for she makes her meows so heartrending that I am forced to believe she was really distressed. I was a fool to do so.

The meadows Jeannie and I were walking among were those we called the Far Meadows. They were beneath an old cairn, ancient meadows which probably had been used for one crop or another for centuries. A great place for adders, it was said. Never put your coat down on the ground, we had been warned. A man once did so, picked up the jacket at the end of his day's work, put his arm down a sleeve, and the adder nipped him.

It is joyous to look at the meadows when the green sheaves of the daffodils are first bursting the soil. Bed upon bed of them, each brimming with hope for us who depend upon them for our livelihood. And part of the fun, sometimes the disappointment, of the stroll is for me to bend down and to pinch with my fingers the collar of the bulbs. Green leaves may be growing but this does not mean that flowers will follow; and you learn to feel whether or not a bud is on the way, and if you have pinched a number of them, spaced here and there in different beds, you come to know long before the daffodil harvest begins whether or not it is going to be successful.

There are words of mine still floating on Minack cliffs. Some belong to one season, some to another.

"Jeannie! There are no buds at all. None at all It's going to be a terrible season."

"Let's not be overconfident . . . but I believe there are more buds this year than I've ever known before."

"I'm nervous, Jeannie. There seem to be plenty of Obs, but the Mags seem terribly light."

Jeannie and I have so many times looked at the meadows, and seen superimposed upon them our bank statement.

That year was the last in which we grew flowers especially for our Cornish posies. Of all the flowers we have ever grown, I think those which ended up mixed in the posies were our favorites. For the posies were so exquisitely arranged by Jeannie, Jane and Shelagh that each bloom therein was a jewel, different from its neighbor. We had forget-me-nots in a greenhouse, long rows of orange marigolds in a field near the wood, freesias in another greenhouse, polyanthus, brightly colored anemones, Beauty of Nice winter flowering stocks and seldom less than an acre of wallflowers. And if you had been there after the three of them had been bunching all day, and saw on the shelves row upon row of the posies, each in a jam jar of water, close together, filling the packing shed with spring, a kaleidoscope of color, then you would have said to yourself as we have done so many times: this is the sight to make the cynic happy.

I remember, or perhaps I comfort myself by remembering, that once upon a time people had the luxury of doing a job they enjoyed, took pride in its craftsmanship and earned enough to cover their expenses. We found with our posies that this did not occur. When we first sent them to market our salesman told us they were the sensation of Covent Garden, and that he could take as many as we could send. CORNISH POSIES from TANGYE, ST. BURYAN, were asked for by every important flower shop in London. And so we expanded, and grew more of all the necessary flowers, and worked harder. Yet, as seasons went by, the prices for our posies became lower; and then one day our eyes were opened when someone told us what had happened. The flower shops had found it cheaper to make up posies on the premises. They bought the various flowers separately on the market, then fashioned the CORNISH POSIES themselves.

We had Obvallaris in the Far Meadows, and these too went into the posies during their flowering time. Obvallaris—such a dull, ugly name hiding the exquisite little daffodils which look like miniature King Alfreds. They were ideal for the posies, but sent away in bunches on their own they could not compete in the market with the fashionable varieties. There were five of these small meadows of Obvallaris, and one of Scilly Whites; and they all peered downward toward the sea. Heaven knows how long the Scilly Whites had lain in that meadow, thirty or forty years perhaps, but they still bloomed their white clusters of flowers, reaching you with scent that rejoices with hope. Of course Scilly Whites are early flowering, and as the name obviously suggests, it is the Isles of Scilly which grow them earliest and best. Sometimes we ourselves had them in bloom before Christmas but on this occasion, when Lama was accompanying us on our walk, the season was a late one; there was no chance of a stem scenting the cottage at Christmas.

All around these meadows was uncouth

country of bracken and boulders, of flamboyant grasses and ominous brambles, of quickthorn and sharply pricking gorse, of the sense of the constant fall to the massive rocks and sea below. All these things wrapped me, when I stood among them, with the knowledge that here was reality. For here too were the trampled paths of the foxes and badgers; and if you stand on one of those paths, then realize that they have been used for centuries, you are a tough, unimaginative soul if you do not feel humbled.

It seemed that Lama knew these paths in the Far Meadows intimately. She scampered up the beaten, foot-wide tracks as if they were giving her a welcome. She crouched on the lip of a stone hedge where a track led from one meadow to another, and when I approached she raced away again. She seemed to be at home. There were no loud protesting meows as occurred when we took her on an ordinary walk. She behaved as if she had gone wild again.

There was a well-trodden track which led across the Scilly White meadow, the green spears of the Scilly Whites bent and bruised, stunted and curling, no time for them to become upright before the pads of badgers crushed them. In this age when the cool calculations of the accountant advise the removal of sentiment from any business, the badgers on our cliffs should have been removed. They do not respect our daffodils. They dig among them if they so desire. If we plant on a piece of ground across which for centuries they have been accustomed to plod, the gesture of man will not stop them from continuing to plod. It's their land, not ours. We are the interlopers. In the end the damage they do does not amount to much.

But enough, perhaps, for the apostles of logic to argue that it is illogical to allow them to continue to roam these glorious, secret, untamed cliffs where we try to earn a living.

Suddenly Lama darted along this track, then disappeared into the cavern of undergrowth at the other end of the meadow.

"Lama!" called Jeannie, "where are you going?"

I myself knew very well.

"Lama!" I shouted, "come back!"

There was a splendid badger set among the undergrowth into which Lama had disappeared, and the undergrowth mainly consisted of a forest of blackthorn. Have you ever crawled on the ground where blackthorn grows? All the growth of the blackthorn is at the top of its prickly wooden stem, and so when badgers make their home among blackthorn, their paths crisscross below as they do in the open. They did here, and I was soon to sample them.

"There's not a sign of her."

I had gone down on my knees and was staring into the gloom, and when my eyes became accustomed to it, I noticed the scattering of dried twigs and clumps of bracken which were the old discarded bedding of the badgers. There it all was on well-pounded paths, slimy soil that never saw the light, pointing to journeys over the years. I sensed I was about to be exasperated. I also sensed that I was the witness of shadows. If I were about to be infuriated by a cat, I was also rewarded by the feeling of continuity in life.

"I can tell you where she's gone," I said.

"Where?"

"Down the largest badger hole I've ever seen."

This was not quite true. I had seen this hole before. It was one of the group of the set which covered several hundred square yards of the cliff. And Jeannie had always said that this set was one of the most desirable badger residences in the country. Well covered, with glorious views of the sea, and immune, it seemed, to human interference.

"Lama!"

The note in my voice had become sharper. It was two o'clock in the afternoon, and we had other things to do than to shout for Lama.

"Lama!"

This time it was Jeannie. She too had gone down on her knees; and there were the two of us, side by side, our backs to the Scilly Whites, growing irritable, at the mercy of a cat in a hole.

"You had better go down into it," said Jeannie.

"I can't go into the hole!"

"You can get into the undergrowth and put your hand down the hole. She's probably just inside."

The hole was only a few feet away but to get there I had to wriggle along the badger path flat on my tummy, the umbrella of blackthorn above me hiding the light, the musk scent of badgers around me; then I reached the entrance, and at the top of my voice I shouted again, "Lama."

The maddening thing about a situation like this can be the side irritations it produces. Jeannie and I, irritated by Lama, began to be irritated by each other. I heard her voice behind me.

"Don't shout!" she said, "you'll wake up the badgers and they'll be after her."

"Stuff and nonsense," I said, my mouth inches from the clammy soil. Then I added mercilessly, "They've probably eaten her already."

There was, needless to say, no response from Lama. Nor when I embraced the entrance, then stretched my arm at its full length down the hole, did my fingers touch any soft fur. Lama had disappeared.

I wriggled my way back to the Scilly Whites and said to Jeannie it would be a good idea if she took my place; and I would keep silent, and she could try the effects of her own dulcet tones. I watched her snake her way to the entrance.

"Lama!" I then heard, whispered, quite different from my own barrack-square tone. "Lama! Come on . . . we're waiting for you."

"Like hell we are," I murmured to myself, and I anticipated that Jeannie would blame her own failure to tempt response on my own brave shouts of "Lama!"

But I was quite wrong. She had also become angry with the cat. She waited for a few moments in the undergrowth, then backed herself out.

"The bread has to go in the oven. I must get back to the cottage."

I watched her go up the path past the cairn, then left to myself I waited a few minutes until I guessed she was well out of earshot. Then I let go; a series of "LAMA!" echoed around the cliffs.

I was quite aware that I had lost my temper, and my reason for doing so had its depths in my long-standing antipathy to cats. They were too independent, too selfish, too stupid . . . all these things I had been told about them. These views were inbred in me. I had been captured by Monty because he was an anchor at a critical time, but what did Lama mean to me? An hour had gone by, two hours . . . the rocks below were passing into shadow, etched by the foam, and we were wasting our time courting a cat—a wild, ungrateful cat, symbol of selfish individualism, and yet so dependent upon us that it would be miserable if we were not there to obey its commands. I was fed up with looking for it. If it were devoured by a mad badger or a hungry fox . . . well, it didn't matter as far as I was concerned. I was going.

I passed Jeannie on my way back to the cottage. The bread safely baked, she was returning with tempting morsels in a bag. Jeannie, the cat lover, had complete faith in bribery. It was now dark, and she carried a flashlight.

"So you're leaving Lama?"

"What else can I do? I've shouted myself hoarse."

"The last five percent. That's what counts."

"Oh, hell," I said, "don't sound so demanding. I've been on my hands and knees after that damned cat for hours; I don't care a damn if I never see her again."

"I'll go on my own."

"Yes, do." And I pounded away from her into the darkness.

I got back to the cottage, picked up a newspaper and angrily began to read it. The cat had put me in the wrong. The story had started so innocently, just a walk with no other intention except to relax. And now hours later it had ended up with friction between Jeannie and me. Perhaps I ought to go and have another look. I rustled the paper noisily. Yes, perhaps I *had* to have another look.

At that particular moment the cottage door opened. Jeannie came in and in her arms was Lama.

"I only had to call her," she said in a tone of victory, "and she came to me."

"Yes, yes," I said quickly though quietly, "just

shows your influence." Then I added vehemently, "But it was the food that got her out. Not you!"

"That's where you're wrong."

"Why?"

"Lama was sitting at the exact spot where you had been shouting."

D o you know," said Shelagh, bunching posies in the flower house, "that it is . . ."

"Yes, yes, I know, Shelagh. It is eight days to Christmas."

"Nine."

"All right, nine," I said.

"One could say, of course," Shelagh went on, smiling at the flowers she held in her hand, "that as we are halfway through the morning, today doesn't count. Then you would be right. Only eight days to Christmas."

"Agreed. Eight days."

Shelagh began this game as soon as a Christmas was over. And it went on throughout the year. Three hundred days, two hundred days, thirty, five . . . And the rest of us—Jane, myself and Jeannie— would bellow in mock horror: "Oh, Shelagh, don't remind us that the year is going so fast!"

Jeannie's mother and Angus were coming again. Jeannie's mother was like Shelagh; long before the rest of us were thinking of Christmas she would be writing kind letters asking, "What would Derek like?" Or to me: "What would Jean like?" Here was an example of prolonging the pleasure of giving. No last-minute gesture of salving of conscience. No extravagance to hide the fact that the receiver had been forgotten. This was a campaign, a considered assessment of hints given and observations made, and ending with all the anxiety that accompanies the edge of victory. Do you like it? Are you sure you like it? And if momentarily you are taken aback, surprised by the way your desires are interpreted by others, the force of goodwill behind the giving stirs you to thank. Wonderful! Fabulous! And sometimes you worry later whether the enthusiasm sounded empty.

One can be tedious about Christmas. One can, in fact, be so tedious that it becomes a bore. In this enlightened gimmick age, it is tedious to accept the idea that there can be one day in the year for which centuries demand goodwill; and so the excuse is made that it is too commercialized. That is true, of course. It is hopelessly commercialized. And yet this is still no reason to treat Christmas as an anachronism. For it will always be the time of old-fashioned kindness, of evidence of truth, of pure unselfishness and, quite often, of unexpected exultation. And so with these qualities as its armor, there is no cause for anyone to consider Christmas as a bore. It demands an effort. That's all.

My own effort has been at its frailest when I have been anticipating Christmas. On this occasion, for instance, I was irked by the prospect of what happens when someone stays at Minack. In spring and summer the close quarters are unimportant because of the season. In winter, at Christmas, there is an inclination for everyone to be on top of each other; and that only means Jeannie and me, and the guest. The guest room, the converted chicken house, is between the sitting room and the bathroom, and with no communication, as a result, with our bedroom. So my toothpaste and my razor lodge for the duration of a visit in congested quarters around the kitchen sink. My clothes too are unobtainable. I do not know where my shoes have been hidden. I yell for socks. I find myself circulating in our tiny bedroom trying to dress, trying to undress. It has been the anticipation of these minor inconveniences that have demanded the effort on my part. They have loomed far larger than reality. The cold winds and early falling darkness magnify the effort I have to make.

A cat, one can well argue, has no right at all to object to momentary dislocation of its habits. Lama, of course, could not worry herself unnecessarily beforehand in the way that I did. She treated the situation as it came, and often she has caused Jeannie and myself much embarrassment by her rudeness. If, for instance, it is beyond her usual bedtime she will stamp up and down in front of the offending visitor as he sits on the sofa discoursing on some matter of great interest; and although the effect on the visitor may be nil, it results in Jeannie and I looking at each other, half laughing, and making us lose the thread of the discussion.

Lama was, of course, now acclimatized to Angus. There was no special friendship but there had been other visits since the first Christmas, and a toleration toward each other had been achieved. Lama clearly would much prefer his absence but, once he had arrived and was clearly at Minack to stay for a while, the truth had better be faced. She would not gain anything by attack.

There was, however, to be another visitor this Christmas, and I myself was apprehensive about this visitor. Jeannie, because she has always been bolder than me, pooh-poohed the idea that any risks were going to be taken. And although I was ready to agree with her, I remained irritated that even the prospect of a risk should have to exist at a time when minds should be at ease. The visitor was to be an Alsatian.

Tara, however, was a very old Alsatian. She belonged to my Cousin Carol, who had a house at Nanquidno near the old mining town of St. Just, five miles from Minack. I had been with him when he first had seen the house, and seldom could a possible new home have been first seen under gloomier circumstances. A thick fog blew up the valley from the sea, so thick that I could not see the pond in the garden in front of the house. Nor see the solid chimneys prodding from the roof. And a wall I saw looming in the grayness proved later to be a high hedge. It was no day to choose a house. No day even to sense its possibilities. My cousin Carol, however, thought otherwise. His Cornish ancestry provided him with the instinct that here was the home of his dreams. "This is it, Tara old girl," I heard him say barely twenty minutes after arriving there, "this is going to be our home." He was a bachelor with an apartment in London, and it took him a long time to break away from his London life. Now, alone, he was now about to spend his first Christmas in Cornwall.

"You must come for Christmas dinner!" said Jeannie. "Come any day, any time, over the holiday!"

"What about Tara?"

"She too, of course," said Jeannie, before I had time to interrupt.

Tara, when I first knew her, was a creature of splendor even in the midst of her breed. Her black marks against the silver sand of her coat, the magnificent head, the glorious way she stood when alert, with ears pricked and intelligent eyes staring at the mystery; all these qualities shone from her, sharing the common denominator of all things with fine breeding. And she was placid too; there was never any question of her becoming over-excited in moments of stress. She was devoted to Carol, and when one thought of him, one also thought of Tara.

But now she was old. She was like a woman renowned once for her great beauty. The splendor was still to be observed, but it was obscured by a lack of luster, a heaviness, a slow and jerky way of moving, eyes that were dull—all the sad accouterments of age. She was also an invalid, and Carol was the permanent nurse. I am certain many people must have considered it ludicrous the way he looked after her. Special pills, special diet, all the inconveniences of semi-illness. And yet it was obvious to anyone that both of them were content.

It was, as it happens, Carol's nature to look after other people. He had had, all his life, the opportunity and the time to be kind in a practical fashion, one of those old-fashioned Samaritans who put themselves to great inconvenience in order to give pleasure to others. He was small and rotund and bouncy; and although when I was a child he was a grown man, he now appeared to be ageless. He set out to be kind and corralled happiness around him. Only the mean-minded could dislike him. He was humorous, but the humor was

153

often derived from his vagueness. He could never, for instance, remember people's names. He would invite a few friends to his house, then flounder in confusion as he tried to introduce them to each other. A comical sight, but his charm easily overcame any embarrassment. He enjoyed life.

My concern about Tara coming for Christmas was due partly to her condition, a selfish reaction on my part that too much fuss might have to be made of her. And this was allied to my doubts as to how Lama and Angus might behave. It was going to be crowded in the cottage. Tara might possess a placid nature when she was treated like a queen on her own, but she might object to sharing the attention with a cat and a Scottie. One snap and there would be bedlam. And it all seemed so unfair to Lama. Her good manners would be tested to the utmost. No cat could be expected to *enjoy* entertaining a Scottie and an Alsatian, and so I think she had every right to complain that we were taking her good nature for granted. After all, two years ago she had been a wild cat.

If she were provoked, if she were annoyed by the invasion of strangers, there might be every justification for her to say to herself, "I'm off!"

In the afternoon of the day before Christmas Eve, Lama arranged herself on my lap. Up to that moment I had been busy. I had promised Jeannie, for instance, to clear my desk, and there were other tasks on my schedule. Then, in a moment of laziness, I sat down on the sofa to glance at the headlines, no intention to avoid my responsibilities. But there on my knees was Lama.

She began to purr. It was not one of those ordinary purrs which one must admit are two a penny in any normal cat-happy circumstances. It was a roar—a glorious anthem praising to the heavens that she was the favored one to live alone with us inside the cottage at Minack. It was a great burst of Christmas wishes. An expression of innocent delight that the three of us were together. And as I listened to her, drawing a finger up and down her black silky back, guilty about the things I should be doing but hypnotically relaxed by the sound of her, I heard a car draw up outside, then footsteps coming to the door.

It is always a challenge if duty demands that you remove a contented cat from your lap. Insensitive people throw them to the floor without more ado. Others pray it will make its decision on its own. I heard the knock, thankfully saw Lama leap away from me, got up and went to open the door.

It was Mr. Murley of Lamorna Post Office. Our letters came from St. Buryan, our telegrams from Lamorna. The telegram he gave me read:

> May I spend Christmas with you unless family gathering.
> Jack.

I hadn't seen him in years. I thought he was in America.

Jackie Broadbent was a legendary figure in the world of newspapermen—partly because of his professionalism, but also as a result of his loyalty to his friends. In a world where daggers are perpetually being sharpened, he risked his own career time and again by supporting an out-of-favor colleague. It was, therefore, a question of the fates mocking him that he should himself have been prematurely retired.

He was a lovable, eccentric character who was frequently the despair of his friends because he would pursue routes which had no end. He was an idealist; and if his heart warmed toward someone or if ethics were at stake, he became a rock in their defense. He was shrewd. His political predictions, both home and international, were often dismissed at the time as too fanciful, yet the years have proved their accuracy. He was endearingly generous in his hospitality. When my mother presented Jeannie at Court, he phoned me a few days before and said he guessed we would want to celebrate when it was all over; and as his apartment was a short distance from the palace, he would like to give us a party. He greeted my mother ebulliently: "A special magnum of Bollinger for you, ma'am,"—ladies of all ages were addressed as ma'am—"in honor of you presenting the prettiest girl of them all at Court today!" And for Jeannie he had a bouquet of pink roses.

He was, despite his many friends, a lonely man. His marriage had gone astray many years before I first knew him, and his life had become a perpetual search for a permanent home. Yet, because of the wandering character of his profession, he lived in hotels and furnished apartments, and so he would soothe himself for having to put up with these temporary surroundings by assuring those who were listening: "You wait for this time next year. I'll have a house of my own by then, and all my furniture and books will be out of storage." Unfortunately each year would materialize and find Jackie going on living in the same transient way. So it was this year. He had been pensioned off, but he still had no permanent home.

"Well," I said, picking up the telegram again after Jeannie had returned, "what do we do?"

"It's a question of where we could put him."

"He could sleep on a camp bed in the flower house."

"He likes his comforts."

"The main thing is how your mother would react."

"She's always been fond of him."

I had a hunch we should invite him whatever the domestic difficulties. These, I believed, would solve themselves when helped by the gusto of the occasion; but this, of course, was a man's view. Jeannie, after all, was going to do all the work.

"Say yes," Jeannie said.

"You're sure?"

"Of course. I've the same hunch as you have."

157

"I wonder why. He'd be self-sufficient without us."

"Isn't that the answer? Because he *would* be self-sufficient, we're touched that he wants to come all the way to Minack. And perhaps we're apprehensive because of this."

I reflect, sometimes, that omission rather than action has provided me with my chief regrets. There is a wilderness about omission. An instant flicks past your eyes demanding acknowledgment, and yet the mind fails to recognize it. There it is, an opportunity with all the shine on it yearning to beckon you, all your desires contained therein, all your striving on the edge of being rewarded, and yet your senses at this very moment of challenge betray you and make you fumble, and leave you with the hunger of what might have been.

When Jeannie's mother arrived we broke the news.

"Jackie Broadbent is coming. I hope you don't mind."

"It'll do him good."

The reply was unexpected, and practical, and refreshing. And if it were short, this was compensated in a few moments when she added, "What a true friend he has been to you both!"

"We'd have sent a wire stopping him if you'd said you wanted to be on your own."

"Nonsense."

There seemed now to be no irking doubt about this Christmas.

I soon realized, however, that Lama had ideas about being a killjoy. She had watched the preparations suspiciously. She had been lifted off the bed in the spare room to make way for the aired sheets and blankets, and had been dumped on the floor half asleep. She had observed the Christmas tree carried into the sitting room, and had been intrigued by the elaborate fuss that Jeannie had made of it, and she did not understand why, when she put out a paw to play with a bauble on a lower branch, she was firmly told to stop. Why this sudden discipline? And why all this brisk efficiency replacing the normally slow-moving, haphazard routine? She went into the flower house and looked for the pile of white packing paper on which it was so cozy to curl and doze, and found it gone. There was a surprising neatness about the shelves. And how was it that the gap in the corner beneath the desk, which had been such a lucrative source of mice, had been blocked up? She had jumped on the camp bed (the same camp bed that Jeannie's father had used in the First World War) and jumped off again quickly. Obviously it was not up to her standard of comfort, but why was it there?

I do not know why it was that this Christmas Lama had hoped to be alone. But there is little doubt that she did. Perhaps it was that it had at last penetrated into her secret animal depths that she had found a home; and now, no longer an outsider, she was jealous of anything or anyone that appeared to threaten her security. She was certainly on guard. And when I remember the wild dangerous time of her kittenhood, I suppose there was reason for her to fear that the comfortable pace of her life was about to be taken away from her.

Anyhow, she was about to take on the role of the killjoy. But there was no ruthless person at Minack who would ask *her* to leave.

The east wind blew on Christmas Day, scything across the sea from the Lizard hidden in gloom. The black easterly. It slashed into our cliff, burning the meadows with the salt which came with it, tearing up the valley to the cottage, cutting into the cracks of window frames, rushing through the wood, screeching a message that bitter cold weather was upon us. And when Lama asked to be let out, and I opened the door and she gaily stepped outside, she suddenly stopped when her whiskers met the wind. "Good gracious, no," she seemed to say to herself, "*much* too cold," and immediately reversed into the cottage.

I heard Jeannie's mother call to me from the spare room: "Merry Christmas!"

"Merry Christmas!" I replied. "Did you have a good sleep?"

Jeannie was with her and I listened to the murmur of their voices, and guessed they had already exchanged gifts. They were always in such a hurry, it seemed to me, and I used to tease them by saying they were greedy. I liked to linger over present opening. I used to madden Jeannie by partly unwrapping a present, then getting up and filling and lighting a pipe and walking about the room before settling down again to the business of discovering what surprise awaited me. I wanted to prolong a pleasure which had taken so long to prepare.

Angus scampered in from the spare room, rushing up to me, then stopping at my feet, pushing his muzzle into my shoes, brown eyes glancing up at me, a gentle, hesitant whoof asking me to play. I pretended a savage kick at him, and he ran away, turned full circle, spread wide his front paws and made again his token whoof. He had been to an elegant dog parlor before he set off on his holiday, and his coat had been trimmed to perfection. He looked particularly handsome. His loquacious stumpy tail, his shiny black coat, the dashing style of his whiskers and beard, proclaimed him as an aristocrat of his breed; and there he was turning full circle again, then pouncing at my shoes and whoofing, and demanding a game which meant a chase up and down the room, a hide-and-seek between tables and chairs, an uproarious dog game of subtle give and take . . . when suddenly I became aware of a presence. Lama, with all the silent majesty of a sphinx, tip of tail flicking, was gazing at us. Not inquisitively. You had only to see her eyes. She was enraged.

I broke off from my toying with Angus and courted her. She was sitting, with restrained fury, on the sofa. There was no comfort in fooling myself by thinking she was indulging in a feline pretense. Her back was straight, like Queen Victoria, and she was burning into the room the message: this is such an intolerable insult to my dignity that I can never forgive it. How dare you play with Angus in front of me!

I forthwith pushed Angus back into the spare room. No touchiness on his part. The game was over. He solidly, obediently returned to his rug. No complications at all. But Lama . . . I tried to lure her into being amused by poking a finger at her. I would gladly have accepted a nip from sharp teeth or a bash from a paw . . . but nothing. Here was a clear example of wounded vanity. No sycophancy from her. She was going to teach me a lesson that I must not take her good nature for granted.

She fell, of course, for my blandishments in the end. Or rather to Jeannie's. "Come on, Lama," she called cheerfully, after I had explained what had happened, "something special for you this morning." And she held a saucer an inch above her little black nose. Aromas! Glorious greed! Let us forget what has happened! There, on the saucer, were the turkey giblets.

It was now my job to take Jackie Broadbent his morning tea. He had arrived in the late afternoon of Christmas Eve, and with him he had brought a leather valise in which were his clothes for the stay, several half bottles of champagne and, carefully wrapped in waxed paper, a plucked pheasant.

There is a hazard about having a stove in the sitting room: Jeannie is watched. We have had guests who, instead of responding to my efforts to divert them, have preferred well-meaningly to give Jeannie advice—a tendency, due perhaps to her gentleness—to influence her to cook *their* way, not hers. There are those who interfere with sauces. I have seen Jeannie happily stirring a long prepared sauce, then heard someone suggest she should add this or that to it, for it seems the sight of her at work, ever dodging our outstretched legs as we sip our drinks, impels good-natured interference. She is so natural, so easy as she goes about her business, that people feel relaxed enough to comment.

It is true that Jeannie usually remains firm. It is also true that she is usually left in peace. But, in any case, it is always astonishing to me how she so serenely, so without fuss, can conduct her preparations so calmly in front of the frivolous rest of us.

Jackie Broadbent's pheasant provided such frivolity. It was a meager bird, already high, and certainly ready to be eaten, so Jeannie decided to cook it right away for dinner.

"Cook it fast in a very hot oven," demanded Jackie.

162

"Cook it slowly," said Jeannie.

"Stuff it with mushrooms and butter," urged Jackie.

"A pheasant shouldn't be stuffed," answered Jeannie.

"Don't forget wafer-thin potatoes, ma'am."

"I agree."

"Agree, ma'am? Agree? Where's the champagne?"

He fancied himself as a cook and as a gourmet. He was one of those cooks who take elaborate care to preserve the stock from his cooking, the expert's base for another dish, and then finds he has kept it so long that it is bad when he needs it.

A cork popped.

"Anyhow," I said, watching the glasses being filled and at the same time thinking of tomorrow's turkey, "this pheasant is a useful trial run over the target." Nobody heard me. Toasts were being drunk. All the wild laughter of easy companionship filled the cottage.

But this was one occasion when Jeannie surrendered the task of cooking. Jackie in due course said the pheasant was ready.

It was the worst cooked pheasant I have ever had.

But it had served its purpose. Jeannie now knew she had to be on her own when she cooked the Christmas dinner.

At midday my cousin Carol arrived from his home near St. Just, holding a red and green knitted tea cozy in his arms. He took great enjoyment from making small incidents into dramas and I sensed that this was one of them. He was highly excited.

"Merry Christmas! Merry Christmas!" Then, the formality over, he hastily added, "I have a surprise for you. Where's Jeannie?"

"But you've given us your presents."

"Ah," he said, still standing in the doorway, "I've got something else."

"Jeannie," I called, "Carol's here with a mystery!" Then turning to him: "We're having the turkey for dinner. Only cold meat for lunch."

Before disclosing the purpose of the tea cozy he wanted a full audience, so he also required the presence of Jeannie's mother and Jackie. Fortunately the three of them appeared from the spare room together.

I watched the delight on Carol's face. Here was the big moment, Harlequin's triumph. The audience titillated into expectation, the mystery still in his keeping; all that was now required was the exact timing of its disclosure.

"Carol," I said gently, "there is a bitter east wind, you're still standing at the door . . . and the sitting room will soon be a refrigerator."

"All right, all right," he said jokingly, and advanced into the cottage, the tea cozy cradled in his arms. Then, as I quickly shut the door, he paused for a second in the middle of the room, looked round at our faces and declared with the dramatic effect of a magician:

"I hold in this tea cozy . . . a blackbird!"

He achieved, without doubt, his triumph. We imagined, I think, that it was to be a gimmick joke, some idiotic foolery which, unless one was in the mood of carnival, deserved only forced laughter. This was indeed unexpected, and there was immediate consternation from Jeannie.

"Here, look at it," said Carol.

Apparently he had been sitting in the ground-floor room of his Nanquidno house when there was a bang on the window. He looked up and was in time to see a bird fall to the ground. He rushed out and found a blackbird stunned into lifelessness.

"The only idea I had," he explained, "was that I must keep it warm. So I tucked it into this tea cozy, got Tara into the car and rushed over."

Jeannie had dealt with many stunned birds before. They sometimes, alas, fly into the clear glass of our greenhouses, especially in the spring when the young are learning to fly. And she has formed a procedure which is infallible in bringing them back to consciousness and healing them, provided no organic damage has been done. She always keeps ready a concoction called Exultation of Flowers, a medicine which comes from the Scottish Highlands, a secret mixture containing the juices from a wide variety of flowers. She opens the beak of the bird, puts a drop or two down its throat and within a few seconds it begins to revive.

And so this was how she treated Carol's blackbird. But the effect on it was so remarkable that within a minute or so it started to struggle, then a moment later escaped from her hand, flew around the room and landed on top of the Christmas tree. It was another five minutes before she managed to catch it again, and she did so when it perched on the mistletoe on the porch. It was easy then, and she opened the door and let it fly out, and for a long time afterward a blackbird with a splendid yellow beak haunted the bird feeder. Clougy, we called it, after the name of Carol's home.

Lama, at the time, was curled on our bed, and she chose to wake up, stretch herself and come into the sitting room at the moment Carol was entering with Tara. The old lady looked at her as if she were saying: "Don't worry, little cat. I'm much too old to cause you any worry." Such condescending good nature would have been effective had Lama been frightened. She was not. It was obvious to us that her only emotion was suspicion. First Angus, now this huge Alsatian. She also observed that Jeannie and I had made an extravagant fuss over the dog; and out of the corner of my eye I caught a dirty look from her, and felt sure she was thinking, Traitor!

But Tara was indeed remarkable. She was now nearly fourteen years old, and so good tempered, so beautiful to look at, that it would be impossible not to admire her; and part of this admiration was due to her owner who never inflicted her on others. She might be very old. She might need special attention. But in one of those uncanny relationships between man and beast, they understood they must share the pain with each other. The outsiders could never understand. Thus, much better to be silent and not try to persuade them. For Tara had often been to Minack but had remained, at Carol's insistence, in his car. Never before had she faced Lama inside her own home.

It was now that Angus scampered in from the spare room, took one look at Tara and scampered back again. Meanwhile Lama had moved to beneath my desk and was crouched there, scowling. I felt certain we were in for trouble. There was Tara spreading herself in the center of the room, Angus becoming excited, and the owner of the premises loathing them both.

"Don't you think," I asked nervously, "that we ought to keep them separated?"

Nobody heard me. Nobody wanted to hear me. Jeannie and her mother were perfectly confident. I was only a fusspot. And as for the other two, they were at the sideboard. Jackie was opening the champagne.

There was no trouble. There was only a certain unease. Tara and Angus tolerated each other; Lama did not attack either of them. But Lama, I well knew, was thoroughly irritated. No room on the sofa, too much noise, Angus nosing at her plate, Tara enveloping the space, *her* space, in front of the electric fire, and a casual attitude from Jeannie and me. We didn't mean to be casual, we were just enjoying ourselves.

And Lama displayed her irritation throughout the afternoon in a most effective way.

"Lama, what *are* you up to?"

I knew, of course, very well. She was at the

window asking to be let out, three minutes after being let in, because she was at a loss to know what to do with herself. Outside much too cold, inside the role of the unwilling hostess.

One moment hypnotizing me with amber eyes through the glass, the next impelling me by a vigorous swishing of her tail to let her out again. It was a shrewd way of emphasizing her displeasure that routine had been disrupted.

Dusk fell early that Christmas Day, darkened by the weather across the bay toward the Lizard. There was the bitter wind, and the huge bank of fog and gloom hiding the distant land, and in contrast the gray heaving sea seemed to have surprisingly white horses, gay to look at, dashing at each other, bursting into spray, regrouping together and advancing in a long line, this ribbon of white which dissolved so soon into the gray, rough mass which was its home. Snow was coming, I felt sure, and if it didn't arrive tonight it would be with us in the morning. There was a menacing cruelty outside the cottage, and I knew that if we had been alone, without diversions, Jeannie and I would have been pacing the meadows, vacantly, uselessly, anticipating disaster, assessing in our minds that there would be no flowers for the posies if snow came.

It was time to shut up Boris, and this time I opened the door and went out with Lama, then down the path across the grass by the greenhouse and into the wood. There in the old chicken house, the size of a palace as far as Boris was concerned, room for thirty Muscovy drakes not one, sat Boris on his perch craning his neck forward and gently hissing. "Good night, Boris," I said, and locked the door. He was such an imperious character that one felt in duty bound to say the words, "good night";

sometimes when I had absentmindedly forgotten to do so, I used foolishly to return and shout the words through the door. As if it were a talisman of good luck to wish him good night.

I had turned and was on my way back to the cottage when, by the entrance of the flower house, I saw a shadow at my feet and there was Lama. I picked her up and began to carry her up to the door. I had not gone far before she began to struggle and to squeak, like the noise of a high note on an out-of-tune violin. "Lama," I said, "you *are* unsociable." I put her on the ground and saw her dash back down the path, then disappear around the corner. She's gone into the old stables, I said to myself, out of the wind.

Inside the cottage was the quiet time of Christmas. Too much at lunch had been caught up by tea; and there was the pause, the interval in which the hilarious gaiety of lunchtime impatiently awaits the start of the preliminaries before dinner. Jackie was at my desk reading a book like a school-boy, hands over ears. Jeannie's mother sat on the sofa knitting a sweater for Jeannie's sister, talking to my cousin Carol beside her, and eyeing Jeannie at the pantry. Jeannie was preparing the turkey.

She followed a Scottish recipe. She stuffed the turkey, made a dough of flour and water, rolled it out an inch thick, covered the turkey with fat bacon and butter, then wrapped the dough around it like a blanket: not a centimeter of the turkey visible. Then the turkey went into the oven for three hours, after which the dough casing was easily lifted off, and the turkey basted and left to brown for half an hour. This was her proven way of doing it.

"Keep Jackie out of the way," she murmured to me.

169

"I overheard that, ma'am."

"Thought you were reading, Jackie."

"No, ma'am."

"It was that pheasant, Jackie. We don't want the turkey like the pheasant."

"No, ma'am."

When Jackie was contrite, one wasn't sure whether he was laughing or not.

"We'll go down to the pub," I said, "then we'll all be out of your way, Jeannie."

"And Carol," she said, "can have the job of seeing you're back by eight."

We were back punctually at eight. We came back and found the cottage lit by candlelight, the Christmas tree in its corner sparkling its baubles, shadows touching the white, rough walls making them appear like crumpled cloth, a single candle in the old baking oven lighting the dome of patchwork stones, the outline of holly in odd places and staring down at us softly from the wall on the way to the spare room was Jeannie's wistful, gentle portrait by Kanelba.

Here was the setting, the everlasting setting of Christmas; unabashed affection for each other, age no hindrance, the intellect momentarily defeated and emotion for the time being supreme, hard men kind, the mean pushed to display generosity, jealousy in abeyance, greed despicable, heightened awareness toward those you love, tenderness toward those taken for granted. This was the ancient shine which suffused the cottage as we laughed and rejoiced and shouted our way through Christmas dinner.

"To Jeannie's mother!"

"To Jeannie!"

"To Carol!"

"To Jackie!"

It was at that moment that my own toast was about to be proposed . . . that I remembered Lama. I had not seen her since I put Boris to bed. I had ignored her existence. First the pub, then our wonderful dinner, and we had all forgotten her. Dogs had been cared for; the hostess had been ignored.

I suddenly, without explanation, rushed to the door.

"Where are you going?"

"Wait," I said, "until I come back!"

"Why?" asked Jeannie.

"I have to find Lama."

I paused and looked at Jeannie. She was laughing.

"Why laugh?" I asked doubtfully, a sixth sense warning me that I was making a fool of myself.

"Idiot!" she said. "I brought her in long ago. She's on the bed deep in a turkey sleep!"

I quickly recovered my composure and went back to my seat. Of course I should have known about Jeannie. Busy as she was, gay as the rest of us, she would have remembered.

I picked up my glass and raised it toward her, smiling.

"To Lama!" I said.

"To Lama!" called everyone else.

At this moment, like an actress making an entrance, she appeared from the bedroom, plump, a sleepy, benign little black cat. She gazed around for a second, then tucking her head into her chest, she collapsed and rolled on her back on the carpet.

She was content.

She too had been captured by the Christmas spirit.

One lovely October morning Lama had come for
a stroll with me, treating it, as usual, as an affair
of fits and starts. She had been at Minack for over
six years and there was now no evidence that she
had ever been a wild cat. Rough edges had been
smoothed. Subtle tricks of domestic cats had been
acquired. And quite clearly she seemed to think
that she was in a catlike heaven where no one ever
meant any harm to each other. No longer was she
on guard for danger every second. She was serene.
She loved everyone and everything. Indeed, her
supreme confidence, her belief that you only have
to offer goodwill for goodwill to be offered in return
often caused us anxiety. I saw her once lying in the
lane beside the stream, while on the other side of
the stream sat a fox cub. Lama looked around and
saw it, then nonchalantly got up and walked toward it. The cub fled.

Our principal concern was her attitude toward
the donkeys. We had acquired Penny, the mother,
by chance. She was black with gray underbelly,
and with a very handsome head; but when we first
saw her in a field adjacent to a pub near Redruth,

172

she looked moth-eaten, bare patches on her coat, elongated hooves like Dutch clogs and an appeal in her eyes which Jeannie interpreted as, "Buy me, please." The publican, who was a dealer in horses and donkeys, and who had only quartered Penny for a few days or so, then gave us a further piece of information. Penny was in foal, and the foal was expected within a month. "Two donkeys for one!" he had laughed. I had gone out for a quiet drink, but when I returned to Minack, Penny was in the back of the Land Rover.

The foal was born according to schedule. He arrived in a deluge of rain on a flat stone in the big field, and he was, of course, enchanting. He was perky and vulnerable, toylike and laughable. He had a pretty head with huge ears like old-fashioned driving gloves, fluffy brown coat, a short box of a body on spindly legs and a look in his eyes that made me smile when I first saw it. He looked so gay. He was so ridiculously happy, and then suddenly, perhaps due to his surprise at seeing us, he lost his balance and collapsed on the ground. Tiny hooves tried to get a grip on the grass, then he gave a lurch and he was upright again. A slight loss of confidence, a sense of indignity, of having made a fool of himself, and then once again he looked mischievous. We called him Fred.

Fred was now three years old. For the first two years of his life he was like a prince with an endless number of courtiers. Children came hurrying down the lane with lumps of sugar and carrots, a party was held for him on his first birthday, cameras were constantly pointing at him, extravagant praises were showered upon him, faces of grownups melted at the sight of him, adulation, the glory of a child film star, innocence, flattery, hardly a day passing without some admirer paying court to him. He reveled in it, and he responded by gently allowing small arms to be flung around his neck and showing no impatience when his ears were stroked and his soft nose hugged. As far as he was concerned this attention would go on forever, but there came the awful moment of truth: a visitor looked at the now gawky teen-ager of a donkey and said, "I prefer the other one." Penny had come into her own again!

Penny was certainly a beautiful donkey with a coat which was now shiny black, and a head which, when alerted, reminded one of an Arab pony. She was placid; when the children came to see Fred, it was Penny who gave them their rides. We would lead her up and down the field, sometimes one sometimes two on her back, while Fred frisked beside her. She was resigned to her duty to give pleasure, and indeed an attitude of resignation was a feature of Penny for a long while after her arrival at Minack. It was as if she could not make herself believe it to be true that she had at last found a permanent home. She had been for so long an itinerant donkey—first in Ireland then in this country, receiving affection only so long as it suited her owner—that she seemed to be daily waiting for her next move. Then it gradually dawned on her that she was here to stay, and that Fred was to stay too; and she began to acquire some of Fred's gaiety.

Lama's behavior toward them was foolhardy.

"Look at Lama!" I had shouted in fright a day or two after Penny's arrival at Minack. Penny, in the middle of a meadow, was peacefully munching the grass, and Lama was gently rubbing herself against a hind leg, treating it as if it were a post.

Penny's detachment on this occasion, her apparent acceptance of a cat behaving in such a familiar fashion, led Lama to believe that she would always be welcome. Here was an opportunity for Lama to display the trust she possessed in such abundance. Why should she worry about a donkey's kick? Or being stepped on by a heavy hoof? This confidence was no doubt justified as far as Penny was concerned. Penny took Lama for granted; to Penny, Lama was just a little black cat which sometimes happened to be in the way. She had no special interest in her.

Fred, on the other hand, was fascinated. It is a fascination which never dimmed from the time we first introduced Lama to him when he was one day old. On that occasion we lifted Lama up to his face, and she licked his nose; and when we put her to the ground again, Fred tried to do the same to her. Such affection, however, had to be balanced by realism; for though Lama remained the same size, Fred of course grew and grew. Lama and Fred might not see the danger in the situation. We did. And therefore Jeannie and I became sometimes distaught by the cajoling antics they displayed toward each other.

Lama had no imagination. If, for instance, Fred was in one meadow and I was taking him to another, I would find Lama sitting directly in our path.

"Out of the way, Lama," I would call, "shoo!"

Not the slightest notice.

At the sight of her Fred would put his head down, and strain at the halter. Then, as we closed within a few feet, his pace would quicken and I would try to hold him.

"Get out of the way, Lama!" I would shout.

And then, as if all the time she had been teasing, Lama *would* dash from the giant which was Fred.

There was no harm in Fred. True, I have known him to behave coltishly, but this was always due to someone treating him too casually; treating him, in fact, as Lama treated him. Fred simply did not know his own strength; and so we feared for Lama when she behaved toward him as if he were a playmate of her own size. We also laughed. It was an absurd sight watching Fred catch sight of Lama on the other side of a field, then go cantering toward her, a frolic of a canter, full of joyous anticipation of a game, while Lama waited for him playing her own version of Russian roulette. Fred was always so ludicrously anxious to reach her. Lama in a field, Lama on a wall within possible touch of him, Lama on the path in front of him . . . Fred never failed to express an extrovert's delight in seeing her; while Lama, trusting Lama, trusted Fred just enough. She was away within a split second of his arrival.

On that October morning when Lama and I were going for a stroll, the donkeys were in a field above the cottage. Fred had now outgrown his gawkiness, had shed his shaggy brown youthful coat and looked like a little thoroughbred; and he was receiving again the attention he so enjoyed. He had grown larger than Penny, and his coat was a cocoa color, and time and again admirers would say "Look at his cross!" It was a beautiful black cross, one line tracing the length of his backbone and dissolving into his tail, the other two branching from it at the nape of his neck, each fingering down his shoulders. "Why is it there?" the few who did not know its tradition would ask. "Donkeys are blessed," I would reply, "because Jesus chose a donkey on which to ride into Jerusalem."

I left the donkeys staring down from their field into the small garden outside the door of the cottage, standing side by side, ears erect, inquisitive. "The donkeys are wanting something," I called to Jeannie. "All right," she replied, "I'll give them a chocolate cookie in a moment." I walked away down the path then right through the white gate to the big field; and then right again along the track toward the small field facing the sea which has been known since time immemorial as the onion meadow. On either side of the track, in early spring, bloomed bed upon bed of daffodils. There was the meadow of a beautiful daffodil with the ugly classified name of Sulphur. (When, as an experiment, we changed the name to Lamorna, the price jumped by a shilling a bunch!) Further on there was a meadow of California and opposite, on the other side of the track, a meadow of the large yellow trumpet called Rembrandt; and beside it, another containing the fragrant white Actaea with its red center. As it was autumn, feet-high grass still covered the meadows, but soon it would be cut and the ground turned over, and by Christmas we would be watching the green heralds of the flowers poking up from the soil.

I paused every few yards, waiting for Lama to catch up with me. When I reached the onion meadow I sat down on a low stone wall, and a minute later she had jumped up on my knees, settling herself like a glossy black cushion, and began gently to purr. It was a heavenly day, very still, an Indian summer day when the sea was a cornflower blue; and fringing the arm of the Lizard across the bay was a billowy line of white clouds. The sun shone on the long stretch of sands at Looe Bar, and below me a few hundred yards offshore there were a half dozen small boats grouped together, with tiny figures leaning over their sides feathering a shoal of mackerel. To my left was Carn Barges, a huge rock balanced upright as if it were a sentinel. Beyond was Carn Dhu which juts out from the far side of Lamorna Cove, sheltering the cove with high, gray boulder-strewn cliffs, this lovely cove which on a day like this has the stillness of a South Sea lagoon, and forever reminds me of Cook's Bay in Moorea. I sat there listening to the curlews calling as they swept across the sky high above me, to a robin singing a sad song, to the sudden laugh of a green woodpecker which seesawed its way inland to my right, to the throb of a French crabber with emerald green hull heading for Newlyn, to the sea touching the rocks like the swish of a gentle wind through trees—and to Lama purring.

This was one of those naïve moments when one would like to tear away from their anchors the sad and the tired and the bored; to refresh and awaken them by the feel of a Cornish day when the sea is a cornflower blue. Here is a gift which has no need of man's interference. Here is permanence, the unending bridge between the past and the present which gives the human soul its base. Brains are no asset at such a moment. All that is required is an attitude of mind which is capable of exultation, a heart that soars as it watches, a human being who has purged himself of aiming to conquer by logic. No brittle questions need be asked. No detached observance. Just the ability to catch the fleeting awareness that there can be moods which do not belong to reason. Another dimension enters your life amid the solitude and the grandeur, and suddenly there is a stranger within yourself.

I had sat there perhaps five minutes when

Lama suddenly became alert, flapping her tail urgently against my arm, and the purring stopped. Thirty yards below me on a rock I saw the cause. A small gray cat was crouched there watching us.

I had seen this cat from time to time over the years. It was obviously wild and I did not see it often; but from time to time one of us would catch it unawares on the cliff, and whoever had seen it would say later to the other, "I saw the little gray cat today." Or when we did not see it for a long time, sooner or later we would say, "I wonder what's happened to the little gray cat."

It never showed the slightest interest in us. Indeed it ran away into the undergrowth if ever we called to it, or even if it only saw us. But on this occasion, as it crouched on the rock, it continued quietly to watch me; and after a while Lama relaxed, the tail stopped flapping, a purr began again.

I wondered why.

M y Aunt Tannie, who was over eighty years old, came down once a year from London for a vacation at Minack. At some other time of the year she would fly by night flight to some corner of Europe for a vacation, and we would receive pithy postcards from places well off the tourist's map. Young in spirit, she was wonderfully interested in modern trends of art, literature and politics, but she was never swayed into overvaluing them by the hysteria of any small influential group. She judged every new fashion on its merits.

She was part of the solidly anticat world I was brought up in as a child. I am quite sure she would never under any circumstances have possessed a cat of her own, for cats all her life had been distasteful beasts; but she was fair about Lama. She thought her very pretty. She went further by saying that Lama had a style about her, a symmetry of limbs and body, equivalent to that of a thoroughbred racehorse. Such a comparison may sound extravagant; but my aunt believed that quality had a common denominator. It might be the swing of a golfer, a small part in a play, always Jane Austen, a final at Wimbledon, a concert at the Festival Hall or the way somebody polished the silver; all these things had a standard in her mind which, if fulfilled, provided pure pleasure.

Aunt Tannie was late in coming to stay at Minack that year. She had taken a motor coach excursion trip to Baden-Baden in the spring, had another excursion for ten days on the Italian lakes in the autumn, and in between had visited Coventry Cathedral, Osterley Park, the Runnymede RAF Memorial, a number of theaters, Kew Gardens more than once, several exhibitions and had remained glued to her television set throughout the two weeks of Wimbledon. She arrived at Minack, elegant, informed and sparkling with enthusiasm for life. She was a lesson in how to grow old—contemporary in thought, historically knowledgeable, self-sufficient, yet a stimulating companion, she had only one flaw. Lama. She and Lama could never come to terms. Neither of them, however hard they tried, could entirely relax in each other's company.

"Pussoo," coaxed my aunt in her usual way on arrival in the cottage, and in what she thought was an appealing tone, "come here, pussoo, come here to me." And she bent down and held out her hand. "Dear pussoo. Be friendly, pussoo."

I silently prayed that Lama would respond and behave like a charming hostess, but I also knew there was a snag. It was obvious that Lama did not approve of the word pussoo. She thought it childish, condescending and overfamiliar. Why should this comparative stranger arrive for a stay and forthwith burble such nonsense at her?

"Now don't be rude, pussoo. Come and say how do you do."

Lama was sitting with her back to the stove, her tail wrapped around her so that the silky black tip gently flicked against a front paw. She stared loftily at my aunt, a cool, superior gaze, like a dowager putting a gauche guest in her place. "I do not obey orders," she seemed to be saying, "I am a cat . . . not a dog."

My aunt, with her affinity toward dogs, was at a loss as to what to do next. A dog would come to her, wagging its tail, smiling, welcoming, at the snap of a finger and thumb, even a dog she had never met before. She liked such friendliness. It was effortless. So much more pleasant than the behavior of a little black cat which defied her well-meaning approaches.

"Selfish breed," my aunt said crossly, thinking of all the cats she had casually known; "you come from a very selfish breed, Lama." Thereupon she left Lama to ponder over such a remonstrance, and retired to her room.

The fact was, however, that my aunt and Lama both had the same basic intentions. Each wanted to win the other on her own terms. My aunt, for instance, longed to see Lama responding to discipline like a dog, a misguided ambition, of course, but one that is common among those who have never understood cats. I once felt exactly the same myself. It maddened me that I should be patronized, defied, ignored by such an arrogant domestic animal; and thus, although no longer that way inclined, I *understood* my aunt.

Lama, meanwhile, had her own frustrations. She observed my aunt's methods of courting and thought them surprising. For she had discovered, in her time, that human beings could be divided into two sections; either they were slaves to her whims or they completely ignored her existence. Yet here was a third section. Here was someone who clearly wished to gain her approval, in fact was most anxious to do so; why go about it in such an unusual way? Lama was prepared to be lured, but not to be ordered; and she also was ready to be flattered, providing the flattery was subtly paid. Hence, had my aunt walked across the room to *her*, pleasing Lama by such a touch of courtesy, my aunt would have been rewarded by some gentle accolade such as a purr or a rub around her legs. Lama, however, did not realize that such accolades did not rank high in my aunt's estimation. My aunt, for instance, would have been horrified had Lama rubbed around her legs, while Lama would have been quite certain she was bestowing a great honor. Indeed, it was this gulf in values that was the cause of the trouble between them.

Both were being thwarted—my aunt by being unable to impose her will on Lama, Lama by being unable to bewitch my aunt.

Both of them, however, were unperturbed by the initial setback. My aunt continued to operate her direct tactics, while Lama set out to *cajole* my aunt into submission. And the cajoling was performed in the most delightful way, delightful, that is, to anyone who appreciated a cat's special attention.

Lama, for instance, would pay my aunt the compliment of jumping on her bed when my aunt was not in the room and curling up in a tight black ball on my aunt's pink satin nightdress. My aunt, when she found out the situation, did not see the gesture as a compliment. In her view Lama, like all cats, was an unclean thing . . . and the sight of Lama on the bed, on her nightdress, greatly distressed her. Get off! Get off! And Lama would find herself unceremoniously dumped on the floor, not understanding what all the fuss was about, but vaguely aware that she had once again failed to bewitch my aunt.

There were other gestures on the part of Lama which my aunt misunderstood. On those days when Lama was left out in pouring rain, designedly on her part because she was on some mouse-catching business, she would in due course reenter the cottage by jumping on the windowsill and staring at us, slit amber eyes in a black face, until she gained our attention. She would then have the pleasure of seeing one of us rush to open the door, and both of us giving her a wonderful welcome. Poor Lama, soaking wet, feel her fur! At this stage she would be immediately aware that we were competing, Jeannie and I, for her favors. She would be about to lick herself dry, a lap was the most suitable place for the exercise, and would it be mine or would it be Jeannie's?

Having observed this competition between us, Lama came to the conclusion that the act of drying herself, of depositing her wet person on a lap, was a gesture which gave considerable pleasure. Why not, then, ring the changes and give my aunt the chance of feeling rain-sodden fur, of watching the busy lick at close quarters, of relaxing in the aftermath of a cat's outing in the rain?

So there was Aunt Tannie, sitting comfortably on the sofa reading a newspaper, and there was Lama like a wet black sponge at her feet. I watched Lama glance up at the skirt which appeared beneath the newspaper. A moment's thought. Yes, I will give her the honor. Leap!

Newspaper, Lama, my aunt crashed together . . . and a second later Lama was on the floor again.

Her most foolish gesture toward my aunt, however, was yet to come. Heaven knows what prompted her to make it because it was exceedingly rare that she ever made it to Jeannie and me. Once during the summer it had happened and I had given her a rapturous welcome, but the circumstances had been somewhat exceptional. It was a hot June afternoon and I had chosen to take pen and paper down the cliff to a meadow which was perched close to the sea. It is a risky thing to do if one intends to work because, instead of working, one becomes seduced by the quiet lapping of the sea on the rocks, and slow-flying gulls, and the hum of insects, and the scent of the honeysuckle which intertwines among the fuchsia, brambles and blackthorn. It is easy to doze. It is easy to forget about writing. I have often set out for the cliff with good intentions, and come back with bare pages.

On this particular summer day I had been lounging in the meadow for an hour or more when to my great surprise I found Lama beside me . . . and in her mouth was a mouse which she proceeded to drop in front of me. Jeannie told me later that she had seen the mouse caught. Lama had caught three mice in quick succession near the barn, and it was the third she decided to give to me. But how did she know I was all the way down the cliff? And why did she think I would so appreciate it?

I was indeed flattered by such a gesture. My aunt, when it happened to her, was not. She was in the greenhouse, protected from a cold autumn wind and catching the warmth of the fading sun, sitting at ease in a deck chair, when Lama appeared through the doorway, pranced up to her and with a wild little cry deposited a mouse, along with the greenery acquired during the capture, at her feet.

"Oh, dear, she's going to eat it," said my aunt, gathering herself in the deck chair, a note of despair in her voice. "Drat you, Lama, I was so enjoying myself. You're a beastly, sadistic cat!"

And off went my aunt, leaving a puzzled, playful Lama in possession of the greenhouse.

These collisions between the two of them, however, were not so disastrous as they might first appear. Lama, in good faith, made misjudgments in her effort to cajole my aunt which might have permanently offended any other cat hater. I am quite sure, in my time as a cat hater, I would have shown no patience at all. Lama would have conformed to my worst opinion of cats, and in those

185

days I would have found no excuse for her behavior. I would have labeled her selfish and disruptive. I would have disapproved of those who fussed over her. I would have been glad to have left her environment.

My aunt was more objective in her attitude. Lama had grace. Lama might have her faults, which, in my aunt's opinion, belonged to all her breed; but she possessed an elusive quality, a subtle femininity, which fascinated my aunt. Thus despite disapproving of her actions, my aunt became fonder of Lama the more she saw of her. Prejudice against the breed did not mean prejudice against Lama. Indeed I found myself thinking that here was a lesson. My aunt, in these lightsome forays with Lama, proved that one should never confuse convictions with individuals. A cat hater can always be charmed by a cat.

Soon after my aunt had returned to London, I saw the gray cat again. Jeannie was with me this time. It was the second week of November.

"We must make up our minds about this year's Christmas card," Jeannie had said at breakfast, "or we'll be in a panic again."

We aimed each year to have a photograph of some part of our life at Minack.

"What do you suggest?"

"Well," said Jeannie, "last year it was the colored one of the daffodils in the stable meadow with the cottage in the background. The year before we left it too late and had to buy a ready-made one. The year before that was me and the donkeys."

I had always liked that one. It was the year Fred was born, and the Christmas card was a picture of Jeannie riding Penny while holding Fred, a very small Fred, by his halter.

"What about a photograph of Lama?" I said. Four years before, the Christmas card had been a picture of Jeannie and me with Lama in Jeannie's arms. It was not a very good photograph. Lama looked like a black spot against Jeannie's white jersey.

"Possibly," said Jeannie doubtfully.

"What's the objection?"

"I just feel," said Jeannie, picking up the egg cups and carrying them to the sink, "that it ought to be the donkeys again. It's their year after all."

It was true that scores of people had come to see them that summer.

"You may be right."

"And I've an idea," Jeannie went on, "of the photograph you could take of them."

"What's that?"

I have no pretensions about my photography. I point my camera at the object, suffer difficulty in focusing, then trust that the automatic light meter will operate correctly.

"I thought we might take the donkeys to Carn Barges," explained Jeannie, "and then you can photograph them silhouetted against the background of our bay."

The bay was a teaspoon of a bay at the foot of our cliff meadows, a crevice of water where often we would find a seal, only face and moustache in sight, swaying with the waves, aware that he was safe as we stood on our rocks and gazed at him.

"It's a good idea," I said, "and we can go right now. The sun rising up above the Lizard will be behind me, and it will be a lovely walk, and we can think of the world rushing to their offices while we have the freedom to set off on this ozone-filled sunny morning with a couple of donkeys along a path above the sea."

Carn Barges, the formation of rocks falling steeply down to the sea which we looked out upon across the moorland from the cottage, was jokingly called by us the near feeding grounds. Around the topmost rocks were succulent grasses which the donkeys much enjoyed. They would nibble away, etched against the skyline while the fishing boats passed by below them; and sometimes a man from a fishing boat would cup his hands together and shout a greeting, and the donkeys would prick up their ears and stare back at him inquisitively.

Then there were also the far feeding grounds. These were farther on, along a tortuous path toward Lamorna, and when the donkeys were in an adventurous mood the walk could be a hazardous affair. We walked in single file, Jeannie and I first, then the donkeys, free of their halters. Usually they followed in docile fashion, leisurely partaking of any greenery they fancied on the way; but there were occasions when they were boisterous, as if they were egging each other on to play a joke on us. And sometimes in this mood they caught us unawares, and barged past us, and in a second they would be racing along the path which led away from the moorland and onto the road which fell down the side of the valley to Lamorna village. Perhaps it was the pub they were aiming for. From time to time we would take them sedately by their halters; and while we sipped beer, they would eat potato chips. But they have never been on their own yet. We have always caught them in time.

At the start of a walk, as they went past the garden and across the expanse of the big field, we always kept them under control by their halters; and only let them run free when they had clambered over the boundary hedge and were on the narrow path which was edged on either side by undergrowth. So there we were on that fine November morning, myself holding Fred's halter, Jeannie holding Penny's, camera slung over my back, when we were joined by Lama just as we had started to set off.

Monty in his time used to enjoy long walks, and he often came with us to Carn Barges. Lama never did. Jeannie explains this by saying that Monty, being born a suburban cat, was innocent of country dangers, while Lama, born a wild cat, was only too well aware of them. Anyhow I never knew her to go beyond Minack boundaries; and that was part of the magic of her. Minack was her kingdom, and that was all she desired.

"I feel a bit guilty about her," I said. Her presence produced a sense of competition; the donkeys were to be the Christmas card, not Lama. And in any case she always looked vulnerable when she tried to join the donkeys on a walk, like a child trying to be grown up.

"She won't come far," said Jeannie; "she won't come any farther than the top of the field."

I led the way, Fred snorting and prancing in excitement, Jeannie a yard or two behind me with Penny, a gay matron of a Penny; and then a few yards behind them the cautious, determined Lama. We reached the field, and I had started to lead Fred down the slope when he suddenly stopped, pricked his ears in the direction of a jungle of grass, then lunged toward it while I tried to hold him back by his halter. And at that moment the gray cat darted out of the undergrowth. It dashed up the path we were coming down, past Jeannie and Penny, past Lama, then leaped to the left and raced down the other path toward the gate at the top of our cliff meadows, then disappeared underneath it.

"I haven't seen her for months and months," said Jeannie.

"Why a 'her'?"

"She's so small. She looks feminine."

"Did you notice Lama?" I said. "She behaved just like that other time a few weeks ago. Took no notice at all."

I looked back again up the path, only for an instant, because Fred was pawing at the ground and jostling me and saying quite plainly that he wanted to move on. Lama had stopped, just as Jeannie said she would stop. She was sitting, watching us in detachment. She was certainly quite unperturbed by the commotion created by the presence of the little gray cat on her land.

The donkeys were in an amiable mood by the time they reached Carn Barges. We had not hurried. It was one of those unexpected mornings when, had I shut my eyes and possessed no sense of time, I would have believed it was a summer morning. The sun warmed my face and there was no breeze to cool it with a winter nip. Gulls flecked the gray rocks below us, and on the point that jutted out from our bay, quite still, a cormorant contemplated. On the other side of the little bay our meadows began to climb the cliff, and in a lower one, upright like a flagstaff, was the palm tree I had planted when my mother died. Small meadows and strange shapes, high hedges sheltering them from the salt and the gales, they looked best in the winter. In the summer the undergrowth grew rampant, smothering the meadows with waist-high green, making it difficult for strangers to believe that in early spring they were ablaze with daffodils.

And up from the cliff, up the clear outline of the path which traced the big field, I could see Lama still where we left her. A black spot of a cat which for some reason—affection, curiosity, mild jealousy of the donkeys—wanted to wait for our return as she had done so many times before. And when we had reached her again she would give us no fulsome greeting as a dog would have done, but instead would lazily stretch herself, begin to stroll slowly ahead of us and then, as if a joy suddenly swept through her, she would race away toward the cottage.

On the roof of the cottage, along its apex, I could see the pinpoints of the two gulls we called Knocker and Squeaker. It had become a habit of theirs to arrive about half-past seven in the morning, force us to get up with their cries if we were not up already, stay until ten, disappear back to the rocks and the sea, and then return to the roof again an hour before dusk. But when the gales blew we never saw them until the storm had abated. Then they would appear again and we would be thankful it was over, one of us calling to the other, "The gulls are back. The weather is on the mend!" And we would reward the gulls with homemade bread.

Fred pushed his nose into my hand. He often did this when we were together, five minutes or so of munching grass and then a gesture of affection.

"Time to go back," I said. I had tried to photograph them with ears pricked, biblical creatures with the rocks beside them in the foreground, and the sea far away below. But they had no interest in posing. Jeannie heaved them this way and that, trying to bring them together for the camera yet keeping them individually apart; and I had no idea whether I had pressed the button at the precise Christmas card moment.

"I'm ready to go," said Jeannie. She said it in a tone of voice which set me wondering, as if she were impatient to return. Jeannie is the sort of person who will go silent when she is hiding her feelings; and although, in the process, she is apparently supporting me in whatever task I am pursuing, I am conscious of this silence. She is biding her time. She is reasoning that in due course, without causing any offense to me and without disclosing what is in her mind, she will gain her objective.

On this occasion, as we stood on Carn Barges and her eyes scanned our cliff meadows, she had an idea which she considered too fanciful to disclose to me.

It was an idea which resulted in the most tantalizing story.

We left the donkeys in the stable meadow when we returned to Minack. Lama had waited for us as expected, raced ahead to the cottage as was her custom and had been rewarded for her patience with a saucer of fish. Then, without saying anything to me, Jeannie disappeared.

I had some letters to write and as usual, being a slow writer, they took much longer than I had hoped. Thus when I looked at the clock, I realized suddenly that nearly an hour had gone by and there was still no sign of her. It was unlike her not to say what she was up to. If there was a task to perform, an adventure to enjoy, we would tell each other what it was we had in mind. Not in the sense it was a duty to do so, for this breeds boredom. Just for the fun of it. Why then had Jeannie not told me where she was going?

I finished my letters and walked out to a spot we called "the bridge," a convenient name for a corner of Minack where there was a spreading view of the moorlands, the sea and the curving line of the Lizard, and where Jeannie and I often sat or stood watching, absorbing the antics of birds, or a fox, or the changing colors of light, or the passing of the seasons, green bracken, brown bracken, flattened bracken.

I was standing there when I heard Jeannie calling me, then saw her running past the old stables, shouting, "Derek! Derek!" She was clearly highly excited.

"Up here," I said calmly, "on the bridge."

"You won't believe it," she rushed out, "it's the most extraordinary thing I've ever known!"

"What is?" I said in a matter-of-fact voice. I was a little irritated that she had disappeared for so long, and I did not feel in the mood to respond to her excitement immediately.

"The gray cat is Lama's mother!"

It was a declaration. It was as if she were announcing that a visitor had arrived. I looked at her soothingly.

"You've been talking with the gray cat, I suppose, and she's told you this."

"You're laughing at me!"

"I can hardly take you seriously."

"You can give me a chance. You can listen to me."

My teasing had reached stretching point.

"All right," I said, "go ahead. I'll listen."

When Fred had disturbed the gray cat and made her run away, Jeannie had made a mental note that the cat had disappeared under the small gate which topped our cliff, and that she ran in that direction with considerable purpose, as if she were going home. I too, of course, had seen her run that way but, as far as I was concerned, she was only escaping from us as quickly as she could. Jeannie, however, with her all-embracing, cat-loving instincts, was curious. She was also, no doubt, wishing to indulge in the customary cat-lover's pastime of trying to make friends with a stray.

And so after we had returned with the donkeys

she had gone off to the cliff, through the gate and quietly down the steps, looking in one meadow and then into another. She then went down some farther steps which brought her halfway among the cliff meadows; one half climbing upward to the big field, the other half falling to the rocks and the sea. At this point, a few yards off the path, there was a small cave. It was such a small cave that a human being could scarcely wriggle his way into it. It was more a crevice, guarded by gray granite with a main entrance nearest the path, and a slip of an exit, an escape route, at its far end. We had always been attracted by it. The interior was cozy, dry debris and rotted bracken like peat, and many times Jeannie and I had thought what a comfortable hideout it would have been for fox cubs, a much more suitable place than the bank not far away where cubs were reared year after year, always to be threatened by man when they were old enough to play.

Jeannie came to this cave and peered into it. She did so without thinking, a reflex action from our past talk about it. She had certainly not looked into it expecting to see the gray cat. She had to stoop, her knees touching the soil, in order to get a clear view, and as she did so she saw that the cave had an occupant. The occupant was neither the gray cat nor a fox cub.

It was a kitten. A black kitten.

"Good heavens," I said.

"You see? Don't you see we've discovered where Lama came from? She was brought up in the cave by the gray cat."

"Well," I said cautiously, "let's leave that fantasy for a moment. What did the kitten do when it saw you?"

"It ran away . . . up through the gap at the back."

"Didn't you look for it?"

Jeannie being such a cat expert, so priding herself on understanding their ways and winning their confidence, must surely have caught the kitten.

"Of course I looked for it," Jeannie exclaimed, though I observed a doubtful note in her voice, "but it wouldn't have anything to do with me. In fact, I didn't see it again."

I was, of course, sure that Jeannie was not fabricating the story. It was not her nature to do so, even as a joke. I was bound to take her discovery seriously.

"How big was it?" I asked.

"Tiny . . ."

"Only a few weeks old then?"

"Yes . . . perhaps a month or six weeks."

"And no sign of any others?"

"Not a sign."

Of course this *could* be the explanation as to where Lama came from. The gray cat was certainly known to us before Lama appeared; and for all we knew she may have been rearing kittens every year in the selfsame cave without us being aware of it.

"Why on earth should there be only one kitten?" I asked, half to myself.

Jeannie was sitting beside me on a wood table we have on the bridge, and as we were talking we watched the *Queen of the Isles*, the new sister ship to the *Scillonian*, passing by on her way to the Scillies.

"There must be a sensible explanation," I murmured again.

"Do we have to have one?"

"Well, didn't you announce that the gray cat was Lama's mother?"

"Yes."

"I'm only trying to think of evidence to prove it."

"I wish," said Jeannie, and at that moment I saw Lama strolling languidly toward us, "I wish you wouldn't be so logical."

"I'm not being logical. I'm only being sensible."

"The same thing."

"After all . . ."

"Of course we can't prove it," Jeannie interrupted; "I'm only telling you what I *feel* is true."

Lama had now come up to my gently swinging foot. She pushed her head softly against it, then looked up at me trustingly, benignly, as if she were saying that she felt in a particularly loving mood and that she hoped I would respond. I did. I bent down and delicately touched her forehead to and fro.

"I tell you what we'll do," I said, still stroking, "we'll go down the cliff together, and I can see the kitten for myself."

Lama, however, had no wish to see us leave. She was now purring, rubbing herself against my leg. Happy, peaceful Lama. No awareness that we were about to court a rival. No knowledge of the thoughts that were going through our minds, that we might at last have discovered her secret. Purr, purr, purr. She was the epitome of a contented cat. A houseful of comforts, endlessly admired, limitless hunting grounds, no enemies, so happy in her life that even the birds were safe. Purr, purr, purr.

"Wait a second," said Jeannie, "I'll put some bread and milk in a saucer. Better still, I'll put it in a jug and pour it out when we get down there."

"And in the circumstances," I said, "Lama also deserves a special helping of something." Then I added, feeling disloyal, "It'll stop her from coming with us."

There was a meadow with a hedge of elders, now bare of leaves, which lay above and to one side of the cave. It was a perfect place for us to hide; and so we went through the gate, down the steps and stood there watching. We had only been there for a few minutes when I grew impatient, and I whispered to Jeannie that we should go straight down and look inside the cave. We had gone a few yards, moving very quietly, when suddenly the gray cat darted out of some undergrowth, raced toward the cave and disappeared into the entrance.

"That's that." I said; "no use having a look now."

"It would scare them still further if we did."

Having been denied a sight of the kitten, I found my imagination awakened. Jeannie's excitement, I realized, was completely justified. And if when she first told me I reacted in a matter-of-fact fashion, I was now as keen as she was. I felt that here was an incident, an elusive fairy story which would have no end, and I was intrigued.

"If you wait here," said Jeannie, "I'll tiptoe down to that trodden patch of earth near the entrance and fill the saucer with bread and milk."

I watched her do so, then when she returned, we went back to the hedge of elders and waited. But there was no sign of gray cat or kitten. Only a robin flew down from a bush, had a look at the saucer and flew back again.

"She knows we're here," said Jeannie; "she won't appear again until we've gone."

We were never to see her or the kitten beside the saucer, but we soon realized it was going to help in another way. It acted as a marker, and while its contents were consumed we knew that they were still around. That first evening, when we went back, the saucer was empty, and Jeannie filled it up again. The same happened the following day, and the next. We would steal stealthily down the steps, hoping to catch them unawares but, although the bread and milk disappeared, our visits had obviously disturbed them. The kitten was no longer in the cave; or at any rate whenever we looked, it was empty.

On the fourth day the bread and milk were left untouched. So also on the fifth. We searched the two meadows closest to the cave but found no clue as to what might have happened; and the only sign of the kitten was a neat, round indentation in the dry debris and peat of the cave where she had lain curled asleep.

Thereupon we began blaming ourselves for having left food so close to their hiding place. We found the day dominated by our questions as to what might have happened, and the concern was for a kitten I had not yet even seen. I would find myself creeping through the gate and down the steps at various times of the day, to stare through the hedge, just to have a look at a saucer on the ground. Had they come back after all? Had the bread and milk been eaten?

On Thursday, the third successive day that the saucer had remained untouched, we regretfully decided the adventure was over. I would have to leave Jeannie alone with her satisfaction that she had seen the black kitten. A mystery that had momentarily titillated us, but would never be solved.

A wild cat, and one small black kitten. There on our cliff amidst badgers roaming around them, gulls at night gathered on the rocks below close together like still confetti, waves edging white around the darkness ceaselessly murmuring. We would leave them to this freedom.

That is what we thought. But on Friday we were to realize that the gray cat had been watching *us*.

Plans had been made, and Lama was to be an ally in carrying them out.

At four o'clock on Friday afternoon we decided to take the donkeys for a short walk. They had, in fact, hypnotized us into doing so. They had been standing side by side at their favorite spot in the field overlooking the cottage garden. They were bored, and they communicated their boredom by staring lugubriously at us when we went in and out of the cottage, and, more effectively still, by impelling Jeannie to watch them through the window as she sat in her armchair enjoying a cup of tea.

"Let's take them to the onion meadow," she said at last, yielding, as they had expected, to the stare. A lugubrious stare never failed them. Sooner or later we were certain to pay them attention.

We put on their halters and led them down the steep path past the cottage, a hazardous few yards, for there within reach was delectable escallonia, early flowering wallflower plants, sweet Williams and various other delights which favored their fancy. We went on our way amid snorts and other manifestations of donkey excitement, heads down to the ground, for instance, with ears back, and frolicking, harmless kicks. An adventurous time, as always at the beginning, a display of great pleasure, putting us both a little on guard.

We turned right to the onion meadow, and instantly I jabbed at Fred's halter, like jamming my foot on a brake. For there, a few yards away along the path, her back to me, every line of her eloquently describing her actions, was the gray cat. She was crouched. Her eyes were intent on some couch grass ten feet from her. She was so certain of an impending capture that she was completely oblivious to our boisterous arrival.

"Hold it, Fred," I said quietly. And then turning around toward Jeannie, I vigorously waved my hand telling her to stop. She had no need for such instructions; she too had seen the gray cat.

The donkeys did not approve of our sudden excitement. At one moment they were gaily setting off on a walk, the next they were returning whence they came. This irrational behavior on our part naturally vexed them, and when they again reached the gravel path by the cottage they anchored their hooves to the ground. A common gesture, of course, when a donkey is not doing what it wants. And it was only when Lama appeared, then collapsed upside down and coquettishly curled her paws to the sky a few yards away from them, that they were spurred once again to advance. The sight of her always entranced them.

"All right, donkeys," said Jeannie soothingly when they were once more back in their field, "we'll take you for a long walk first thing tomorrow." The promise did not impress them. They felt cheated.

But Jeannie and I were imbued with the enthusiasm of amateur detectives. We had been offered a clue and we were intent on following it up. If the gray cat was still roaming our land the chances were that the kitten could not be far away, and so if we could watch the gray cat, if we could shadow her movements, she might lead us to the new hideout. So we now quickly returned to the spot where we had left her and found her gone.

The light was now beginning to fail, and a wind from the south was rising. The sea was noisy, ominous, and fishing boats were hurrying across the bay toward Newlyn as if they were frightened of what was behind them. Blackbirds hoarsely chattered while they searched for roosting places, and gulls soared in the sky uttering human cries of warning. The magpies, over in the brush of the shadow valley, clattered their harsh sounds together like castanets, and looming above us, sweeping in from the sea, were the billowy dark clouds impatiently waiting to let loose their contents. A dirty night ahead. That was certain.

It was my idea that we should go down the cliff

and have another look at the cave. I did not really expect to see anything, but the prospect of looking seemed to give us a purpose now that the gray cat had disappeared again. We went down the steps, glanced out of habit through the bare branches of the elder and saw the gray cat, a few yards from the cave, sitting alertly with her back to us.

We were, of course, very surprised. Almost a week had gone by without a sign of her, and now within ten minutes we had seen her twice in widely separate places.

"She must have raced down from the path," I said.

"She was probably in a hurry to take the mouse to the kitten."

"She certainly went fast."

"I'm *so* relieved," said Jeannie; "the kitten can't be far away."

We were content, as it was getting dark, to leave it at that. If we decided to search for the new hideout, we would do so tomorrow, and so we went back up the steps to the field. At the top of the steps to the left, there is what is called the skol meadow, and beyond it there is another meadow where grew a patch of soleil d'or. Only a few of them and not enough to send away commercially, but as they were the earliest bulb flowers of all they gave us much pleasure. Here was spring before even winter had begun, and from time to time we would stroll to the meadow and see how the green spikes were progressing. We did so on this occasion. A whim on Jeannie's part took us there despite the growing darkness, and it was five or six minutes before we got back to the big field and had reached the path which led us fifty yards to the cottage.

Two or three yards up the path, close to the

left-hand bank, we saw Lama. It was not unusual for her to be there. It was her sentry box. She would post herself at this spot, awaiting our return, whenever she had spied us going off for a walk and had been too late to catch up with us. There she was, a black shadow in the gloom, about to receive a loving, rapturous greeting from Jeannie and me, when suddenly I saw her leap a couple of feet in the air, heard her utter a jungle battle cry, then watched her disappear at speed up the path toward the cottage. The sound of battle cries faded and all was silent again except for the rising wind.

"I don't think," said Jeannie, "that all that noise and fuss seemed very genuine." A cat connoisseur's remark. An experienced observer's assessment of a situation which was suspect. Lama had put on a show. A flamboyant temper had been meant to impress us. A cacophony of empty noise, a sawdust gesture of bravery, a display of feline exhibitionism aimed at pulling the wool over our eyes. The *other* cat, so the elaborate pretense went, was *not* a friend. *That* is why I am chasing it.

But while Jeannie sensed what had happened, I had seen. I had been a little ahead of her, caught sight of Lama and simultaneously had observed her companion, and they were side by side, a black shadow and a gray one. It was bewildering.

"Unless I'm dotty," I said, "it's the gray cat again."

"It can't be."

"What she's been doing, racing up and down from the cliff like this, is beyond my comprehension."

"And Lama behaving like that!"

"We'll see if we can find them."

We hurried up the path and first went to look in the old stables. There was no trace of Lama, and we went outside again, and across to the trees on the other side of the lane beside the greenhouse. The donkeys caught sight of us in the dark and Fred began to trumpet a song, then Penny joined in with her terrible groaning contralto.

"She's here!" I heard Jeannie suddenly shout, "and what's more, the gray cat is on a branch just above her!"

It was an old elm, spreading its branches behind the packing shed, a fat trunk in which green woodpeckers had chiseled nest holes over the years.

"But they look friendly!" I said in surprise when I saw them.

They were within paw-striking distance of each other, ten feet from the ground, Lama balancing on one branch while the gray cat was just above her, her tail encircling the branch she was sitting on like a monkey. They were watching each other, dozily, no sign of animosity. They were not even stirred into action by our upturned faces. No imaginary temper this time. They were clearly content in each other's company. Indeed Lama was rubbing her head against the branch in such a way that she appeared to be purring, but this we could not hear because of the wind rushing through the trees.

We put Boris to bed, shutting the door of his house in the wood and bidding him good night as he sat on his perch, then we went indoors. We had not been there long before Jeannie's curiosity got the better of her, and she picked up the flashlight, and went back again to look up at the tree. They were there still, communing with each other, a few feet apart; and when Jeannie shone the light directly on the gray cat, she showed no fear. She was a little cat with a neat, small head, a short body and the plush fur of the semi-Persian. There was no doubt, in Jeannie's mind, of the similarity. Rain had started to spatter, and the wind was growing angry, and the sea was beginning to roar. But up there in the tree Lama and the gray cat continued their silent, feline conversation.

"Have we solved your secret at last?" said Jeannie by herself to Lama in the darkness. "Have we?"

Lama returned to the cottage in due course, and she spent the night curled at the bottom of the bed. In the morning the wind and the rain were still lashing the windows, making a noise like the rattle of drums, and I was good-naturedly annoyed when Jeannie said to me after breakfast that she was making a stew . . . and would I fetch an onion from the string in the stables?

I put a raincoat over my shoulders and ran down the path, and my hand was on the bottom part of the stable door to open it when I saw something inside on an old sack in the middle of the cobblestone floor.

Asleep on the sack was the black kitten.

e were living again the time when Lama first came to Minack. A black cat in the offing, uninvited, imposing its personality upon us from a distance. No Jane and Shelagh this time to help Jeannie in her maneuvers. No vacancy for a cat to fill.

Hence, although my first reaction was to hasten to tell Jeannie, my second was one of vague concern. A kitten which had arrived in such magical fashion could not be denied a home, and what would Lama say to that? I doubted too my own behavior. Lama had taken the place of Monty in my life, and I viewed with apprehension the prospect of having to divide my loyalties. I was still a one-cat man.

I was, however, anticipating a situation which had not yet matured. I was so enchanted by the thought of the kitten clambering up the steps of the cliff and on up the steep field toward the stables that I was taking it for granted that the journey had been made with a purpose, and the purpose was to win our approval. Jeannie thought so too.

"Easy now to understand why the gray cat came to see Lama," she said. I guessed what she was thinking. The situation provided excellent material for her fantasy-weaving. "She asked permission," Jeannie went on, "for the kitten to stay at Minack."

"Booking accommodation from the landlady?"
I joked.

"Very funny."

"So you think Lama has agreed to share her home?"

"Some understanding took place."

"Rubbish," I said. "Anyhow, come and see it."

We went down to the stables and Jeannie once again hopefully carried a saucer of bread and milk, but when we reached the stable door I foolishly coughed, and the kitten woke up and, with the instant reaction of an animal caught off guard, dashed into a corner under a fat bale of peat. We made no attempt to lure it out, for not even Jeannie expected to be friends right away. Its confidence had to be slowly won. It would have to be the same story as that of Lama: the growing trust won not by a gimmick but by time.

"Put the saucer down just here," I said, "and we'll go around to the lane and watch through the window."

I had never before watched a hungry, wild black kitten ecstatically devour a saucer of bread and milk. There had been no pause, no frightened wait for us to disappear. We walked around the building and looked through the window, and in those few seconds the kitten had made up its mind. Fear was not going to interfere with hunger. And so when we put our faces to the glass there was this tiny black daisy of a face hugging the saucer, tiny pink tongue shooting at its contents.

"It's so small," I said, "do you think it could have walked here on its own? I wonder if the mother carried it?"

"We will never know," said Jeannie.

Small as it was we could see the resemblance

to Lama. The neat little head, the short body, the firm cup handle of a tail and the black velvet of its fur.

"When it grows up," I said doubtfully, "we won't be able to tell the difference between the two of them."

"Your tone suggests you're regretting it."

"I'm only thinking . . ."

"I know what you're thinking," said Jeannie, laughing; "it's always the same with you . . . shying away from a new arrival. Just as you did with Monty and the donkeys, and Lama for that matter. It's your nature to be like this in the beginning."

"Oh, well," I said, "it's only that I can't help wondering how Lama is going to like sharing her kingdom."

But Lama's mood during the coming days could not be faulted. I had foreseen the possibility that she might storm the stables and put the kitten to flight. There was nothing to stop her doing so except her good nature; the gap in the door was still open as we had no wish to cage the kitten inside, and so the kitten, so to speak, was at her mercy. Lama, however, seemed not to be aware of it. She pursued her customary peregrinations. She fenced with Boris. She dozed in the packing shed. She helped Jeannie to bunch freesias by pushing her head in the blooms as they lay on the bench. She displayed no sign of knowing that there was a possible heir apparent within meowing distance. There was, in fact, an air about her which suggested she was a lady sure of her position.

Nor did the kitten behave in the way we expected. Instead of responding to our attention, it hid from us. We would arrive at the stable door, look inside and be just in time to see the tiny figure

209

dash to its fortress, a fortress of the bale of peat, sacks of fertilizers, an old table, a disused motor hoe and a bundle of wooden stakes. Out of sight and out of reach, it was as safe as a rabbit in its warren, and it would only emerge to eat the food we had left for it, long after we had gone. We would watch through the window, half an hour or more, before we saw it creep from its hiding place to the saucer.

So we watched, myself in a detached way, Jeannie in the hope that the kitten would one day show its appreciation of her efforts. We watched, for instance, the peculiar way it drank the milk from the saucer. The usual cat drinks neatly. The kitten, however, buried its face into the milk so that when the saucer was dry, its face looked as if it had been dipped into snow. We were amused, but saw no significance in it.

After ten days of such behavior I began to feel thwarted. Moreover the kitten was forcing us to lead a double life, and so when Lama came purring around us we both had a guilty conscience. What right had we to flirt with a wild kitten when Lama was so trusting? We had done our best to win its affection but it had spurned us. It clearly did not want our company. And if that were the case, so we argued, we could justifiably attempt to satisfy our curiosity. We would open up the fortress and see the kitten at close quarters.

On the December morning that we decided to reach the kitten's hiding place, Lama's attitude suddenly became frivolous. We walked out of the cottage and found her skittishly playing with a pebble from the gravel, and before we could stop her, she dashed gaily down the path to the stable door.

"Now there's going to be trouble," I said.

"You stop here," said Jeannie, "I'll catch her."

Lama, however, had no intention of being caught, and as soon as Jeannie approached her, she jumped on the wall out of reach.

"Let her be," I said, feeling guilty again that we were deceiving her; "I'll block up the gap in the door. . . . The kitten won't get out and Lama won't get in."

We quietly began dismantling the fortress. The motor hoe was lifted out first, then the old table and after that the bundle of wooden stakes.

"I should say it is behind the gap between the peat and the fertilizer bags," I said, realizing I had now to be on guard. The heavy part of the moving was about to begin.

"Be careful."

"I will."

I shifted the bale of peat about eighteen inches, and I pushed aside first one then a second bag. I had moved enough to see the corner which we believed was the fortress. It was empty.

"It hasn't dashed away while I was moving this?"

"I can't see it."

"It's not here," I said; "there's not a sign of it here."

At this moment there was a rattle behind me. Lama was poised like an acrobat on the edge of the stable door. A black cat edged against the daylight. A cat which a second later was on the cobblestones of the floor beside us, an upturned tummy of a black cat, white whisker distinct among the luxuriant others, a happy black cat.

"Why so coquettish, Lama?" I said, bending down and stroking her. Then I paused, and turned to Jeannie, laughing. "Do you know," I said, "I believe you were right, Jeannie."

"How?"

"Lama has been making fools of us."

"I never said that."

"You said that the gray cat was Lama's mother, and that she asked Lama a favor concerning the kitten."

"I said that more or less."

"That's what *did* happen, I reckon. Lama agreed to let the kitten stay in the stables until it grew strong enough to go away and find a home of its own."

"You ridiculed me when I suggested it."

"I take it all back. But there's one thing I want to know . . . What has happened to the gray cat?"

We had not seen her since that night when she was in the tree. It was indeed many weeks before we saw her again.

"She felt her kitten was safe. She could do no more for it, so she went off. After all, Lama was safe after she came here. . . ."

Lama had had enough attention, and had got up, and was sauntering away.

"Dear Jeannie," I said, as we too left the stables, "I'm glad you've got a fey mind."

"Are you laughing again?"

"Certainly not. A fey mind makes unreasonable facts convincing."

"Well," said Jeannie, unsure whether I was paying a compliment, "whatever my mind may be, there is a job of work to be done. We must send out the Christmas cards today. Will you help?"

"Certainly."

"Let's go."

As we went up the path, we passed Lama. She

was sitting on a rock, a huge rock embedded in the ground, a rock which had been anchored there through the ages. She sat with tip of tail flicking, her Oriental eyes blinking serenely, and, had it not been for the breeze, I would have heard her purrs.

A cat with a mission achieved.

We were alone at Christmas. Jeannie's mother had died three years ago, and Angus three months before her. We were alone except for Boris and the gulls, the donkeys and Lama, and the kitten we never saw.

It was still in the neighborhood, no doubt about that. Every evening after Lama had come indoors, Jeannie would go out into the darkness and leave a saucer in the stables. It didn't matter how stormy the night, she still kept her appointment.

And now on this Christmas morning, Lama herself was about to perform an important duty. I was lying comfortably in bed when I heard Jeannie call from the sitting room: "Lama is coming to you with a present!" Then I heard her add urgently in a whisper: "Go on, Lama! No, not that way . . . through the door!"

Then Lama appeared, almost at eye level, and I observed that around her silky black neck was a red ribbon, and attached to the ribbon, dangling against her chest, was a decorated narrow box which suggested the container of a fountain pen. It was indeed.

"Lama . . . thank you!" I said, grabbing her and lifting her onto the bed and holding her, firm hand on soft fur, "just what I want."

This was the game of Christmas. The relish of absurdities which enrich momentarily the act of giving, and within a few minutes of Lama's presentation I was up. I pulled a heavy sweater over my dressing gown. I did not bother about socks as I pulled on my rubber boots. Then I was off into the chill morning to fetch the donkeys, collecting on my way the two placards I had already prepared. The placards were the lids of old cardboard flower boxes, and on one I had scrawled MERRY CHRISTMAS! and on the other WITH LOVE FROM US BOTH. I hung the first around Fred's neck, the second around Penny's, and on each was attached a large envelope.

"Come and see the donkeys!" I shouted when I had led them back to the cottage. "Hurry, Jeannie!"

I had pushed them ahead of me, and I feared they might become restless as they stood on their own by the porch, two shaggy heads side by side waiting to deliver their presents—a silk scarf from each.

"Donkeys!" cried Jeannie, "whatever have you been up to?"

They both had their reward soon after, and when I took them back to the field they were still munching the carrots Jeannie had given them. I shut the gate, watched them amble away, then hurried down to the wood to let Boris out of his house. It was to be his last Christmas.

I was late, and he was cross that I had kept him waiting, and I heard him hissing before I had even turned the key in the lock. "Sorry, Boris," I said, as I opened the door, "it's Christmas. Merry Christmas, old Boris!" He came out of the house flapping his wings and followed me back, waddling from side to side until he reached his pond in front of the packing shed. He always had his breakfast there; nowhere else would do.

On the way back to the cottage I had a look in the stables and saw that the saucer of bread and milk had been left untouched. Usually it was clean by the morning.

"No kitten last night," I said when I returned.

"That's the second night running," said Jeannie; "it'll be back tonight." It was true that we had noticed that the food could go untouched for two nights but was always eaten on the third.

"It's still looking for a vacancy," went on Jeannie, "and until it finds one it will always come back."

"Well," I said smiling, thinking of the old lady in Penzance who, when Monty died, assured me the vacancy would soon be filled, "let's have breakfast and then have a wandering walk around Minack with the cat which *did* find a vacancy."

Lama, fortunately, was in the mood for a walk, and as we moved off toward the cliff she kept only a yard or so behind us. There were to be no delays on her part on this occasion. She wanted to remain close to us, jauntily enjoying herself, finding a feline delight in sharing the pleasure of the day with us. And when we reached the cliff gate she dashed ahead underneath it, like the gray cat had done that day when Fred had disturbed her.

"Back where she came from," I said to Jeannie, watching Lama scamper down the steps. Then I added, "You remember how Monty never liked coming down here?"

"But, Monty," replied Jeannie, "was not born within sound of the sea."

The only entrance to our cliff was through this gate at the top. It was no place for strangers. There was a deep cleft biting into the land, a sheer fall to the sea below, guarding one boundary of the meadows, and the other boundary disappeared into boulders, brambles, gorse and, in summer, a forest of bracken. Below were the rocks, granite and blue elvin pitted with fissures, huge ungainly shapes, each part of the whole which sloped without plan inevitably to the sea. Here the seaweed, draped like an apron, thickened the water at low tide, and gulls, oyster catchers and turnstones poked among it, uttering wild cries. There was the sense of loneliness, and yet of greatness. This was unmanageable nature, the freedom man chases.

And to us the cliff reflected our endeavor since we came to Minack. It was a part of ourselves. We had seen it those years ago when it was untamed and envisioned the meadows we would carve from the undergrowth, the rich crops we would grow, the sure future we would build. Here we had been a part of some victories and many defeats. We had seen harvests of early potatoes lashed by a gale and destroyed in a night.

We had rejoiced in the flower season at the sight of the daffodils, dazzling yellow against the blue sea, gulls high above, gannets plummeting offshore, then gladly endured the steady task of picking and gathering. Such as this was our victory. Here in remoteness, a sense of communion with the base of beauty. Not victory in a worldly sense. We produced. We were two of the losing originals. When our efforts left our environment, so did our control. Far away people, cool in their calculations, undisturbed by our hopes, beset with their own problems, decreed our reward.

We had our shield. Moments like the quiet of a Christmas morning when Jeannie and I were together, with a cat called Lama who was born within sound of the sea.

Part 3
Ambrose & Oliver

Lama was with me while I wrote my books about Minack. She planted her muddy paws on the first page of the manuscript of this book, and I treated it as lucky that she had done so. Even in my anticat days, as I have said, a black cat was an emblem of good luck. I was never superior about this superstition, and I always felt happier if a black cat crossed my path. A nanny may have planted the idea in the first place, or perhaps it was my mother. My mother disliked cats, but she had an intuitive mind, a mind which could dispense with hard reason. All through my growing up she shared my hopes, talking on my behalf in family councils, giving me confidence in practical ways and displaying more than once the queer power of the spirit which has influenced me ever since.

My father, when he was a child, had a nurse called Miss Lewin, and after Miss Lewin had completed her life of looking after other people's children, she retired to Ilfracombe. For what seemed many young years of my own life, we were always about to visit Miss Lewin, but for one reason or another there was always some good cause for the visit to be postponed.

Then at last the great day arrived. Today we *will* visit Miss Lewin, and it was my mother who decided this, for my father at the time was away. Perhaps my mother, in her wish to provide a diversion for a school vacation, believed it would provide me and my two brothers with an adventure. Unfortunately she had lost Miss Lewin's address.

It is vague now in my mind as to how we reached Ilfracombe, except I seem to remember my mother at the wheel of our four-seater Morris open touring car, repeatedly blowing the horn at cattle blocking the way as we careered up the north coast of Cornwall into Devon. My mother was an excellent driver, and she was one of the first women ever to drive a car from London to Cornwall . . . although at the time she was incapable of reversing.

We reached Ilfracombe, and I was impressed by the Victorian heaviness of the place. Solid houses with porticos, solid streets, solid shops, solid people in the streets. But where was Miss Lewin?

There then occurred the event which impressed me forever afterwards. . . . We had wandered around for an hour or more when suddenly my mother pointed to a solid house in the center of the town, one in a long avenue, and declared, "If we knock at that door I'm sure we'll find her."

We did. Miss Lewin was in the sitting room, ninety years old and blind, but I had been so amazed by my mother's intuition that I remember nothing of the old nurse herself.

The incident left a profound impression upon me because it was the first time I became aware that intuition was stronger than logic. We may draw up sensible plans, proliferate our lives with rules and regulations, have years of study and training, and yet it is intuition which holds the key. A doctor's diagnosis, the success of a political leader, the achievements of a businessman, the skill of a teacher—all in the final instance depend on intuition.

"What are you looking at?" Jeannie asked.

A warm, late October afternoon, and we had taken our saucerless cups of tea to the terrace close to the cottage we call "the bridge."

"There's something black in the corner of Bill's field," I said, "over by the hedge on the right. I thought it was a carrion crow at first. . . ."

"What is it then?"

"I need my field glasses."

"I'll fetch them."

Jeannie ran back to the door of the cottage, passing Lama curled like a black cushion in the cup of an old rock, one of the rocks which formed the foundation of the cottage. A rock which had been there since the beginning of time, solid witness of history . . . Athelstan, Middle Ages, the Spanish Armada, Marlborough, the loss of the American Colonies, the Bastille, the Prince Regent and Beau Brummel, Trafalgar, William the Fourth and the Reform Bill, Melbourne, youthful Queen Victoria falling in love with Albert, the unorganized emotions of the Brontës, the Great Exhibition, Oscar Wilde, Mafeking, Edwardian grace, Bleriot, Passchendael, Marconi's first message across the Atlantic, horses leaving the land, old values fading, jumbo jets penciling the sky, ocean liners discarded, cement, highways, over-population . . . the rock where Lama curled was the same as in the beginning.

"Here they are."

I looked across the narrow valley to Bill's field and to what I thought for a moment to be a carrion crow, and I now saw clearly that I was watching a black cat.

"A black cat," I said to Jeannie, "which is about to jump."

Its body was quivering, paws were shuffling to gain the feel of a comfortable springboard, a mouse was about to be its victim, then a leap . . . and failure. Too soon or too late I would never know, because all I could see was a spread-eagled posterior and obvious frustration.

"Let *me* have a look," said Jeannie, and I handed her the glasses.

"He's pretending it never happened. He's found a tuft of grass to be interested in."

At that moment, if I had known it, the step had been taken that was to change our life at Minack.

And that of Lama.

My mind went back to the gray cat, whom we had named Daisy, and the black kitten in the barn. The kitten had stayed in our barn for ten days; and then one morning after the saucer of milk had been left untouched, I said to Jeannie that I was sure the barn was empty and that I felt we would never see the kitten again.

Perhaps we never did. Perhaps the kitten died or wandered miles and miles away. I will never be sure. All I can tell you is that a black cat with a thin tail, and the habit of burying its face into a saucer of milk, *did* one day come back to Minack.

Jeannie had given the name of Rosebud to the kitten, and so during its brief stay in the barn there were frequent remarks such as, "I'm taking the saucer down to Rosebud." Or, "Let's look through the barn window and watch Rosebud." And then later, after the kitten had disappeared, there were such musings as, "I wonder what happened to Rosebud?" Or, "Do you think a fox caught Rosebud!" Rosebud, therefore, had become a ghost personality in our household.

Jeannie's interest was, of course, greater than mine. Cat lovers' vanity is easily wounded, and I am sure she was irked by the manner in which Rosebud had ignored her. One evening, during the stay in the barn, Rosebud had, however, touched her. It was at night when Jeannie had gone down to the barn, and she had almost reached it when she was aware that something was, for a brief moment, brushing her leg, and then a second later she saw a black shadow dash away from her. This was the first physical contact with the kitten who had the habit of burying its face in a saucer of milk, and Jeannie was never to forget it. She was tantalized by this contact and by the mystery of Rosebud's disappearance. And from that moment on she was always looking for Rosebud.

I was too.

One of the charms of living in the country is the possession of time in which to delve into trivial mysteries. It was always so. I imagine the questions of those who have lived in Minack cottage . . . What is that strange ship sailing past Carn Barges toward Newlyn, and where has she come from? Why have the badgers abandoned the set down the cliff this spring? Who is that walking through the bracken on the other side of the valley? Did you hear the chiffchaff this morning, first one of the year? What killed the moorhen, was it a hawk? Why was a dog fox calling outside the cottage for the second night running? Why do gulls float from the west at night to rest on the rocks facing east?

I can imagine these people who lived their lives at Minack puzzling over these minor problems. Such events served no purpose except momentarily to occupy their attention. A diversion to their day which possessed no significance. They were pursuing the languid journey from birth to marriage to death, uncluttered by the side issues which fill, or empty, the society of today. They were enjoying, and quite unself-conscious that they were doing so, a natural life.

These ghosts of Minack have left their impression. I sense their presence. How, I sometimes wonder, would they face the problems which Jeannie and I face today? For although we may still possess the kind of freedom which is denied those who are forced by circumstances to lead routine lives, we are aware that the theorists are catching up on us. We have become, like everyone else, units in the national computer, and we are now the servants of Mr. Average; we no longer can sentimentally pretend we are isolated from the herd. We gaze wondrously at statistical reports and discover what we do. We play Bingo twice a week, eat more bananas than we did two years ago, drink more beer, and are unfulfilled because we have no telephone in the house.

Such examples of Mr. Average may seem trivial, but there is an underlying significance about them which is disquieting. For the cult of Mr. Average fools people into believing that we are all equal; and we are not, whatever the politicians and union leaders may say. The cry of fair shares for all is as futile as the expectation that all horses have an equal chance of winning the Derby. We can't all be a Gauguin or a Churchill or a Mozart or a Nicklaus or a Jane Austen or a Margot Fonteyn.

Yet the mood of this age urges us to be indignant or full of self-pity if we are not, and the result is a barren philosophy of envy which leads people to believe that rewards come as a right, and not as a consequence of talent, endeavor, and luck. The cult of Mr. Average taunts us to disregard ourselves as individuals. Our contrariness, our complexity, our special likes and dislikes, our subtle emotions which often surprise ourselves, are ignored when the computer does its work.

One observes Mr. Average in detachment until one becomes involved with him. Jeannie and I suddenly became aware of our involvement when it was decreed that the wage of the agricultural worker, being below the national average, was to be increased by £7 a week within a year; and with the promise of similar annual increases in the future.

Such a wage program is admirable in theory. Many concerns, of course, counter by higher prices, higher fares, higher rates, and higher charges for other affected services . . . with consequent squeals from the very same people who pressed for the higher wages. But there is a host of small businesses that cannot cope with this sudden rise in annual wages and their end is in sight.

It is sad because small businesses can often offer job satisfaction which is impossible in large concerns; and job satisfaction, although a dirty phrase in the minds of some, as if it reflects a pleasure which has been deceitfully invented by an employer to dupe his staff, offers a base for a happy life. Those, for instance, who work on the land have this job satisfaction. The sky is their factory ceiling, they do not have the expense and weariness of traveling to work on crowded trains and roads, they breathe unpolluted air, and they have nature around them to provide them with diversions.

But we still have to be realistic, and try to make the market garden pay . . . and market gardeners, unlike farmers, have no Price Review which helps to compensate farmers with guaranteed prices to cover their increased costs. Market gardeners, instead, are dependent upon the open market, and the weather; and, although prices for their produce may have risen substantially in the shops, their own returns have actually declined, not risen, in recent years.

Nor can market gardeners mechanize their methods of work with the comparative ease that farmers can. There is no machine to pick an acre of daffodils, then bunch and pack them; or a machine which is capable of pinching out unnecessary growth in tomato plants, or of picking the fruit when they ripen. Market gardeners have no alternative to hand labor; and hand labor is pricing itself away from reality.

It was a year after Rosebud had disappeared from the barn that we had our first false alarm. I looked out of the bathroom window into the field we call the donkey field, an acre of green grass where the donkeys spend much of their time, and saw the little black head of Lama peering from a thicket of coarse grass which the donkeys, for pernickety reasons, had decided not to eat.

"Lama," I called to Jeannie, "is in the donkey field hunting rabbits."

"She isn't," I heard her call back, "she's on my lap, and she's stopping me from putting the bread in the oven."

"How extraordinary," I called back again, "the cat I am looking at must be the double of Lama."

"A moment and I'll be with you."

I could see in my mind how "the moment" would be spent . . . the careful transfer of Lama from lap to sofa, and the murmur of sweet nothings as she did so. Jeannie might be inquisitive about Rosebud, but Lama would always be her queen.

But, as I said, it was a false alarm. Just as Jeannie reached me the cat moved away from its grassy hideout, and though the body was black it had a dirty white leg. It was also a large cat.

"Too large for Rosebud in any case."

"And Rosebud didn't have a spot of white."

I watched the cat move away down the field, then over the hedge alongside the wood. I had never seen the cat before, and I didn't expect to see him again, nor did I want to do so. I was, for Lama's sake, apprehensive about large tomcats. I remembered the warning, given me when Lama first came to Minack, that farm tomcats were notorious for the way they hunted neutered females, and killed them if given the chance.

"It isn't one of Walter's cats," said Jeannie, "I'm sure of that."

There is a higgledy-piggledy collection of farm buildings at the top of our lane on the way to the main road, and two small farmhouses. In one of

227

them live our friends the Trevorrows, and the name of Trevorrow is one of the oldest in Cornwall. For many years Mrs. Trevorrow has taken in visitors during the summer, and she is famous for her good food, and when we have a girl from afar to work for us during the flower season, Mrs. Trevorrow gives a temporary home to the girl. A hundred yards away is the farmhouse of the Cockram family. Jack Cockram was an evacuee from London during the war and learned his skills as a farm worker at a farm not far away; and then one day I was able to help him become a tenant farmer, and his farm now spreads out from the higgledy-piggledy farm buildings, the haphazardly placed fields, mingling with those of the Trevorrows. Both these families have been wonderful friends to us. I remember asking Bill Trevorrow very early on when we came to Minack if he could help us out by plowing a steep piece of ground in which we wanted to plant potatoes. Next morning he was there, and I took a photograph of him as he sat poised on his tractor before beginning his task. I remember at that moment thinking how wrong it was of me to ask him as a favor to take on something so seemingly dangerous. Yet he knew what he was doing. He would not have offered to do it unless he had the measure of it. In the many years I have known Bill Trevorrow, I have learned that that is the criterion by which he is guided.

Walter Grose is the third farmer at the top of the lane, and for many years he was tenant of yet a third farm which spread out from the higgledy-piggledy buildings, but after Jack Cockram came along they joined up together in partnership. However, Walter, a bachelor, did not live at the farm; his house was in St. Buryan village, and he used to

travel to work by van early every morning and return late at night. A long day among the fields and
his cows . . . and his cats.

He had numerous cats which lived around the
farm buildings, black and white cats, cats with
brown smudged faces and brown and white
bodies, patchy gray cats, and, of course, numerous
kittens, half-grown cats and somnolent elderly
cats. They waited expectantly for his arrival in the
morning, then gathered around the van as he produced their breakfast, and they gathered around
the van again when he had his coffee break, when
he had his lunch, when he had his tea. Walter was
a Pied Piper of cats.

Of course, so many cats could cause problems.
Mrs. Trevorrow, for instance, though devoted to all
animals including cats, was naturally perturbed
when a Walter cat appeared on her kitchen windowsill. Jack Cockram, I suspect, also viewed the
cats with apprehension. But what could anyone
do? Walter would sit in his van having his tea out
of a thermos, or munching sandwiches, and there
were his cats . . . on the hood, around the wheels,
comfortable and purring, aware that here was a
man who would look after them, feeding them
with a continual supply of fashionable tins of cat
food.

Naturally other farm cats were attracted to
the scene. Eager tomcats stepped across the fields,
and from time to time the great barn which housed
the hay became a maternity home for kittens, and
corners of it would nurture small families of Wal-
ter-fed cats.

I came up the lane one April morning at the
time of our first Rosebud alarm, and saw Walter
bending down, fingering the leaf of a Hart's

229

Tongue fern which was growing in the bank. This fern is named after the tongue of a fully grown deer, and it is pale green, delicate in texture, with slender tongue-shaped leaves.

"Lovely," he said, without looking up, "man couldn't make anything as lovely as this."

"They pay to have it in their gardens up country," I said practically, "and yet we can see it growing naturally, taking it almost for granted."

"Never," said Walter, "never can take nature for granted."

An old countryman like Walter is caught between his proved contentment in the way of life of his past and the necessity of being on the bandwagon of twentieth-century progress. Any countryman, for that matter, is in the same trap. He distrusts city-type standards, yet seems to have little power to resist them. The cement-based apostles of progress have a charisma which the countryman cannot match. The countryman, rich in the minor matters of life, has no persuasive answer to those who demand more land, more land, and still more land for housing developments, highways, schools and factories. The countryman watches the badger sets, home for a thousand years of badgers, demolished within an hour by a monster machine. Or a fox's lair, or the site of a long-used heron's nest, or hedges and undergrowth where warblers, chiffchaffs, whitethroats make their nests after flying thousands of miles to do so. But what arguments can he produce to prove that the preservation of such minor matters is more important than yielding to the materialism of the human race?

"When I was young," said Walter, "we went looking for plants like these, and wild flowers, and there was excitement in finding them. It wasn't just the few who did this; most of us felt the same way."

"You didn't have the advantages, Walter, of television and cars and motorcycles."

"What advantages? Are they happier racing back to watch a program than I was finding a patch of wild violets mixed with primroses? Funny thing," he went on, "I remember when it all changed."

"How do you mean?"

"Milk," he said, "never used to be collected on Sundays, the Sabbath being what it was."

"But the cows had to be milked, didn't they?"

"Ah, yes, but that was the only work that was done; no kind of business was ever conducted."

Thus the churns of Saturday evening milking, and of Sunday morning and Sunday evening, were kept back for the Monday collection.

"Then one day Grandfather heard a rumor there might be Sunday collection before long, and I remember him solemnly saying to me, 'The day they change to collecting milk on a Sunday . . . all else will follow.' "

Walter hadn't changed much at any rate. He still worked seventy and more hours a week, always had a pleasant word for any passerby, still replied to the question, "How are you, Walter?" with the answer, "Poor but happy," and still had his cats.

The black cat with the dirty white leg didn't belong to him, as Jeannie had said. We never knew where it came from. It would roam around Minack for a day or two, then disappear for weeks, and when it returned, when one morning I would see its face peering among the grass in the donkey field above the cottage, I would call out to Jeannie that the tomcat was back. And immediately I would be on guard about Lama.

The second false alarm had more substance. A girl from Nottingham had called on us, and wanted to look at the cottage that had figured in one of my earlier books. I gave her directions how to get there, ten minutes away, through the Pentewan meadows.

An hour later the girl returned from her pilgrimage and surprised us by saying she had met a black cat by the old quarry. Jeannie and I reacted to the news in predictable ways: I ignored it, Jeannie insisted she had to make an investigation. She went off the same evening to look for it.

She found nothing. The next day we walked over to the quarry together, then the following day and the day after that. Not a sign of a cat. "The girl imagined it," I said to Jeannie.

But Jeannie was persistent. There was a full moon the following night, and once again she set off for the quarry, alone this time, leaving me to wallow in a bath. Then twenty minutes later I heard her call excitedly, and I clambered out, wrapping myself in a towel, and found Jeannie in the sitting room holding a saucer in either hand.

"I've found it," she cried, as if she had found a mislaid valuable brooch, "and it's outside there in the garden!"

I looked around for Lama and saw her in a deep sleep on the sofa. She was unaware of the unfaithfulness.

"What happened?"

"It just appeared out of one of the meadows, and came up to me, and when I turned to come back it followed. It's a he, that I'm sure, and I shall call him Felix."

Still wrapped in my bath towel, I stepped out-side and peered at Felix, who now was devouring a saucer of fish which Lama would have had for breakfast in the morning.

"That certainly is not Rosebud," I said immediately, and rather crossly, "and he certainly isn't one of Daisy's offspring." Daisy, the neat, small gray wild cat, mother of Lama and Rosebud. "He's leggy, and bony," I went on, "and he has a small head, and he's very skinny . . ."

"He's starving!"

"Don't fool yourself that this is Rosebud returned. This is just a black cat which has been abandoned . . . and he's looking for a new home. We'll have trouble unless you get rid of him quickly."

"How quickly?"

"Tonight!"

This was, of course, bravado talk on my part. It was too late to do anything. All we could do was to shut the door on him, and pray he would be gone in the morning. He wasn't. He had made himself a nest in the tractor shelter, enjoyed an excellent sleep after his first decent meal in weeks . . . and now was ready for more. There he was, looking at me, while Lama was at my feet rubbing against my leg.

"Jeannie," I said authoritatively, "we couldn't get rid of him last night, but this morning . . ."

There are people I know who have thick skins. They simply refuse to accept the fact they are not wanted, and they will mooch around or bossily try to take charge without taking note of any hint that they should buzz off.

Felix was one of these. During the course of the following five days, he resolutely refused to take note of my obvious distaste for his presence.

233

He had found a home, and nothing was going to budge him from it . . . and budge him we certainly tried.

Our first step was to discover that he belonged to a recently sold farm which was now empty. Adjacent to this farm was another farm, and its owner was a good friend of mine and a lover of cats. Both farms were a mile or so from Minack as the crow flies, across a number of fields, and out of sight. We called on my friend, and he happily agreed that he would look after Felix if we brought him back.

This we did. We picked Felix up, sat him on Jeannie's lap in the car while I drove and took him around to his benefactor. That was Monday afternoon. By Tuesday midday he was back at Minack, his radar system guiding him across the fields. Once again we picked him up, put him in the car and took him to my friend. Wednesday afternoon he was back again. Once more we returned him. Thursday there was no sign of him, and I felt relaxed. Friday he suddenly appeared just as some visitors were taking a photograph of Lama . . . and the subsequent print included him. Felix was clinging to us, and I had become desperate.

"We must telephone his previous owner," I said to Jeannie; "he may be so distressed by the story that he will have Felix back."

We drove to the telephone booth at Sparnon on the way to Lands End. I sat outside the booth with skinny Felix on my lap while Jeannie talked to the previous owner, and I watched her through the glass gesticulating with one hand, and I guessed she was getting nowhere in her plea that he should take possession again of his abandoned Felix. Jeannie can be persuasive, and determined, but she was bluntly told that the man's new home was too small for a cat, and that she could do what she liked with him.

But just after she had given me her account of the conversation, I suddenly saw coming along the road toward us a tractor and trailer, and driving the tractor was the young man who had become the new owner of the farm. This was a blessed moment of good fortune, and I seized it. I jumped out of the car, ran across the road and stopped him.

"I need your help!" I cried.

The young man was not going to live at his new farm, for he already had another. His plan was to cultivate the fields, and sell off the farmhouse as a private residence.

He needed no persuasion.

"O.K.," he said, looking down on me from the tractor, "as I bought the farm I reckon I am responsible for what went with it. . . . We have enough cats as it is, mind, but I guess the children will be glad to have another."

So ended the Felix saga. The second, and last, of the Rosebud false alarms.

hen one March morning I came out of my office, which used to be the stables, and was faced by a startling sight.

On the near side of Monty's Leap was crouched Lama.

On the other side was a black cat.

They sleepily looked at each other, and they were both identical in size and shape.

They reminded me of bookends.

We were rushed, at the time, by the beginning of the peak period of the daffodil harvest. The California, most prolific of daffodils, were coming into bud so fast that we had difficulty in keeping up with them before the buds burst into unsalable full flower, and we had much of the earlier Joseph Macleod still to pick, and the Lamorna, and Dutchmaster, apart from other varieties.

I hurried over to the small greenhouse where Jeannie was packing the bunched daffodils. It is a job that requires concentration, and Jeannie does not like being interrupted. She counts each bunch that she is packing in a box, and often when I address her at these times, she does not answer.

"There's a black cat the other side of Monty's Leap, and Lama is this side. They're staring at each other."

Jeannie was not listening. She had to pack perhaps a hundred boxes a day, and each box had to be perfect.

"There's a black cat the other side of Monty's Leap," I repeated.

In order to keep the bunches in place during the journey to market, a horrid metal rib is lanced into each side of the cardboard box over the stems of the daffodils; do it carelessly and you can cut a finger. Jeannie safely completed this task on a box and then, as if she had suddenly come alive to my presence, turned around to me:

"*What* did you say?"

"Come quick," I said, "I believe the real Rosebud has come at last."

Jeannie ran ahead of me, past the big greenhouse, then through the gap into the lane leading down to Monty's Leap. Then she stopped, and when I reached her I saw Lama strolling peacefully toward us.

"I don't see any black cat," said Jeannie.

"It was there, I promise you. It was lying just by the gate, and Lama was this side by the violets."

The violets were a patch of Ascania, the original Cornish violet; I had stuck a root or two beside the lane, and they had spread. Sweet smelling on warm early spring days.

"Perhaps it was the shadow from the gatepost you saw."

"Don't be silly. It was a black cat, and it had a head like Lama's, and it looked small."

"Lama doesn't seem to have been upset by it."

Lama, true, looked serene. She had reached the small lane-side well where a frog was croaking. This well, which was no more than a shallow hole beneath a great rock, was used by past inhabitants of Minack cottage during the winter. Land water collected there. But when summer came, and the land became dry, there was no water in the hole, and the inhabitants carried their pails farther up the lane to another well.

Lama paused.

"Croak, croak."

She put out a paw, a gesture full of doubt, and nowhere near the frog. The frog was out of sight, half submerged in the safety of his home.

It is sad that frogs are disappearing from the countryside. I have known summer evenings at Minack when the lane in the neighborhood of Monty's Leap was so covered by dancing frogs that I would not walk that way for fear of treading on them. Tadpoles too abounded in the little stream from which, in the beginning of our life here, we filled our jugs with water . . . and tadpoles. Indeed on one occasion when my mother was staying with us she found a tadpole in her morning cup of tea. She was kind enough to make no fuss, and smiled away our apologies. But when she returned to London she hastened to Harrods, and bought us a china contraption called a Cheavin's Saludor Filter, and thereafter we emptied our jugs into it, then returned the captured tadpoles to the stream. We still possess the Saludor, and we use it as an ornament in a corner of the garden.

Fred once involved himself foolishly with a frog. Fred has a thrusting personality compared to the ruminating character of Penny. Penny approached a mystery with care, Fred with no care at all.

Thus Penny would have avoided the incident which resulted in Fred looking so foolish. Penny would have noticed the rustling in the grass on the bank close to the small reservoir, stood there patiently observing it and then turned away. Not so Fred.

I was standing close by at the time so that I saw the incident in detail. Fred heard this rustling in the grass, and for a moment he stood still with his ears pricked, resembling, as strangers often remark, the epitome of a thoroughbred. He has a very noble head when his ears are up and his eyes alert, and he deserves all the compliments he receives. This donkey of dignity, however, was about to lose his dignity.

He pushed his white nose down into the grass . . . and a frog jumped out and sat on it.

We went back to the small greenhouse at the moment Geoffrey, our help, appeared, a jammed-tight basket of daffodil buds in either hand.

"Mr. T.," said Jeannie, "swears that he saw a black cat, the double of Lama, down by the leap."

"It's true, Geoffrey. They were facing each other. I couldn't believe my eyes."

"But when I got there," interrupted Jeannie, "there wasn't a sign."

"Too many pasties perhaps," he said, winking.

Pasties, for some reason I cannot remember, had become a joke word for drinks in a pub. "Too many," therefore, meant I had seen double.

"Not at this hour."

"Anyhow," I said, "we'll miss the train unless we hurry."

Jeannie glanced at Geoffrey.

"I ask you," she laughed, "he behaves as if *we've* held things up!"

We fetch our milk from Jack and Walter's farm—rich milk which Jeannie first scalds, then skims the surface so that we always have our own Cornish cream. We carry an aluminum can up the lane and hitch it on a nail outside the farm gate, and Jack fills it after the next milking, usually a morning milking because that is the best one. Jeannie had taken the can up to the farm one evening, and had reached Monty's Leap on her return when she saw the black cat.

"I just couldn't believe it," she rushed at me when she saw me, "a black cat, the exact double of Lama. I wouldn't have believed it possible. It's Rosebud! It's Rosebud!"

I looked at her with amusement.

"A week ago I told you that I had seen it," I said, "and you didn't take me seriously."

"I was too busy . . . but now I have seen it I am amazed! It is obviously a Daisy cat . . . the same shaped body as Lama, the same shaped head . . ."

It was at this moment that I had a sense of apprehension. I could not place what it represented at first and, in such a situation, one often can shrug such apprehension away. Your mood, you say to yourself, is responsible. Or perhaps the weather. You therefore console yourself by saying that exterior circumstances are responsible for the unpleasant, fleeting sense of sadness. In any case, on this occasion, I kept my feelings to myself and, instead, was outwardly enthusiastic that Rosebud at last, after the false alarms, had returned to Minack.

But had she?

It was four and a half years since Daisy, the gray cat, had brought the little black kitten up from the cliff into the barn. But Daisy had made it quite plain that she wanted nothing to do with us. She scorned Jeannie's blandishments, and I watched amusedly Jeannie's failure. Jeannie was not accustomed to being rebuffed by cats, even a wild one like this gray one. Yet in the years ahead it was to be proved that she had in some way established an understanding. Daisy found her way to Minack when she was dying, and in the last few days of her life, though still refusing to sacrifice her independence, let Jeannie try to help her. She hung around by Monty's Leap, sheltering among the heliotrope leaves that border the bank, refusing the food Jeannie offered her, but in the end allowing Jeannie to pick her up and carry her into the greenhouse, the only time Jeannie ever touched her. That day I gave her a saucer of water and Daisy, as if to show how angry she was with herself for asking help from a human, violently brought a paw down on the saucer and broke it. An hour later she had died.

Where had Rosebud been in the meantime? Why had we never seen her around except for that time when we looked across the valley, six months previously, and saw the black dot in the corner of Bill's field? Why, if she had a good home somewhere, would she want to come back to Minack? She had been a frightened, unfriendly little kitten, and except for that moment when she had brushed against Jeannie in the dark, she had never been in physical contact with either of us. Our only contribution to her welfare, in fact, was the saucer of milk we used to give her in the barn, and which she splashed all over her face. . . .

"Jeannie," I said suddenly, "I have an idea that will help to prove it is Rosebud."

"I think I've had the same idea."

"Milk?"

"Yes."

"Then let's set the trap."

We proceeded to do so the following morning. We were lucky. We had not long to wait. We had placed a saucer of milk in the lane on the other side of Monty's Leap when the black cat appeared and walked cautiously toward it. We were thirty yards away by the barn with field glasses at the ready.

And when the cat had cleaned up the saucer and moved away, we clearly saw her face. It looked as if she had dipped it in snow.

now started to keep a diary of Rosebud's appearances. Her visits, for a long time, had no pattern. We would see the smudge of black on the other side of Monty's Leap, then wonder where Lama might be. Lama was the queen of Minack. Any challenger might be tolerated, but never accepted. Rosebud had better disappear again if she thought she might be able to usurp, or share, Lama's throne. There was also the question of Rosebud's sex. There began to be doubts. A significant scent was smelled on occasion, and suspicions began to be raised that Rosebud wasn't a Rosebud. But let this short extract from my diary explain our dilemma:

April 9 . . . Rosebud at Monty's Leap staring at me.

April 10 . . . Rosebud was across the leap and was outside the stable section of the barn.

April 21 . . . Haven't seen Rosebud for days.

May 2 . . . Rosebud back. Where on earth has she been in the meantime?

May 7 . . . Visitors came to the door, saying that they had seen Lama in the lane. They hadn't. Lama was indoors. Rosebud had played the part of Lama.

May 10 . . . No sign of Rosebud.

May 18 . . . Rosebud around these past few days, but seldom across Monty's Leap. A very nervous cat.

June 1 . . . Rosebud shows no sign of letting us touch her. We approach and she scuttles away into the undergrowth.

June 4 . . . Problems. Is Rosebud a he after all? There was a strong smell of a tomcat by the leap this evening. This would be serious.

June 15 . . . Rosebud has been away for some days. Then this morning Lama came running around the corner of the cottage and dashed past me inside. A second later Rosebud appeared at the corner, and I shouted her away. I've never seen them so close together before. And Lama was *frightened*.

June 17 . . . This morning I walked down to the

leap and saw Rosebud sleeping on a bank of dried grass. As usual she fled as I approached. Then I went up to the patch of grass. . . . There is no doubt Rosebud *is* a tom.

The discovery jerked us into reality. We had to be sensible and make up our minds what our intentions were going to be toward the cat. We were, I realized, secretly flattered that he had chosen to hover around Minack because, after all, we never asked him to do so, and in any case we would have been pretty heartless if we had not been impressed by his apparent desire, after such a long absence, to come back to the place where he was born. Yet he had to go. We couldn't risk anything happening to interfere with the flow of Lama's life.

"We mustn't take any notice of him," I said.

"I'll try not to."

"We must shout at him whenever we see him."

"That won't be easy."

"He'll go back whence he came if we frighten him."

"I don't want to frighten him."

"Which is worse . . . he being frightened, or Lama?"

"What a silly question."

"All we have to do then is to starve him. It's perfectly straightforward."

Then I added as an afterthought: "In any case we'll have to find a name for him . . . the days of Rosebud being over."

Jeannie looked at me in astonishment.

"I thought you said we were never going to have anything to do with him again . . . so why give him a new name?"

"Well," I said, "we'll probably talk about him,

won't we? So it's better to have a name which fits the sex."

"If you say so."

The maddening thing about the situation was that the cat had infiltrated into my mind. He had touched a soft spot, my awareness that loneliness is pitiful whether a human suffers it or an animal. Against my will I had found myself from time to time *thinking* about him, and I was moved by his perseverance which he had pursued without brashness. This black cat did not have the thrustfulness of a Felix. He wasn't barging in on our lives. He was hovering on the perimeter, watching, nervous, and, except on that occasion when he chased Lama around the corner of the cottage, he had done no harm. I had a hazy interest in the cat, like that of a man who wants to know a girl better when he shouldn't.

"So what shall we call him?" I asked.

We had been able to observe him closely enough to distinguish the differences between him and Lama. From a distance, even a short distance, they looked amazingly similar, and at first glance one couldn't separate one from the other. Both had the same dainty head of Daisy, their mother, and this was the reason why we thought Rosebud was a Rosebud, for it is usually easy to tell a tom from a lady. Lama, however, was more compact, and there were her extraordinary eyes which were amber, though deepened in color by browny flecks. The other's eyes were pale yellow, and his body was thinner. There were also differences between their whiskers, and between their tails. Now that she was growing older, Lama's white whiskers had become a permanent feature. Her tail, however, had always remained the same plush, silky plume, and it was admired by all who saw it. But the tail of the other was a miserable affair. . . . It was very thin, and looked like a black, elongated twig.

"Let's call him Twig," I suggested.

"I was thinking of Oliver."

"Why Oliver?"

"After Mike."

Mike Oliver was a friend of ours who kept a cat and dog home near Newquay.

"All right. . . . Rosebud has become Oliver."

Oliver by now had disappeared. A week went by, two weeks, three, a month, and there was never a sign of him. It was as if he had overheard our discussions and had decided it was better to vanish than to be scared away by our shouts. We were glad he had done so because no one could enjoy making a frightened cat more frightened, and his voluntary absence meant that we could enter again the quiet rhythm of our summer days with our consciences clear.

We no longer, for instance, concerned ourselves about Lama. She was able to wander sleepily from nest to nest without us worrying that Oliver might suddenly appear and disturb her summer thoughts. She would be absent for hours on end, and be deaf to our calls when someone arrived who wanted to meet her. This was her idea of a perfect life though, suddenly feeling adventurous, she would sometimes wander up the lane, across Monty's Leap and beyond, passing the spot where Oliver used to watch us, and continue to stroll, sniffing this tuft of grass or that, sublimely confident that she was queen of all she surveyed. It was peaceful for us to watch her. This was the unrattled mood which we loved most at Minack.

This mood, however, had its dangers, duping us into believing that our world was full of pleasant people. It lulled us into forgetting that the rat race still existed. When we lived in London we were always on guard, always ready to try and counter the double cross if it took place.

Yet if you develop an attitude of distrust toward those who appear to be friends, a light goes out of life, and so it is better to be cheated occasionally rather than to be inherently suspicious. Our trouble is that we sometimes behave with such innocence. The peace of Minack is the cause of it. We become so involved in the beauty of our surroundings that we forget the world orients around money, greed and power. We forget that people are so consumed by the stresses of material self-survival that they do not concern themselves with ethics, and that the transatlantic philosophy of believing any dirty action is justified if the objective is gained as a result is now a part of life. We forget these things as we stare out at the view from Minack across the green bracken of the moorland in summer to the blue expanse of Mount's Bay lined by the ribbon of the Lizard, or watch swallows sweeping the sky, or lazily listen to the bees feeding on the pink flowers of the escallonia up by the bridge or smell the scent of the musk rose beside the great rock in front of the cottage. We forget that the true values have become distorted in the pursuit of man's mania for materialism. We forget these things, and are therefore vulnerable when someone beams a false friendliness. We foolishly believe he is under the same spell as ourselves until later we discover the truth.

On August 10 we saw Oliver again.

He was a little way up the lane on the far side of Monty's Leap, and he was sitting neatly in the middle, staring down toward Minack.

My feelings were mixed. His absence had made me wonder, and worry for that matter, whether something harmful might have happened to him. Gin traps are no longer legal, but there are still the snares. Snares, in my opinion, are diabolical, and it is sad that the RSPCA appears to approve of them. A snare can slowly throttle a rabbit or a cat, and when sometimes a cat is caught with the snare around some other part of its body, it becomes so ferocious that the trapper, instead of releasing it, kills it. I was therefore relieved by the sight of Oliver. I was also upset. We had been enjoying the old peaceful times during the past few weeks, and Lama had been able to roam as she wanted. This return of Oliver could only interrupt her comfortable routine.

"We'll ignore him," I said, puffing at my pipe.

"Yes," Jeannie said, "I certainly won't feed him."

"Well," I said, still looking down the lane, "we can't waste our time staring back at him. We have work to do."

We were in the last stages of the tomato season, and we were grading and weighing the tomatoes after Geoffrey had picked them. He would bring the baskets into the small greenhouse and empty the contents onto the long bench. Then Jeannie and I would pick out the very small ones and put them into one tomato box, or tray as it is called, and put the rest in two other trays, one of them being for the ripened fruit, the other for the half-ripened. Each tray had to weigh twelve pounds, and when this was done, the outside was labeled with the number of the grade the tomatoes were supposed to represent. I have to admit, however, that we cheated on these Common Market-imposed grades. We cheated because we objected to the fact that the three grades were only concerned with the size and shape of the tomatoes, and took no account of the flavor. Hence Grade One tomatoes might fulfill the legal conditions to perfection, yet have the taste of soap, and so we put all the tomatoes, except the very small ones, into Grade Two. Then we stapled a special card on the side of the tray which had printed in large letters: GROWN FOR FLAVOR! This accurate description worked wonders. We were saved the trouble of specially grading the tomatoes, and at the same time caught the imagination of the buying public. Thus our wholesaler soon found he was able to obtain a premium for all the tomatoes we sent to him.

Not that this meant a fortune for us. The growing of tomatoes occupies the greenhouses in one way or another for ten months in the year. In November the soil is sterilized, and for eight weeks the greenhouse vents are shut, and nothing must be grown during the course of this time. True, we might use another sterilizing chemical which completes the sterilization within forty-eight hours, but the one we use is unpleasant enough. It has to be respected by anyone using it and its fumes can easily cause distress. But the other method of chemical sterilization can kill.

After the sterilization comes the stringing. Each plant has to have its own string to climb up and, because we are busy with the daffodil harvest when the plants arrive, Geoffrey does this stringing ahead of planting during the slacker time of January. Each string of our two and a half thousand plants is attached by hand to an overhead wire, and to a small galvanized stake which is pushed into the ground after the planting. Then, during the first week of March come the plants, and the oil heating begins, and every ten days or so a mammoth oil truck is squeezed by its driver down our lane, and its contents pumped into the two tanks, and conveyed by pipes to the five heaters, providing us with the opportunity for the following six months to watch our money go up in smoke. All the while there is the endless pinching out of unnecessary growth in the plants which takes up many hours of hand labor, and the less time-consuming tasks of opening and shutting the glasshouse vents in relation to the reigning temperature, and mixing the liquid manure for the automatic watering. Thus, when at the end of May the tomatoes begin to ripen, we have a vast amount of expenditure to retrieve before we make any profit out of our efforts.

Yet I have no good cause to grumble. We are not being ordered to grow tomatoes. We could stop doing so, pull down the glasshouses, sell the heaters and be spared the sight of an oil truck ever coming down the lane again. Thus if we choose to struggle on as we have done in the past, it is our own fault. We are wishing to pretend the present situation is as it was when we began at Minack, when the prospect of possessing glasshouses and heaters promised the lure of an assured future. The trouble is that we invested large sums in this future, and we now cannot afford to give it up.

"You'll have a two-thousand-pound turnover from tomatoes," the Ministry of Agriculture adviser had told us at the time, and I had enthusiastically believed him.

He was wrong. That figure has never materialized though we have never thought of blaming him for his faulty optimism. The world has changed since he gave us his advice, and we have come to realize that we do not possess the sharp minds of business people. Our form of profit is the pleasure of living life in a slow way, amidst untamed, undisciplined, uncomputerized nature. We compromise. We have to be satisfied with trying to earn just enough to make the market garden pay.

There is, however the other side to us, a leftover from our London days. We both have luxury tastes: tobacco from Simmons in the Burlington Arcade, shoes from Raynes, wine from the Wine Society, books from Hatchards, and other foibles which have no place on supermarket shelves. . . . Yet, when I look at the list in my accounts, each item seems to be modest, none of them wildly extravagant, and I thereupon marvel that the total is so large. True we sometimes have to go to London, but the occasions are few and far between. No gambling debts are on the list, no Continental vacations, no large-scale entertaining, and still the money has disappeared. The puzzle, of course, is commonplace. People all over the world are in the same dilemma. Where has the money gone?

I did, however, once have the opportunity of becoming a millionaire, and it was only due to lack of zest, and of courage, on my part that I didn't take it. Toward the end of the war, as I walked around London, I observed there were many streets with their buildings festooned with For Sale signs. In Park Lane, for instance, the lovely though bomb-battered houses between Brook Street and Marble Arch looked at me as I passed, begging me to give them my protection; and I soon became so obsessed by the sight of them, by their past, and by what seemed to me to be a great future once the war was over, that I went to see the real-estate agents to ask the price. It was a Friday, and when I reached their offices it was twenty-five minutes to six, and the doors were shut. Had I been five minutes earlier the manager might have greeted me with open arms, and I would have been launched as a property dealer. As it was, my enthusiasm dimmed over the weekend, caution prevailed and the houses had to wait for another buyer.

Oliver continued to haunt Minack, and we continued to ignore him. It was not too difficult to do so because he never, until one day in late September, crossed to the cottage side of Monty's Leap. He would sit for hour upon hour beside the granite post of the white gate, staring up the lane as if he was willing us to pay him attention. He certainly was not begging for food, so he was no doubt having enough from somewhere. Yet what compelled him to come to Minack despite our rebuffs?

He was now such a fixture on the other side of

the leap that we became careless about Lama, though she herself seemed content, showing no fear of him when she wandered down to the stream and saw him on the other side. She roamed the immediate area of the cottage as she always had done, settling in long-accustomed nests, sleeping in a curled black ball, queen of the world she had known so long. But visitors were confused.

"We were coming down the lane, and we were very lucky. We saw Lama! We took a picture of her."

"That wasn't Lama."

"Oh?"

"No, it wasn't Lama, it was . . ."

I soon gave up explaining who Oliver was. It was too complicated. Nobody would believe or understand me. And anyhow I didn't want to talk about him at the expense of Lama.

"That was not Lama," I would say therefore, "that was her understudy."

At the end of September, however, the understudy caused serious trouble. We had taken the donkeys for a walk along the cliffs, and down the road to Lamorna and the pub. On our return we left the donkeys in the stable meadow, walked through the wooden gate and saw two black cats staring at each other a few feet apart close to the white garden seat.

"Don't move," I said to Jeannie, "let's see what happens."

It was absurd how alike they were, except for Lama's compactness and the tails.

"Perhaps they're going to be friends," said Jeannie.

"I doubt it."

Their eyes were unblinkingly staring at each

other, and I was reminded of a game we played at Copthorne, my preparatory school, called the stare game. Two small boys would stare at each other and the loser was the one who dropped his eyes first. Then the winner would take on another small boy and another, until he was declared champion starer of the form.

I am afraid Oliver was the champion starer on this occasion. Lama suddenly turned and bolted up the path, then disappeared around the corner of the cottage.

"Damn," I said.

Though Oliver had not moved, Lama, queen of Minack, had panicked on her own territory. Oliver had imposed his personality upon her, and I was angry.

"Shoo," I said, advancing toward him, shuffling my feet on the gravel so that I made a noise like a tire spinning. "Shoo," I hissed, "shoo, shoo, shoo . . ."

And Oliver raced down the lane.

"Good riddance," I said firmly.

The incident, as it turned out, was of benefit to Lama. We often used to leave her out at night until we were ready to go to bed, and then we would bring her in. Sometimes in winter she was out for hours, and we would not bother about what might be happening to her. She was capable of looking after herself. Born a wild cat, she was accustomed to the adventures of the night. She had never caused us concern. Rain, snow or a howling gale, we took it for granted that she was able to look after herself.

But what we had forgotten was that she was growing old. Three years before she was quick enough to catch a stoat, and mice galore, and a

rabbit or two. Now, we realized, she had eased off
on her hunting, and she was sleeping more, and
contemplating more, and in any case she now ran
away from an intruder.

A few evenings after that incident I was standing by the bridge having a drink when I heard a
cacophony of catlike screams down by the leap. It
was dusk, and I could see nothing from where I
was, though I immediately jumped to the conclusion that Oliver was causing trouble again. Lama
loved to take an evening walk down by the side of
the greenhouse, through our small orchard to the
gap in the hedge where the stream runs and which
is framed by the elm trees and which leads into the
main greenhouse field. Lama loved to walk this
way, then turn right past the compost heap to the
lane, and back to the cottage across the leap. Sometimes she would stroll one way, sometimes the
other, but the route was always the same.

I put down my glass on the slate ledge which
serves as a table on the bridge, and ran down the
lane shouting like a wild man. I was finished with
Oliver. We hadn't asked him to come to Minack.
We hadn't fed him for weeks, we owed him nothing, and yet he was completely upsetting the
rhythm of our days.

Just as I reached the leap I saw Lama on the
other side in the shadow, and it wasn't Oliver I
saw crouched close to her, spitting. It was a large
gray and white cat with a small head and big ears
which looked like those of a fox. It reminded me of
pictures of the devil. It didn't stay a second when I
arrived.

So I had been wrong about Oliver. I was glad.
He may have been upsetting our routine, but he
had never given the impression of being a fierce

cat. On the contrary there was something forlorn about him as if, like a lonely person, he was looking for love. At the same time he *might* attack Lama, and we were certainly not going to risk this happening, nor risk a repeat of the attack by the gray and white cat; so from then on Lama was kept indoors as soon as dusk fell.

I also decided that the time had come to take more seriously the question as to where Oliver came from. We had lazily let the question lie fallow because it did not seem all that important, and we also did not want an answer to the question which might cast doubt on our firm belief that Oliver was the original Rosebud. Yet it was nearly six years since Daisy had brought her black kitten up from the cliff and deposited it in the barn. It must have found a home somewhere. . . . Was it possible that, after the ten-day stay in the barn, Daisy took it away again and left it at one of the farms nearby? An extra kitten among a farm population of cats and kittens might not be immediately noticed.

We already knew he did not come from the two farms at the top of the lane, the Rosemodress farms, and we therefore decided to ask the owners of Tregurno when we next saw a member of the family. The Jeffrey family were old friends of ours though we seldom saw them, despite the fact their farm was only a mile and a half across the fields in the direction of Lamorna. When we first rented Minack, and before it was habitable, we used to stay at Tregurno, a splendid old Cornish farmhouse with front windows facing farm fields, moorland and the sea, and it has today a fine reputation as a farm guesthouse.

The Tregurno farm, at the time, used to take

their milk churns to the milk stand at the bottom of the lane on the edge of the main road; there they were daily collected by the milk truck and taken to the milk factory at St. Erth. One morning, when I was driving into Penzance, I arrived at the milk stand when young Roger Jeffrey had just unloaded his churns.

"Have you ever had a black cat your way?" I said, stopping the car beside his tractor. He leaned forward from his seat, a good-looking Cornish face with black hair.

"You mean Blackie? Oh, yes, I've seen him down your place from time to time. All the others at the farm go for him. I don't know why. He's the odd one out."

"I can't understand why he comes down to see us," I said. "We don't encourage him; in fact it's the opposite. We want him to go."

I had stopped the engine of the car but the tractor's engine was still ticking over, and it was difficult to hear what Roger was saying. Then I added, and it was, I afterward realized, the sixty-four-dollar question: "How long has Blackie been with you?"

"Nearly six years," said Roger.

It was nearly six years since the kitten had disappeared from our barn.

"Thank you, Roger," I said, and drove off.

I felt vaguely pleased. I would not have liked him to have said, "Oh, yes, that's our Blackie . . . he's only two years old." That would have spoiled the game. I wanted to continue to believe that the black cat and the kitten were one and the same, and I was therefore suffering from conflicting emotions. One part of me was enjoying the mystery of a cat who wanted to return to his original home,

257

the other was wanting to be free of his persistent attention.

Awhile later I saw Roger's mother and I brought up the matter again.

"That's our Blackie down your place," said Mrs. Jeffrey, "no doubt about that. . . . You feed him I expect?"

"We haven't for ages."

"He comes back to us for a day or two, then off he goes again. I've even tried shutting him up in a room, but it doesn't do any good. I'm very fond of Blackie."

The mystery became more puzzling. Why should a well-fed, well-loved cat ever wish to leave its home for the sort of treatment we were giving him?

"Perhaps he goes," went on Mrs. Jeffrey, repeating what Roger had told me, "because the others attack him. They don't seem to like him."

I then put to her the idea which had long been in my mind.

"We had this kitten which disappeared from our barn," I said, "and it was about the same time as your Blackie arrived at Tregurno. You don't suppose Daisy, the mother, carried it across the fields to your farm, just as she carried it up from the cliff to the barn, and for some reason left it with a foster mother with kittens of the same age?"

Mrs. Jeffrey couldn't accept this. She was sure she knew the litter in which Blackie was born.

"I just wondered," I said, "whether the others attacked him because they knew he didn't belong to the Tregurno cat dynasty."

We both laughed.

"Anyhow," I added, "you can be sure we're not trying to keep him."

The situation had now become more complicated. Oliver, in his original name of Blackie, was
yearned for by Mrs. Jeffrey to go back to Tregurno.
Oliver, in the role of his Minack name, had this
mystical desire to haunt Minack. Lama would like
to see him gone forever, and Jeannie and I agreed
with her . . . until we caught the look of Oliver
staring at us up the lane. Then we couldn't help
sensing that there was some curious magic being
performed. Heavens, at this stage we had no no-
tion of its meaning. There was nothing logical
about it. Only a mood, like the scent of a flower on
a summer's evening one cannot place.

The rains came at the beginning of November.
We were thankful for them. The level of our well
had sunk so low that we had been rationing ourselves.

The rains fell, and Oliver did not mind.

He made himself a niche in a pile of old grass
and bracken trimmings which was heaped beside
the lane just beyond the leap and the white gate.
Above it were the bare branches of an elm and a
may tree, and they gave him little shelter. His shelter, for what it was, was a small umbrella of
bracken covering the dent in the grass on which
he curled. He might be there for two or three days,
then away for the same period, and if we walked
up the lane he would lift his head and stare at us
as we passed, an intent though timid stare.

At the beginning of December I found him
lying there at night, and, though the sky was clear,
a gale was howling through the trees, and a small
branch fell in front of me as I walked. His unusual
faithfulness had begun to get on my nerves. We
were conducting a war with a cat who refused to
be defeated. There we were ignoring him, refusing

to feed him, and yet by a Gandhi-like meekness he was putting us in the wrong. Now, having seen him lying there at night, I began to doubt whether our toughness was justified. Something compelled him to behave in this manner. What could it be? I had no answer to this at the time, though I felt the moment had come when he might have a reward. One had to be pretty heartless to ignore such re-mote-control devotion and, provided it did not inter-fere with Lama's life or stop him from returning to Tregurno if he wished, it didn't seem foolish to offer him again a saucer of milk.

Jeannie laughed when I suggested it.

"After all these weeks of sanctions you give in!"

"Sanctions never are of any value," I an-swered, "if the opposition is determined."

So Oliver had his milk again, and again dipped his face in it, as if he was eating the milk and not lapping it. And more important, of course, he re-joiced in his victory.

Not that he embarrassed us by displaying af-fection. He ran away when Jeannie advanced up the lane with the saucer, then would only reappear when she had gone. First a saucer of milk, then as Christmas drew near, a saucer of fish or chopped meat. But Jeannie still had to leave it on the ground, as if she was leaving it for a wild animal, then disappear before Oliver would dare to come out from his hiding place.

Soon he had another victory.

"There's an old wooden box in the barn," Jeannie said, "and if I put it down there near where he's sleeping, and put some straw in it, he'll have some protection from the weather."

Oliver moved in the same day without any encouragement from us. He was there on Christmas Eve, then absent during Christmas Day, but back at nightfall when Beverley Nichols paid a call on him.

Wise, witty, self-deprecating Beverley was spending the daytime of the holiday with us though staying at a hotel in Penzance. He had a devotion to cats which was similar to that of the Egyptians in the time of the pharaohs. His attitude, therefore, was in tune with that of Jeannie and so, when they were together, they indulged in that kind of cat worship which I still find a little distasteful. I will give an example.

I took them for a drive in the car around Zennor, Gurnards Head, Morvah, Pendeen, Trewellard and St. Just . . . and I had to be ready to pull up and stop whenever they saw a cat which caught their fancy. At Trewellard, for instance, there was a huge tabby sitting on a garden wall, sitting peacefully, eyes half closed, when he was suddenly awakened from his dreams by Beverley and Jeannie jumping out of the car, hastening toward him with arms outstretched and cooing those curious noises which are peculiar to cat worshipers. The tabby, however, I have to admit enjoyed it. He was still being rocked in Beverley's arms when the startled owner appeared, and by chance he was the coalman who delivers our anthracite. "My friend," I said nervously, "loves cats. He writes about them, you know."

On the other hand there are also cats which do not succumb to these extravagant blandishments, and Lama was one of them. Lama liked to maintain her dignity. Lama did not favor those who threw flattery at her as if it was confetti, and then expected her to yield submissively to their wishes.

Hence, when after the Christmas lunch Beverley expressed a desire to rest and invited Lama to share his bed, I doubted whether the union would be a success. Lama, for instance, squeaked when she was picked up from the sofa and carried into the bedroom, notwithstanding Beverley's protestations of devotion. And when the door shut on the bedroom, I wondered what kind of rest Beverley would enjoy. Ten minutes later I had the answer. The door was opened a few inches, and Lama flew out.

"They have had words," I said to Jeannie.

That night an easterly was blowing, and we put on coats before walking down the lane to visit Oliver in his box. I carried the flashlight, Beverley a saucer of chopped turkey and Jeannie a saucer of milk. Oliver was about to have a feast, and we only hoped he would be there.

He was there all right. I shone the light toward the box, and it lit the pinpoints of his eyes. But would he answer our calls? Would he respond to the most inveigling noises that Beverley and Jeannie could devise? Certainly not.

Like Lama, he was immune to flattery.

he first daffodil was in bloom by the middle of January, and by the beginning of February we were gently picking a basket or two. This was the most pleasant part of the daffodil season. The rush hadn't started, expectation existed and as always Lama came with us as we wandered among the meadows close to the sea.

She would walk up and down between the beds, the black plume of her tail mingling with the green spikes of the daffodil leaves, and sometimes when I was bending down to pick a stem, she would come to me, pushing her head against my hand, and then I would cease to pick and proceed to pay her the attention she expected of me. Or I would put a basket down at the edge of a meadow, go on with my picking, then look back and find her sitting in the basket. Or suddenly I would see her alert, stalking a noise in a bank of young grass, the sea as a background, a gull floating overhead, a robin observing from a branch. Moments like these made a mockery of the faraway world where fanatics throw bombs for narrow causes, where politicians maneuver for personal power, where strikers bellow defiance at reasonableness out of boredom, where earth-moving machines destroy a thousand years of history in an hour. Moments like these place the jargon of words like "rationalization," "productivity," "growth," "monetary crisis," "differentials," "price index," and "progress" in their true perspective. Such moments offer the Grail which man seeks.

"All life," I said, "except this instant is a dream."

"Why do you suddenly say that?"

I was standing in a tiny meadow which borders an area of blackthorn within which are the homes of both a fox and a badger family. One of the most desirable sites in Cornwall, we say, because they are safe from the humans who would like to kill them. Jeannie was beside me, and Lama was squat at our feet, black tail around her paws, swaying her head, utterly at peace.

"Well," I answered, "what do you remember of this morning?"

"I got your breakfast, the mail came, I wrote a letter to my sister, I wrote half a page of my book . . ."

"All hazy now in your mind."

"I suppose so."

"That's what I mean. Half one's life is dreaming of the future, the other half dreaming of the past."

"I understand."

"Our sophisticated years are now a dream, all the times at the Savoy, a bottle of champagne on ice in our room, a first night . . . Cholmondeley House, Mortlake Cottage, glamorous parties in your office with Danny Kaye and all the others. Only the instant was permanent."

"Like now."

"Yes . . . you and I and Lama, and that robin,

and the gull sailing down into the bay, and that wave moving in to smack the rocks. . . . This is the instant which is real."

Jeannie laughed.

"And now it's over!" she said.

I was being too serious, and she was bringing me back to my senses.

"All I meant," I finished by saying, "is that one mustn't take these instants for granted."

The wind began to blow that evening, coming from the south, first the scudding clouds, then a spitting of rain, then a torrent. It is a pleasing experience to be in a Cornish cottage with feet-thick stone walls, listening to the elements roaring and screaming, pausing to take breath, then at it again, tearing at the old granite weathered by ages of such storms. There is the atmosphere of coziness and safety, and the marvelous sense of being attacked by forces outside man's control. A storm is a sign of my freedom. In the final instance I can laugh at a militant, an economist, a television commentator or a headline writer. They can mouth their opinions about how I should conform to their theories . . . but I am free. The rain and the gale sigh and shout and fling their strength against Minack, and faith is restored. The cockiness of humans is in perspective.

I lay on the side of the bed nearest the door so I was favored first when Lama decided to jump on the bed. She jumped up and nestled close to me, and I woke up, suddenly finding her presence. And when I put out my hand and touched her, her purrs joined the roar of the gale and the rain. As I lay there in the dark with my hand cupped around her I found myself wondering about Oliver, then felt a twinge of guilt. I was being unfaithful. There was Lama beside me, blissfully confident in the affection she was receiving, while my mind revolved around her rival. Where was Oliver in this storm? Was he safe in his box down there beyond the gate? Similar twinges of guilt are felt by errant husbands and wives when, although keeping up the pattern of normal behavior, they are thinking of another.

There was no easing of the rain and the wind in the morning. The cottage windows are small, and so when the clouds are low it is dark in the sitting room. It was very dark that morning, and we had our breakfast with the standard lamp switched on.

"Lucky," Jeannie said, "we don't have to worry about the daffs. Another two weeks and we might have been in trouble."

"What are you going to do today?"

"First I have to make bread. There is only a crust left and I'll give it to the donkeys. Then I'm going to try to finish my chapter. That will be six."

"Halfway."

"I am so slow."

I am too. I envy those writers who spill words onto paper with the speed of sand poured from a bucket. If I write five hundred words in a day, I am ready to celebrate. Such a celebration, however, is rare.

"I read the other day that Arnold Bennett wrote five thousand words of *The Card* in two days . . . then retired to bed with a migraine for three. It was a week before he was ready to write again."

"I would put up with a migraine," said Jeannie, "if I could do that."

I had finished my breakfast, and I went over to my desk and picked up a pipe and filled it. But I paused before I lit it and looked at the rain lashing against the window from which I could see the barn and the land leading down to the leap.

"I think," I said suddenly, "that before I do anything I will go and see how Oliver is getting on."

"I'll come with you. I'll take him the fish that Lama's left."

We put on our yellow oilskins and went outside and down the lane, and as I did so I glanced at the stable meadow and saw in the far corner the donkeys with their bottoms to the hedge. Heads down, mournful, yet I knew that nothing would move them from their positions. They enjoyed their masochism. They would remain there, despite the warmth of the barn which awaited them, the rain drenching their winter coats, until Jeannie brought them that crust of bread. For a minute they would then become alive. Then back they would return to their lugubrious manner. They were martyrs of the weather. They made certain we realized it.

We reached the leap, and the stream was a yard wide and gushing toward the sea. We half jumped to cross it, and a few yards on we came to the spot in the copse beside the lane where Oliver's box was placed, and found it awash.

"Idiots," I said, "we should have remembered this gully was sometimes flooded."

No sign of Oliver. No sensible cat, in any case, would remain in a place where there is no shelter. If Oliver was wise, he might have had dreams of a nice warm farmhouse, and given up his siege of Minack. That would have suited me. I would like to be rid of my twinge of guilt.

"I'll leave the fish here in any case," said

Jeannie, her voice almost inaudible in the noise of the storm.

"Better not, it'll be drowned in the rain."

So I took the saucer from her, and we started back to the cottage.

On the other side of the leap, a few yards up on the right and close to the little land well is a gorse bush. It is a large gorse bush with gnarled branches and dense prickly foliage, and in early spring it has a resplendent display of yellow, scented blooms.

We were about to pass it when we heard a meow. A sharp crack of a meow, like the sound of a rocket fired from a boat in distress.

We both darted to the gorse bush . . . and there was Oliver crouched on a wristwide branch three feet from the ground.

"Oliver!" Jeannie cried out, and I added, "Couldn't you have found a better place to be in this weather?"

He could have done so. He could have gone back across the fields to Tregurno.

"Funny cat," said Jeannie.

"I'll put the saucer down here."

He sat on the branch staring at us, and I knew if we went any nearer he would flee away.

"I'll make you another house," I said solemnly, "and I'll make it above high water."

Later in the day I proceeded to build it. I gave it a foundation of rocks and a covered entrance. On the rocks I placed a new large wooden box, then roofed it with plastic and filled the inside with hay. The whole was camouflaged with old bracken, as if it was a thatched cottage. It was a splendid house, and this prompted Jeannie to make a joke, saying that Sir Christopher Wren could not have done better; and so Oliver's new home was christened the Wren House. He was delighted with it. He moved in the same evening, and he continued to use it for several weeks until an injury prompted him to move.

In the meanwhile came the daffodil season, and the daffodil season that year was enhanced by the presence of Fran, an Australian girl from Burnside, Adelaide. She was just twenty-one, fair and small, sturdy, affectionate, occasionally moody, indefatigable and very willing, and had a wonderful way with Geoffrey.

Fran was on a working tour of Europe. She had been in this country a few weeks and had a job in Reading when her sister, with whom she was staying, proposed that she should write to me. They had read a book or two of mine. Fran wanted to see Cornwall . . . and she preferred the outdoors to a shop counter. So the two of them concocted a letter to me, and before I had time to answer it, Fran arrived at our door one Sunday morning.

"Couldn't wait," she explained, "to find out whether you wanted me."

She had arrived in an ancient two-seater car, and she had driven from Reading, and it was January, and the forecast that morning said heavy snow was on the way. I said she was welcome to work during the flower season, and we fixed a date when she should come, and I said I would ask Mrs. Trevorrow whether she could stay with her.

"In fact I'll ask her," I said, "whether you can stay there tonight. You can't drive back to Reading with snow coming."

"Oh, yes I can."

She spoke defiantly. Why is it there are those who grate when they speak their mind, while there are others who give no offense? I took Fran's attitude without concern.

"See you on February twenty-first," I said.

"Sure."

We sent her into the Lama field, the first day she arrived, to pick Joseph Macleod. The Lama field was a new acquisition, a rented acquisition, and it had a curious history as far as Lama was concerned. The field was almost as close to the cottage as the donkey field from where the donkeys looked down upon us when we were on the porch. It was adjacent to the bridge where we had our meals on summer days, and for years it had been cultivated by a neighbor. During all that time Lama never went into it, tempting though it must have been for her to do so. Yet the very day after it came into our possession she was wandering around it, inspecting it like any new owner of a property, and as we watched her we decided that we would call it Lama's Field.

Fran preferred picking daffodils to bunching them, and after the first few days she proved to be a very quick picker. She would arrive in the morning and off she would go to join Geoffrey, and from time to time we would hear peals of laughter if the meadow in which they were picking was near, and we would be thankful that the flower season was going to be a happy one.

On the big daffodil farms the daffodils are picked *and* bunched in the field. I never understand how this can be done satisfactorily, but the reason for doing so is the paying of labor by piecework. Finding labor to pick flowers becomes more difficult every year, and piecework allows a big grower to employ all and sundry without losing money on some of the types who come. Yet there are physical difficulties about bunching in the open which I find impossible to surmount, and Geoffrey agrees with me. For instance, if there is a howling gale and rain, how do you slip a rubber band on a bunch of ten blooms without it taking a minute or two fiddling to do so? And how, with such amateurs involved in the piecework, can you guarantee that each bloom in the bunch is perfect? The truth is that with the arrival of some big growers from up-country in Cornwall, the standard of daffodils sent to market has dropped. Often poorly bunched, always crammed too tight in a box, such growers have helped to reduce the price received for daffodils, and in any case they are not interested in flowers. Their main interest is the marketing of the bulbs.

We ourselves have pride in each box dispatched, and we have an unfashionable kind of pleasure out of doing a job, though sadly underpaid at factory standards, which will give people happiness. Thus it is vital not to have any harsh element during the flower season which will bite into our enthusiasm. We may only have two or three extra helpers from time to time, but they all have to love their work. A sulky intruder spoils everything.

Fran, occasionally, was sulky, but she was never an intruder.

"Geoffrey, Mrs. T. and I like you," I said after a week or so, as a way of teasing conversation.

"You're joking!"

By that time, although I did not know it, she had decided to paint the inside of a small hut that stood in one of the meadows. It had been erected years before and used for "shooting" potato seed; later I had used it as a study, and had written one of my books there. She had an hour for lunch, and instead of spending part of it with Geoffrey she would disappear. It never occurred to me what she was doing until I discovered it by chance. I passed by the hut one morning, decided to look in to check that all was well . . . and found to my astonishment that the inside had become rejuvenated. Instead of the workaday, dismal, cobweb-ridden interior, there was a sheen of fresh brown paint on the walls and ceiling.

"Why didn't you tell me?" I asked Fran.

"Surprise, Mr. T."

"But the cost of the paint . . . You can't possibly afford it."

"How do you know?"

"It's obvious. You wouldn't be here if you could."

"That's a beaut."

"Why?"

"You don't know anything about me, Mr. T."

I was to know enough that we were all sorry when the flower season came to an end, and she left to go on a solo exploration of Britain, and we made sure that she came back to us during the summer for a month to help with the tomatoes and the digging of bulbs.

eanwhile Oliver appeared to be enjoying the Wren House, and he displayed increasing signs of losing his nervousness. Jeannie, for instance, on several occasions had succeeded in stroking him. No longer had she to drop the saucer on the side of the lane, then run and hide behind the hedge of the greenhouse field if she was to watch him emerge and consume her offering. He now did not mind her standing beside him in the lane. We observed also that he had a companion, a robin, which watched him constantly from a branch a few feet above his house, though he himself took no notice of its presence. We therefore wondered whether, like Lama and Monty, he did not chase birds.

Early one morning, a week after Fran had left to go on her travels, I looked out of the bedroom window and saw Oliver near the white garden seat. The sight of him so close to the cottage was a surprise, though it was not this that caused me to call out to Jeannie. What prompted me to do so was that he looked to be in trouble. He was hobbling on three legs. His back two legs were sound, so was his right front one, but the left front leg was dangling. I watched him hobble out of my view in the direction of the garage.

"Oliver's had an accident," I said; "he's cut his foot."

"How?"

"You'll have to examine it."

"He'd never let me."

I paused.

"I know. I'll get my field glasses, and we'll see if we can focus on the damage . . . and we might get a clue as to what has happened."

When we went outside we found that Oliver had gone into the garage and had curled up on an old sack at the far end beside the front wheels of the car. I couldn't possibly train my field glasses on his foot. It was obscured by the car.

"We'll have to wait for him to come out," I said.

I realize, in retrospect, that this was the turning point in our relation with Oliver. Up to now we had kept him at bay. We had treated him with goodwill though in distant fashion. We had succeeded in pursuing a policy of moderate kindness without taking upon ourselves any responsibilities. Our role had been that of do-gooders who were anxious not to become involved. But now our role was about to change.

Oliver slept all morning on his sack, and it was not until after lunch that he appeared again, hobbling on the gravel. I fetched my field glasses and stared. For a half minute I had the chance of seeing the trouble quite clearly. There was a deep cut on his left paw, and the fur of the paw had been rubbed away. An inch or more of it was bare to the skin.

"A snare, Jeannie," I said. "I guess he's been caught in a snare."

We afterward joked that he deliberately caught himself in a snare in order to gain our sympathy. He certainly received such sympathy, and he responded as any grateful patient might be expected to do. Instead of the frightened cat we had hitherto known, he meekly accepted Jeannie's nursing, and he displayed no objection as, twice a day, she bathed his paw. The cut was deep, and he must have struggled for some while before he was released by the arrival of the trapper. If a cat is in a snare for a length of time, this length of time can be an advantage despite the physical suffering; the cat is exhausted when the trapper comes, and he doesn't struggle.

Jeannie bathed Oliver's paw every day for a week before he put it to the ground again, and she bathed it with Exultation of Flowers, the amazing potion we used to revive my cousin Carol's stunned blackbird. And what is Exultation of Flowers? The description on the bottle suggests an old wives' tale brought up to date:

Electrical impulses in stable suspension, obtained by potentising the following flowers by an entirely new method and in harmony with cosmic radiations:

Oak, Eucalyptus, Water Crowfoot, Sunflower, Bean, Daisy, Birch, Mimosa, Dandelion, Violet, Rose, Larch, Vetch, Marigold, Gowan, Bulrush, Dahlia, Gladiola, Tulip, Hyacinth, Pansy, Spiraea, Heather, Gorse, Broom, Aconite, Daffodil, Larkspur, Cornflower, White Clover, Red Clover, Wallflower, Forget-me-not, Pentilla, Viburnum, Syringa, Olive, Lotus, Bluebell, Coreopsis, Periwinkle, Mesembryanthum, Pink, Carnation, Iris, Mathuiloa, Fig, Star of Bethlehem, Ageratum, Petunia, Mustard.

This, of course, is not a miracle potion. I have, however, witnessed some remarkable results, and it certainly helped to cure Oliver.

Oliver now proceeded to move from the Wren House and make his headquarters in the garage. Doubtless he had been impressed by the care Jeannie had bestowed on him and he sensed it would be foolish not to make use of it. She had not only looked after him but, more important still, she had shown affection. Thus he had won three victories since the initial rebuffs in his campaign to return to Minack . . . saucers had been put down for him beside his adopted home beyond the leap, the Wren House had been built for him and now at last he had experienced the first signs of the love he wanted. No wonder he decided to move closer to the cottage.

Thus he now introduced another crack in the routine of our life at Minack. He hadn't brazenly intruded as in the case of Felix, but had instead infiltrated by gentle persistence. It was a maddening situation. Deep down inside me I remained anticat, and yet I had to admit to myself that my anticat defense broke down whenever an individual cat chose to entice me with its charms. First, Monty, then Lama, and now here was Oliver hovering on the brink. It vexed me that I should have been put in such a situation. It vexed me that my loyalty to Lama should be challenged. Why couldn't Oliver abandon his pursuit of us? Why couldn't he return to the comfort of his former home?

He had no intention of doing so.

"Don't let Lama out," I now had to call periodi. cally to Jeannie; "Oliver's around by the water butt!"

Or:

"All clear. Oliver's up the lane."

As the summer went by there were periods when Oliver continued to disappear, sometimes for several days on end, and we would be relieved by his absence, and once more become forgetful about him, and Lama would take up again her natural routine.

He was, for instance, absent during the week a BBC 2 television unit came to film us for a program. Oliver's absence from Minack during this week helped to ease the task before us. It was unnerving enough to wake up in the morning knowing that we had to try to appear pleasant, intelligent and pictorial, without also worrying whether Lama might have an involuntary meeting with Oliver.

There are, of course, those who blossom on such occasions, and I envy the confidence they display. Jeannie and I have been involved in a half-dozen television programs, and each program has produced its moment of terror. In one scene I was supposed to talk ad lib into the camera. I was sitting on a garden chair with my back to the escallonia, and the bridge to the left of me. Cameramen, the sound man and the director were facing me three or four yards away in the patio which is covered by an umbrella of blackthorn. My idea was to put forward my theory that anyone today who intends to give up town life and go to live in the country should first take courses in bricklaying, plumbing, gardening, carpentry and any other vocation which would give him practical independence. However, each time I started my dissertation I forgot what I was going to say after a minute, and my mind went blank. The director would then try to coax back my confidence.

"Now, Derek," she would say, smiling sweetly at me, "look at *me* while you're talking."

The trouble was that Derek received no inspiration at all by looking at her, and charming and delightful though she was, I remained tongue-tied. I thought of the scores of people in my life to whom I had been able to babble without effort . . . and now on this important occasion I was dumb. There had been similar occasions in the past nevertheless, women whom I have wanted to enchant but with whom I have been silent. Years, years ago, and I still remember them.

"Now, Derek, we'll try again. . . ."

It was not until the autumn that the program was shown on BBC 2, and as it was in color Jeannie and I proceeded to rent a color television set which was delivered on the morning of the day concerned. This was a mistake on our part. We should have had it delivered days before, so that we could become accustomed to the knobs and the various strengths of color and light which they control. We sat side by side, the room in darkness, the screen before us . . . and there we were. We looked awful. We were the color of oranges.

There is a postscript to the program which needs telling. I was up there by the bridge, stuttering out my words concerning my theories as to how those who want to leave town life should prepare themselves for the country, quite unaware what was going on behind my back. The director was murmuring, "Now, Derek . . ." but behind me on the blue slate of the bridge was Lama, and she was calmly, exquisitely, washing herself. She stole the scene.

Fran breezed back into Minack in the middle

of June. She had careered around Britain, up the east coast and down the west, in her little gray car, living on bacon sandwiches. In retrospect I don't think we really needed her help. One can so easily make jobs for people unless one is on guard. Geoffrey could have picked the tomatoes without Fran. A lot of bulbs would also have been dug. But we would have missed the gales of laughter, or the sudden silences.

The arrival of the mailman was an event of enormous importance for her. Like many a distant traveler, however content in their passing environment that they might be, she was homesick at mail time.

I would meet the mailman and there was an air mail letter from Adelaide.

"Fran!"

She was with me in an instant, to seize the letter and hurry away with it, like a crow with a trinket. Awhile later, I would ask what news she had had from home.

"Haven't read it yet."

"Oh," I would answer, remembering myself when on a world tour, caressing a letter from home until a secret, suitable moment.

At the end of the month, she went off to join the Vyvyan family at Trelowarren, one of the most beautiful estates in Cornwall. Amanda Vyvyan is my goddaughter, and we were of course responsible for Fran going there. The day before she was due there came a crisis.

"I'm not going," said Fran.

"Why?"

"Not in the mood."

"You'll let us down, you know."

"Shall I?"

"Yes."

"Oh, well," she said, and the Australian accent seemed more pronounced than usual, "I suppose I'll have to."

Just as well she did. Or am I wrong in thinking that? She was introduced into a new kind of life at Trelowarren, and she loved it. She came into contact with a far wider social world than she had ever known before, and as a balance she was able to enjoy the quiet loveliness of an estate which belonged to centuries of time. She was a great success at Trelowarren, and sometimes she would come over to Minack with Amanda.

"Come on, Mr. T., be sociable."

At the time I was writing a book, had put my typewriter away at half-past nine in the morning when they had arrived, had spent morning, lunch, afternoon and tea with them, and then heard her say, "Be sociable, Mr. T." But it was her birthday and so I forgave her.

She left Trelowarren to look after the child of a rich couple in Paris, then the child of another rich couple in Switzerland. There was a visit in between to Spain, and letters to Minack. She is now back home again in Burnside, Adelaide.

During her stay with Mrs. Trevorrow, Fran reported seeing Oliver up by the farm from time to time. His absences during the summer had been fairly frequent though they never lasted for more than a day or two, and Fran's information gave us the clue as to what he was up to.

He was attracted to one of Walter Grose's many lady cats who maintained their crèche in various corners of the farm buildings. Periodically, however, the kitten population became so large that Walter, kindhearted though he was, had to enroll the help of the RSPCA to dispose of them. These periodical clearances no doubt caused much maternal anguish, and it would seem that the more experienced mother cats would sometimes change their routines and have their families away from the farm buildings where they could not be found. This, I think, is what happened in the case of the lady cat who was particularly favored by Oliver.

I first saw them together one afternoon in late summer, a few hundred yards down the lane between the farm and the main road. They were sharing a gateway into a field, Oliver at the hinge end, his lady at the other, and there was a gentle, adoring look on Oliver's face which showed no change when I called to him from the car as I passed. The lady was not pretty. She was brown, black, gray and white, with a slash of orange across her face, and, though I believe most people would pass her by, Oliver was enraptured. Several times afterward I saw them together, and the mood between them was always the same; they were deeply in love.

At the beginning of October I saw the lady at the Minack end of the lane, close to Monty's Leap. I am sorry to say I hissed at her. I also shuffled my feet hastily on the gravel so that the noise frightened her, and she ran away. Oliver was causing trouble enough without also having to cope with his girlfriend. After this incident she disappeared, and I did not see her again.

In the middle of October, however, an event occurred which is one of the strangest I have ever known in my life.

It was a Sunday morning. Jeannie had taken the car to St. Buryan to mail letters and collect the Sunday papers, and after she had left I had strolled down the lane to Monty's Leap.

Oliver suddenly appeared as I stood there and,

with the confidence he now had gained, came up
close to me. As he did so I heard a tiny cry in the
undergrowth to my right from the direction of the
Wren House. An instant later I could not believe
my eyes.

A tiny ginger kitten, the exact color of Monty
when he was a kitten, stumbled out of the autumn
leaves which had gathered beside the lane.

And Oliver ran toward it, and began immediately to lick it.

I left them together—Oliver licking the kitten as
if he were the mother—and hurried up the lane.
Jeannie would soon be back, and I had to stop the
car before she reached the gate, and tell her what
had happened . . . and warn her that we would
have to get rid of the kitten forthwith.

"Stop!" I cried.

I had reached the well, halfway up the lane to
the farm, when I met her. She looked bewildered. I
had never before confronted her and the Sunday
papers in such a fashion.

"Bad news?" she asked anxiously.

"Terrible news," I replied, "Oliver has brought us a kitten."

The engine was ticking over, Jeannie's side window was down, and I was appalled to see her face mellow into gentleness. No sign of shock. No sign of disapproval, and I realized I had been an idiot to expect from her any other reaction. Her record provided enough evidence that she wouldn't be on my side.

She switched off the engine, stepped out of the car and said, "I'll walk very quietly, not to disturb them." Then added, "What is the kitten like?"

Her question could have been parried if the kitten had been a tabby or some other color which had little significant distinction. Had this been so I could have laughed the matter off. I could have said that Oliver had produced a kitten out of the undergrowth, and I had frightened it away. "Oliver ran off also," I might have been able to add. But the kitten was ginger, and it had miraculously appeared close to Monty's Leap, so how could I dismiss the matter casually?

"Well," I replied, "it is a very odd situation. There I was standing with Oliver by the leap when there was a meow from the undergrowth just beyond the gate, then out on the lane appeared this tiny ginger kitten."

"Ginger?"

"Yes, ginger. That's the extraordinary thing."

As it happens I never called Monty ginger. I described him, after I had first met him in Jeannie's office at the Savoy Hotel, as the size and color of a handful of crushed autumn bracken. I could have described Oliver's kitten in the same way. I didn't do so to Jeannie because it might have suggested enthusiasm on my part.

283

Then she saw the kitten.

We had reached within twenty yards of Monty's Leap, and there in the shadow beside the lane were the two of them. The kitten was nudging Oliver.

"It's Monty!"

The damnable part of the situation was that I couldn't argue with Jeannie. The kitten *was* Monty as I remembered him as a kitten. The little white shirt front, a smudge of orange on each paw, a tail with dark rings against cream, the rings graduating in size to its tip. There was only one difference, and an important one at that. Monty, on that afternoon at the Savoy Hotel, had immediately set out to woo me by endearing antics. His double, so many years later, behaved in exact opposite fashion.

As we approached, he fled.

I was thankful. It is easier to be tough if affection is not being used as a weapon against you. Monty tried to climb up the inside of my trousers, Lama came to the door in a storm, Oliver wanted to come home to Minack . . . Such demonstrations of wishing to know me dented my obduracy. I yielded.

But a kitten which was as wild as an autumn leaf had no claims on me, and though I had to admit that the circumstances were extraordinary, I believed on that Sunday morning I would be able to deal firmly with the situation.

"Now, Jeannie," I said, "we have to think of Lama. No soppiness on your part."

My tone was a mistake. I sounded aggressive, anticipating a mood which I knew was there but which was not yet on display.

"I'm not being soppy."

"I know you're not, I didn't mean that, but you know how you *can* be . . ."

"*You* found the kitten, *you* were standing by Monty's Leap . . . I wasn't."

My intentions were good, but I had maneuvered myself into being in the wrong. This can easily happen. One slip, and the other is at you. You try to retrieve yourself, make a counterblast, and before you know where you are, there is an argument over a matter quite different from what you began with.

Jeannie went back to the car, and I walked on to the cottage. All my fault, I said to myself. It's always the same. . . . I object to the arrival of a Monty, Lama, Oliver, Penny or a Fred, and am then proved wrong. It is as if I am trying to cling to an independence which fate no longer intends me to enjoy. I splutter my objections, give in to Jeannie and am pleased in due course that I have done so.

I arrived back at the cottage as she drew up in the car. She was laughing.

"You *do* get unnecessarily worked up sometimes," she said.

A remark I could not deny.

"My apologies," I said, making a mock bow. Then jokingly added, "Nevertheless I'll leave you if you feed that kitten."

I had never envisioned the time when Lama would grow old. Lama, I foolishly thought, would always be with us. I never doubted it. And yet concern now began to creep into my mind. Attempts were being made to intrude on her life which were beyond normal understanding. First Oliver, now this kitten. She was no longer free in the way she had been for all her years at Minack. We had to be her sentries and her scouts. We were guarding her so that she would think nothing had changed. We were pretending. We wanted to pretend that Minack was her domain as it always had been since that day she cried at the door in a storm.

Yet no one was deliberately trying to oust her. I have known people ousted from their businesses, from their farms and from their homes. I have known people buy another dog or a cat because they were frightened by the age of those they already had. But in Lama's case no one was trying to oust her. Lama, we both believed, was immortal, no substitute was wanted. A comfortable feeling, had it not been for Oliver.

Oliver watched, hung around and waited. What was going on in his mind as he stared at us? Did he realize that Lama was growing old and he was young? And what was it which prompted him to produce a ginger kitten from the undergrowth so close to Monty's Leap? There was no logical explanation for the coincidence. This was a magician's trick. It was uncanny. And although I had made my customary noises about keeping the kitten at bay, I knew in my heart that if it played its cards correctly I would not be able to send it away. First Oliver, now the kitten. Both uninvited. Both a threat.

For three days the kitten remained on the other side of the leap, and we would watch it playing with fallen leaves in the shadow of the trees. Then on the fourth morning, I found Oliver in an unusual mood. Instead of keeping at a distance I saw him advancing toward me from the direction of the white garden seat and the verbena bush. Then he self-consciously turned on his back, in Lama's endearing manner, and with legs in the air he watched me coaxingly with his yellow eyes. I took no notice, whereupon he jumped up, rushed past me and disappeared under the car in our garage. It was then that I saw the kitten. It was asleep, curled on a patch of old straw between the wall and the rear wheel. I did not disturb it and went into the wood to see Geoffrey. When I returned, the kitten had gone.

I had, a few weeks before, created a bedroom for Oliver in the shelter where we kept the tractor. It was a large cardboard flower box laid on two boards several feet from the ground. I had lined it with hay, placed the lid of the flower box at right angles so that it served as a draft-proof wall on the open side of the bedroom, and left an opening above the packing case containing greenhouse spare glass from which he could jump in. It had met with his favor. It met too with the kitten's favor. The following morning, instead of its being on the floor of the garage, I found it in the shelter in the bedroom, and Oliver had a black paw lying across its tiny body.

It was very young, so young that its eyes had not yet changed their color; they were still blue. One would have thought it still required the attention of its mother. However it seemed happy enough snuggled up to Oliver, and I left them together to go and fetch Jeannie. When we returned, they both had vanished.

We saw Oliver again that day but not the kitten, though the following morning the kitten was once again snuggled up to Oliver in the bedroom. This time, however, we were more circumspect. I only glanced at the two of them. Jeannie placed a saucer of bread and warm milk flavored with sugar close to the wheel of the tractor; we then both retreated to the shed opposite. We watched the kitten jump down from the bedroom, then dip his face in the saucer. This moment, I thought, was an excellent moment for a photograph, and so I stepped out of the shed, pointed the camera at the kitten and clicked. The print showed the blur of a running ginger kitten.

There now began a frustrating period during which the kitten made it quite plain that it did not want anything to do with us. It ignored Jeannie's blandishments, except to consume the contents of the saucers offered. This was no cuddly kitten. This was no kitten saying to itself how wonderful to be welcomed by members of the human race. It intended to be free, from the toddler stage onward. "If you are idiot enough to feed me, and give me a bedroom," it seemed to be saying, "that's all right with me . . . but I don't owe you anything."

Nevertheless it owed Oliver something. As the days went by, and the kitten kept aloof from the attention we were ready to offer, its attachment to Oliver was touching. We also observed, from a distance, the behavior of Oliver in the role of an anxious, loving parent . . . taking the kitten on walks, slapping its face when it became cheeky, and watching carefully when it wobbled off on an adventure of its own. The kitten in return plainly respected Oliver. It realized that though it might treat Jeannie and myself with disdain, it had to obey Oliver. Oliver, it seemed, was one of those old-fashioned fathers who was able to impose his personality on his offspring.

The kitten, after a few weeks, had to be given a name, and as Jeannie is a natural name giver I left the task for her to do. The first step was to discover whether it was male or female, and so, since it was impossible to catch it during the daytime, one night we stole down to the shelter with a flashlight. I put my hand into the bedroom, seized a wriggling ball of fur and held it up while Jeannie investigated. It was a boy.

"Ambrose," exclaimed Jeannie almost immediately, the light still shining on him; "we'll call him Ambrose!"

"Why," I asked, letting him escape from my hand.

"It's simple," she explained illogically; "when the flashlight lit up his face it softened the ginger color of his fur, and it looked amber. Then his little face made me think of the amber musk rose in the garden, and so I put two and two together and there's the name Ambrose. . . . Amber Rose. See?"

We were walking back to the cottage, and she couldn't see my face in the dark. I was smiling tolerantly.

Later I was to learn of another Ambrose, a St. Ambrose who lived in Italy in the fourth century. He was a distinguished lawyer who became a Roman Catholic priest and a great preacher, and he took special pains to attack the dogma of the Roman Catholic Church that animals have no souls, that man alone is a spiritual being. This dogma, he believed, resulted in great cruelty being inflicted on the animal world, and he preached a series of sermons which have recently been republished in Italy urging his hearers to treat animals with kindness, and as part of the oneness of life.

I know quite a few people who should be forced to read these sermons and learn them by heart. People, for instance, who discard dogs and cats when they are bored with them, as casually as if they were empty cigarette packs. People who set

289

snares at random, or use similar devices to catch birds. People who horde wild animals in confined spaces on land, in ships and in long-distance aircraft. People who spray chemicals indiscriminately, turning the hedgerows brown and killing the wild flowers, the butterflies and harmless insects of the countryside. People who persecute badgers, badgers which were here before man arrived. People who dupe themselves into believing that the human race has a divine right to exploit nature. People who are leading future generations to live in a cement-covered world where the only animals will be in zoos, the only green spaces in municipal parks.

Thus the name of Ambrose has a significance beyond the physical one described by Jeannie on the night she christened him.

A westerly gale blew the bedroom in the shelter asunder at the beginning of December. The wind bashed flat the flower lid which was serving as a draft-proof wall, and shifted the flower box which served as the bed as well. And so we decided that Oliver and Ambrose should have two bedrooms . . . the one in the shelter which was cozy when the easterlies and the southerlies were blowing, and another in the small greenhouse where they would be safe from the westerlies and the northerlies. This greenhouse bedroom also had other advantages. Both Oliver and Ambrose took a great liking to the two hay-filled boxes we provided for them . . . and they were content, therefore, to be shut in there for periods during the daytime. This meant that Lama could then wander at ease around Minack.

It was easier to shut in Oliver than it was Ambrose. Oliver we now could pick up without much difficulty. Ambrose was so elusive that we could never come within a few feet of him. We had to lure him into the greenhouse, bribing him with whiffs of freshly boiled fish.

There was of course no harm in Ambrose, but we set out to keep him and Lama apart because we did not want her to be annoyed by such a juvenile newcomer. There was another reason too. Ambrose had such devotion for Oliver that he became distressed when he could not find him. It was better for them to be shut up together.

The day came, however, when we could not find Ambrose, and Oliver was shut up on his own. Ambrose had set off on an adventure soon after breakfast, and we did not see him again till lunch-time. We were sitting on the garden seat, the verbena bush beside us now bare of its scented leaves, and Lama lying like a pocket Trafalgar Square lioness a yard or two from our feet.

Suddenly Ambrose appeared, coming under the donkey-nibbled gate in front of us, and he proceeded to make a pathetic mistake. He came scampering toward Lama, a loving kitten smile on his face and an eager readiness to nudge head against head. But instead of the welcome he expected, he was greeted by a threatening growl, followed by a hiss which sounded as if a long-surpressed steam engine had found its release. Ambrose raced away. For the first time he had discovered there were two black cats in his life.

This incident fortunately did not leave its mark on either of them, and indeed Lama was to become intrigued by Ambrose. A few days later Ambrose came walking up to her under the elder tree in front of the barn where she was sitting up-right, like a cat replica of Queen Victoria. Ambrose may have mistaken her for Oliver again, but I think not. He had learned his lesson. His approach was not so bold as on that first occasion, suggesting he realized that here was someone who deserved a well-mannered respect.

"Hello, Auntie," he seemed to say, then walked on.

He was, however, to find as time went by that Lama could be unpredictable. He might offer to greet her with a friendly nudge of the head and receive a short hiss as a reward. He would then look surprised, hasten away, pause and look back. What had he done wrong? But there were other times when Lama would watch him as if she were mildly amused at the sight of him discovering the world of Minack. . . . Ambrose trying to catch a moth in the dusk, Ambrose becoming unbalanced on a branch and holding on with his front paws, swinging like an acrobat, Ambrose looking up at Penny and Fred as if he was thinking they were mountains on the move. There was no friction between Lama and Ambrose. Her attitude was one of tolerance, the attitude of the elderly to the young, and she was only gruff with him if she thought his ebullience was taking her for granted.

I wish I could say the same of her relationship with Oliver. She was frightened of him, and we no longer could pretend otherwise; and although most days we were able to keep Oliver out of her sight, there were inevitable confrontations. They would then have their staring matches. They would be several yards apart, crouched, and I would not dare to intervene in case I set a light to a fury between them. Instead I would watch, and will Lama to win the staring match, or better still try to will them both miraculously to break off the match and be friendly with each other. But the match always ended the same way, and suddenly Lama's nerve would break, and she would turn and flee back to the safety of the cottage.

There was one moonlit night shortly before Christmas when Lama wanted to go out, and I escorted her up to the Lama field. Across the bay were the sparkling lights of Porthleven, and the flooded lights of Culdrose, and those of the upturned mushroom dishes of Goonhilly tracking station pointing toward their satellites. A glorious, keen night, salty sea air to breathe, myriad stars winking above me and silence. No passing boat to break the silence, no aircraft screaming, only the murmur of waves on rocks and the sudden coughing bark of a dog fox to remind me the natural world was continuing as it has done since the beginning.

Lama was ready to return, and so in the manner of a Special Branch man guarding the Queen I scouted ahead, down the two steps from the field to the bridge, then left with the huge escallonia on my right, and down past the water butt to the door of the porch. At the side of the water butt is a bush planted a few years ago and now so large that it hides the water butt. A splendid windbreak, and scented in summer with tiny bells of white flowers. Underneath it, the shadow is very dark. As I went past I did not see Oliver sitting there. Thus Lama, hastening back to the warmth of the indoors, came face to face with him, and there was an explosion, and after that they scattered, and I couldn't find either of them.

We found Oliver first, and he gently let me pick him up and carry him into the greenhouse. But there was no sign of Lama, and for an hour or more Jeannie and I searched the area, calling,

calling . . . in the wood, back in the Lama field, down the path toward the sea, to Fred's Field, the field in which he was born, then up the lane beyond the leap. Lama, Lama, we called, and became every minute more worried. Not that, as it turned out, we had any need to feel worried. We had reached a stage of near desperation when, with the moon penciling the finger branches of the orchard trees, Lama approached us . . . nonchalantly, mistress of the occasion, a queen who put her Special Branch man in his place by her dignity.

Jeannie and I were on our own at Christmas, and when Geoffrey set off at lunchtime on Christmas Eve to have fun with his family, we opened a bottle of champagne and toasted the holiday to come. No decisions to make, an embargo on trying to solve problems, no cause to move away from the environment of Minack. This was a sweet moment. The world would peal its bells, the people worship in their churches, and boisterous bodies would dance and shout, wearing paper hats and throwing streamers, and television programs would yell their jollity, but here it would be quiet. Clouds skimming over the bay, a gull crying on the roof, a magpie chattering in the wood, a fan of wind breathing through the trees, a woodpecker laughing at dusk, and the sea murmuring, always the sea murmuring.

"What are you going to do with Oliver and Ambrose this Christmas Eve?" I asked Jeannie.

"We might give them something special in the greenhouse bedroom."

The greenhouse bedroom had its door kept ajar, a tiny entrance large enough for Oliver and Ambrose but small enough to deter intruders. It was a better place for a Christmas Eve banquet than the muddy floor of the shelter.

The donkeys always had mince pies on Christmas Eve, munching them one by one in the barn after we had tantalizingly held each pie in front of their noses for a second or two, and they munched in the light of a candle softening the ancient, rough granite walls, gray white with whitewash. Lama, meanwhile, the saucer in front of the fire, would be rejoicing in the turkey giblets, and this was a routine that both donkeys and Lama had been involved in year after year.

"What special something?"

"I've got a John Dorey."

John Dorey was Lama's standard fish until it became too expensive, and she became accustomed to ling instead.

"They'll like that."

We went down the cliff after lunch. We have a holly bush growing there in a corner overlooking the sea, and though it never produces berries, the curly leaves are dark green and spiky, and they look well decorating the cottage. So, as we needed another armful to complete the decorations, we set off to collect some. We hadn't walked a dozen yards down the path toward the sea to Fred's Field when I looked back and found Lama trotting behind us.

A Lama walk was both an honor and a comforting pleasure. An honor because it was her own personal, secret decision to come with us, and a comforting pleasure because of her antics. It was comforting too because the three of us were on our own again, far from any possible interference by Oliver and Ambrose, and it was especially comforting to have such a walk on Christmas Eve, for we had shared many memorable Christmases together. I had too a reason for this one to be perfect. I had a restless, niggling feeling that this one would be her last at Minack. I was to be proved wrong, proof how foolish it is to be swayed by menacing premonitions.

We reached the bottom of the field, and she rushed in front of us under the small gate at the top of the cliff, and down the steps, and through a little meadow where the pointed foliage of the Magnificence daffodils was already showing in rows. We followed, and as we did so a band of long-tailed tits took off from the fuchsia hedge to our left, a score of them perhaps, and they flitted away toward the blackthorn which covered the cliff to our right. Only in mild winters do we see long-tailed tits, restless, tiny pink cushions; and in a hard winter they die as easily as the redwings which sweep down from the north in search of warmth and then, when not finding it here in the far west of Cornwall, career up the south coast, north again, dropping away all the while from the mainstream to die in snow-covered coverts and frost-hard fields, until there is no mainstream left.

"We're lucky," I said.

"Lucky, lucky."

We paused by the little cave where first Lama, then Oliver was born.

I laughed.

"I wonder how many times we have spoken that word," I said.

"Thousands!"

In a world in which so many people are chained to routines they detest, or waste the hurrying days of their lives protesting against imaginary injustices, or conscientiously live their years but fail to fulfill their youthful dreams, it is sensible to appreciate one's luck.

I am always touching wood. We both are. We have had long periods of failure in our lives, and so we are always on guard. Many occasions when expert advice has led us astray, or we have made stupid misjudgments, debts have mounted as a result, far exceeding our bank balance. I am always remembering these financial terrors, and the long, early morning wakes which came with them.

"What is it," I said to Jeannie, my eyes on two gannets offshore, "that we most value in our life here?"

The gannets dived, disappeared for a second or two, then reappeared, flapping in the water, gorging their fish. Then up they went majestically into the sky.

"The taste of freedom in its purest sense," she replied.

I knew what she meant. Freedom was once governed in this country by common sense, just as behavior was governed by conscience. Laws were then limited to guarding the framework of freedom and these laws were respected, just as the rules of behavior were respected. Of course there were abuses, but the offenders had to risk the moral condemnation of their comrades, an intangible punishment which hurt. Today there is no such condemnation. We have become instead bemused by cynicism and by the overwhelming mass of legislation which, although enacted in the name of freedom, is eroding it. Freedom is no longer synonymous with fair play for the conscientious, the loyal, those with pride in work well done, and the man who cherishes his chosen way of life. Instead, in this affluent age, freedom relishes the chip on the shoulder and the couldn't-care-less brigades, blackmail of the public by striking minorities, high wages without responsibility, obliteration of the corner shop and the small farm, and a creeping destruction of the values which eons of time have proved to be the base upon which our inward happiness depends.

Thus when Jeannie said "the taste of freedom in its purest sense," she was thinking (as Emily Brontë was thinking when she roamed the moors above Haworth) mankind and all its chains banished from her mind; the glorious awareness that there are dimensions in living which wait to be discovered by those who are prepared to discard their man-made prejudices, open their eyes and ears and have the patience to be quiet. Quietness is the secret. Quietness opens the door to sensitive pleasures. Noise lovers will never understand, never know them. They may see, but will not feel.

Such pleasures as the freedom of a Red Admiral butterfly on a sunny September afternoon, red and black patch of velvet touched with white against the pale cliff green of an ivy leaf, about to migrate across the Bay of Biscay to Spain and beyond. Young badgers on moonlit nights whimpering in play. The fragrance of a Peace rose with dew-covered petals on a June morning. A lizard motionless on a sun-baked rock camouflaged by gray lichen. Swallows saying good-bye, with see-saw flights over our small reservoir. The summer hum of a bee busy within a cup of a flower. Exquisite spider webs across rarely used paths. A chiff-chaff on a prickly, white-blossomed blackthorn branch proclaiming on an April morning its arrival from Africa. Grasshoppers hopping in dry summer grass as if playing games. Gales, blocked by summer leaves on trees, taking their revenge by blackening the leaves before their time is over, gales hissing and roaring when there are no leaves to check them as they rush on their way. The cottage listens, and we are warm inside. A gull calls on the roof. "It's Philip," I say when I look up through the glass top of the porch. Philip who has been with us for many years, and receives special treatment. "I shouldn't," says Jeannie, "but here's a slice of the beef." And she throws it up on the roof, and Philip skids down its side, and gobbles the beef. Salt, sticky on my face as I walk the cliff, the wind off the sea. The donkeys competing with us as we pick blackberries. Lama pouncing upon a daddy longlegs during an October afternoon. The earthy smell of wet, dying bracken. The weird, beautiful cry of the curlew, the poor man's pheasant, as it flies in packs over the August countryside. Nothing to do except to watch. The timelessness of nature, yet the remorseless passing of such timelessness. Here at Minack we are lucky enough to belong to the secret beginning and the secret ending. We do not know what has happened. We are only aware what is around us has a value beyond rational explanations.

We collected the holly and lost Lama. It was the usual temporary loss when we went down the cliff. She thought it funny to hide from us, and listen to us calling against the sound of the sea below, and when at last she decided to appear from the undergrowth in which she had been tolerantly watching us, her game had not yet finished.

She proceeded to tantalize us by walking very slowly up the steep path, then would pause to sniff the sea air, as if she was saying, "I've got plenty of time even if you haven't."

"Come on, Lama, come on," I would call, and she would look in another direction.

The game always ended in the same way. I would advance toward her, be thankful when she didn't race away, pick her up and carry her up the field. I would carry her in my arms as carefully, Jeannie has always said, as if I had been carrying the Crown jewels. This may be so. No Crown jewel, however, could make such an ill-tempered whine of protest as this little black cat who was being carried up a cliff against her will. Nor was this the end of her show of independence. Once in the field, she wanted to return to the cliff. If I put her down too soon, if I was halfway up the field instead of being within sight of the cottage, her compact little person would dart away, heading for the cliff again. This wild, lovely cliff, where the only man-made things are the meadows Jeannie and I have created from the undergrowth, where hunted foxes can aim to reach when they run, where badgers can nose inquiringly from their sets for danger, and find none.

I kept a watch out for Oliver as we neared the cottage but there was no sign, and Lama was able to saunter up the path and into the porch without incident. The Christmas tree was on the porch. It was placed in the corner by the door on the seat top of the cupboard where we keep our boots. It was, as usual, a small Christmas tree given us by our old friend Fred Galley who was foreman of the wholesalers which sell our tomatoes. The gift, along with a bunch of mistletoe, was donated with customary Christmas aplomb. Jeannie had to

fetch it. Jeannie willingly indulged in the customary boisterous Christmas jokes. Jeannie was
kissed, Fred Galley holding the mistletoe aloft
above her head. It was always a happy occasion.

The Christmas tree was carefully decorated by
Jeannie and even now, long after she first played
with one of the red baubles, Lama was always
ready to play again. In that long ago first Christmas the tree was a big one, and it stood in a corner
of the sitting room, and it was easy for her to play
with the baubles. Now she had to wait until one
fell off onto the floor, and when this happened, anyone who was watching was treated to a fine display of high-class football. We had the usual tem-
peramental Christmas lights—ten lights on, one
off, all lights on, then all off. However at this moment when we arrived back with the holly and,
because dusk was beginning to fall, I switched on
the lights, all of them blazed. It was a pretty sight
both indoors and out, and the lights shone on the
green leaves of the climbing geranium that clung
to the wire fastened to the old stones of the cottage
outside.

"I think," I said, "Oliver and Ambrose ought to
have their feast. Feed them now, and we won't
have to bother about them for the rest of the evening."

Jeannie had a piece of holly in her hand.

"You go and find them. I'll finish putting the
holly up. Then we can feed them together."

The John Dorey had already been cooked, and
it was divided between two saucers. Delicious,
fresh fish—a wonderful feast for any cat.

To my surprise, I had no difficulty in finding
them. They had already gone to bed in the flower
house. I went down there where their two boxes,
each full of hay, stood side by side on the flower

bench, and found them together in the larger one. Silky ginger fur merged with black fur, paws around each other, two sleepy inquiring faces looking at me with strands of hay upon their heads.

"Are you ready to have a feast?" I said.

A silly question, but their look forced me to say something.

"Stay there." I added, "We'll bring you one."

But as I finished this sentence, Ambrose jumped out of the box and ran along the bench toward where the lemon tree grows as if the devil was chasing him. No devil chased Oliver. Oliver was relaxed, and looked at me sleepy-eyed, and stayed in the box. He needed no feast to make him happy. He was happy already. Last Christmas he was in the Wren House with mud outside. This Christmas he was in the dry flower house, and his offspring was with him. He had no complaints. He was advancing. He had no reason to behave as if the devil was chasing him.

Nor, ostensibly, had Ambrose any reason. True, he was barely three months old but already there were signs that he possessed a neurotic nature. There was a mind barrier between him and us, and although he gladly accepted our practical approaches in the cause of his comfort, he was not going to pay any rent for them. No cuddles, no games, no purrs. Ambrose was not going to conform as Monty and Lama conformed once they had come into our lives. He wanted to keep his distance. For some reason, even at this early age, he distrusted the human race.

So Jeannie, in due course, concocted an explanation for his attitude, and although practical people might say that the explanation is nonsense, I believe it has some substance. It is simply this. The mother of Ambrose had become obsessed over

302

the years at the way her kittens had been taken away from her. This terrible fear had been communicated in cat language to Oliver who proposed that she should bring one of her kittens to Minack where he promised to look after it. Hence Ambrose's mysterious arrival, hence Oliver's devotion to him, hence Ambrose's inborn fear of the human race.

We never saw any sign of his mother around Minack, and although Oliver continued to disappear from time to time, it was now only for a few hours, and not for the few days which once had been the case. He behaved as if he now had a purpose in his life, and that his roaming days were over, like an erratic husband who had become a devoted father. Jeannie, with her profound knowledge of cats, said she had never known such a situation before—a tomcat who had taken charge of a kitten, who would play games with it and take it for walks, who would huddle close to it and help lick it dry after being out in the rain. Oliver loved Ambrose. There was no doubt about that.

Indeed it was Oliver's capacity to love which was our problem. He had now reached a stage when he would burst into a roaring purr whenever we came near him as he lay in one of his hay-filled beds, and he would nudge his head against our outstretched fingers, and his yellow eyes would look meltingly at us. This put me in a particularly vulnerable position. Jeannie could be expected, as a chronic cat lover, to be impressed. I, on the other hand, yearned to ignore his affection, but couldn't. I was like someone who, content in the comfortable routine of life, had met a potential lover. Conventionally happy at one moment, but intuitively aware at the next that the stranger you had just met was already a part of you. That, because of some alchemy, you belonged to each other. An affair which might bring a period of pleasure if you had the patience to sustain the deceptions, or a sense of frustration for many years afterward if you hadn't.

Oliver, I realized, belonged to Minack. Here he was at peace, as far as a cat who was forbidden indoors could be at peace, and it was this acceptance of ourselves on his part which caused me increasing concern. I have never been able to consider animals as soulless objects because I believe that animals are as sensitive as human beings, more so in fact. A human being can always throw up false defenses when his ego is threatened. An animal, however, can only react with truth. Hence when Oliver purred he was expressing unadulterated pleasure. He was not deceiving. He was not behaving like a human being who calculatingly flatters in order to gain a personal advantage. On the other hand I was unpleasantly aware that, as a tomcat, he was capable of sudden and savage behavior, and that, although he did not appear to be a very active tom, he remained a permanent threat to Lama. Lama would scent him and bolt back to the cottage. Lama would see him in the lane and would not dare to walk down to my office where she had spent so many hours of her life. It was a dilemma which would soon have to have a solution. We could not indefinitely continue under such tension.

We brought the saucers of John Dorey down to the flower house, waved one of them in front of Oliver's nose whereupon he jumped out of his box in excitement, then put them side by side on the floor. There was no sign of Ambrose but we guessed he would soon arrive after we had left, and so we went back to the cottage to begin our own Christmas Eve evening. A quiet evening, for that matter. We had a drink or two, Jeannie spent an hour wrapping packages in the spare room, and we both wracked our brains for pungent little verses which would accompany the presents to each other, and the presents we organized for each other from the animal and bird inhabitants of Minack. An absurd game which amused us, and with results which always proved Jeannie the most pungent.

We had dinner on the porch by the lights of the Christmas tree and then began our wait for the ceremony of the mince pies. Of course we had no true cause to wait; the donkeys would have delightedly eaten them at any time, but we had started a tradition of waiting until a quarter of an hour before midnight, and we were determined to maintain it. The ceremony had been inspired by another tradition, the tradition that donkeys the world over go down on their knees as the clock strikes midnight on Christmas Eve, an act they are also supposed to perform at midnight before Palm Sunday. Such a tradition, I believe, is best left to the imagination. We have never set out to establish its reality because we always leave the donkeys to themselves a few minutes before midnight. We leave them in the stables quietly savoring the last of their mince pies, and although we have been tempted to watch through the window which faces the lane, we have never dared do so. We prefer fairy stories to keep their magic.

Lama meanwhile, during the course of our wait, had retired to bed. She had chosen the cupboard in the spare room, curling herself among my shirts, and betraying her presence by regular, gentle snores. It was a favorite place of hers, although she had other favorite places according to her mood.

Soon after half-past eleven I said to Jeannie it was time to prepare for the mince-pie ceremony, and I was glad that it was so. Neither of us like to stay up late, and all my life I have relished nine hours sleep. Of course quite often I wake up half-way through the night, and this period is sometimes productive of ideas, and so I console myself that I am not really wasting too much time in bed. Nevertheless it is a salutary thought that, in every ten years, I have my eyes closed for nearly four of them.

"I'm ready," said Jeannie, "you carry the plate . . . I have the matches for the candle."

She was standing on the porch, the Christmas tree and its lights beside her, putting on a coat. I was about to join her when she turned and looked out through the glass door into the night.

"Derek," she said, and the tone of her voice was enough to show that something had startled her, "come quick . . . just look outside!"

There they were, Oliver and Ambrose, faces upturned toward the lights of the Christmas tree. Two Christmas Eve outsiders, side by side, one with the look of a choirboy, the other as if he had an unbearable desire to join us.

We never wish to go away from Minack. Sometimes I regret our lack of enterprise, and I realize that those who live in cities and noise-filled streets have an advantage over us in this respect. They *have* to go away. They *have* to find places where they can recover from the tediousness of their environment. We have no need to do so because we live in surroundings we love. We are content in our compound. We do not have to say, as so many have to say, "I must get away from this cement world I live in, from the traffic and the noise, from the strain of my job and the *pressures*."

On occasion, however, we do have to go away, and one such occasion loomed in front of us not long after Christmas. We were invited to stay at the newly built Berkeley Hotel in London for its opening party, the last, probably, of the truly luxury hotels which will ever be built in London. And one reason for the invitation was, of course, Jeannie's past position in the luxury hotel world, her life as public relations officer of the Savoy Group.

The years she has spent at Minack, helping to dig potatoes, weeding anemones and violets, cooking in the tiny cottage, her clothes becoming green as she tended the tomato plants, shoulders growing tired as she heaved the daffodil boxes . . . had not kept the top professional hoteliers from knowing her worth. She might live in the country but she would never adopt provincial standards. She had a sophisticated hotelier mind, and this was recognized. *Gourmet* magazine of New York, for instance, had recognized this and had proposed she could go anywhere she liked and write for them (the Berkeley was one such place and she wrote a world-quoted article about it). But, as far as Jeannie was concerned, most important of all, her onetime chief Sir Hugh Wontner, chairman of the Savoy Group and lord mayor of London, appreciated her flair as well. Hence his personal invitation to attend the Berkeley opening party.

The invitation, however, posed a problem. A luxury-class hotel might have an opening party, but we first had to consider the welfare of Lama. Always before when we had gone away she had had no rivals ensconced at Minack, and although naturally we had never liked leaving her, we knew she was safe wandering around on her own with Geoffrey keeping an eye on her and shutting her up in the cottage when his working day was over. But this time she might not be safe. Geoffrey would not have the time to guard her as we guarded her. Nor was it fair to expect him to do so, because one lapse on his part and she might be face to face with Oliver, or she might sniff the tomcat scent and be terrified, as we had already seen her terrified. It was an impossible project.

A decision is often postponed until circumstances force you to make one, and for weeks we had been wavering about having Oliver fixed. The time had now come when we could waver no more, and so I contacted our vet, and one morning he collected both Oliver and Ambrose, bringing them back a couple of hours later, whereupon they both buried their faces in saucers of fish. They have been content ever since.

As for Lama, she was changed by this new situation in that she soon showed no signs of fear, no signs of sniffing a tomcat around. Of course this eased our minds, though we were not so foolish as to think that they would ever be friends. When we were away Geoffrey would have to watch that they did not meet, and while Lama was out he would have to make sure that Oliver and Ambrose were secure in the greenhouse. But we believed that the threat that Oliver might ever attack her was now over. She would be vexed by his presence, and that would be all. She would no longer be scared. Indeed, and this in due course turned out to be correct, she would impose her personality upon him by her haughty demeanor. Oliver, in fact, was to be made to feel a second-class citizen.

We set off for London, therefore, without qualms, and proceeded to enjoy the transfer from cottage to luxury, and it was luxury on a scale that was unusual. The Berkeley was not yet open for ordinary guests and we had, except for one other couple, the whole hotel to ourselves. Nobody else on our floor, or the floor below, or the floor above. It was as if we were Arabian oil potentates. It was as if I had had a mad dream in which Jeannie and I owned a luxury hotel in which nobody else was allowed to stay. There we were, a few hours away from Lama, Oliver, Ambrose and the donkeys which at that moment would be munching the grass in the stable meadow . . . and we could press a button, and sophisticated hotel staff would hurry to fulfill our demands because there was no one else to hurry to. It was comic.

The opening party was in the evening after we arrived. It was scheduled to begin at six o'clock, and we decided to ask my Aunt Tannie to tea beforehand. My aunt, now ninety years old, was an old friend of Lama and has always shown an endearing interest in Lama's activities.

Thus when she came to tea, she was soon to ask, "And what about Lama?" We then explained the predicament in which we were in, the divided loyalty, the mixed-up emotions which occur when love is offered you when you do not want it. I found myself becoming quite unsettled until my aunt interrupted in practical fashion, saying, "These kind of problems solve themselves."

My aunt was late in leaving after tea. We escorted her downstairs and into a taxi, then panic. I found the time had gone so fast in her company that Jeannie and I had less than half an hour to change and be ready to join the distinguished company in the ballroom, and after such a special invitation we did not want to arrive late.

We hurried back to our suite, and while Jeannie began her changing, I threw off my clothes and rushed into the bathroom for a shower . . . too hastily, too hastily. I turned on the taps, stepped into the bath and stood up. Bang! I had misjudged the height of the shower, and the top of my head had made contact with the metal shower head. My predicament was obvious. Twenty minutes to go and a cut on my head. I shut off the shower, seized a towel and wrapped it around my middle, then held my sponge under the cold tap of the sink, placed it on my head as if it was a pad of cotton wool and walked into the bedroom.

"I've cut my head," I said excitedly, expecting sympathy.

Jeannie took no notice. I saw she had a needle and thread in her hand, and the black dress she was to wear lay neatly on the bed.

"I've cut my head," I repeated. It was most unlike Jeannie not to rush to my aid in such circumstances, and the sight of me standing there with a sponge on my head should have been enough to tell her that something seriously was wrong.

She now had the needle in one hand and the thread in the other.

"A button has come off my dress," she said.

"Oh, my God!"

Fifteen minutes to go.

"And I can't thread the needle . . . Please, please will you do it for me while I get on with my dressing? . . ."

Such a moment as this, I thought, as I took the needle, was feminine indulgence . . . a button off a dress being infinitely more important than a cut head.

But I screwed up my eyes, held the thread in my fingers and lanced it toward the eye of the needle. I missed. I missed again. And again.

"Damn," I said.

Then I caught a look of myself in the mirror. I was reminded of African ladies who balance pottery jugs on their heads, except that I was balancing a sponge.

"There!" I said at last and in triumph. "I've done it!" and handed Jeannie the threaded needle.

She dropped it.

There are times when I am amazed at my patience. I, often an impatient person, can suddenly find myself so serene that a stranger meeting me at such a moment would come to the conclusion that I was constantly phlegmatic.

"Let me try again," I said gently.

Jeannie was so impressed by my behavior that she suddenly displayed interest in my injury. Naturally, at this stage, I laughed it off. The shock of it was over, and although the sponge was still perched on the top of my head, I sensed the worst was over. I had cut it, it had bled, but the cold water in the sponge was healing it.

Five minutes left. Needle in left hand, thread in right, and I lunged.

"I've done it again!"

My cry of triumph echoed around the room. This new, marvelous luxury hotel might echo many cries of triumph in the years to come, but seldom one so triumphant as this. My second threading of the needle had been achieved at the first attempt.

We joined the line waiting to be received by Sir Hugh Wontner, Miss Bridget d'Oyly Carte, granddaughter of the founder of the Savoy, and Mr. Charles Fornara, general manager of the Berkeley. None of them, of course, could have guessed the domestic drama in which we had been involved as we smilingly shook hands.

Unfortunately for myself, the ceiling of the ballroom where the party was held was of glass, and astonishingly beautiful. As the party progressed, however, I was disturbed by the number of people who remarked to me, "I've just seen your head up there. . . . How did you cut it?"

We returned to soothing Minack, and as soon as we were off the train at Penzance, Geoffrey meeting us, we were asking, "How's Lama and the others?"

"Lama slept all the time . . . hardly came out. There was no trouble at all."

"And the donkeys?"

"Fred hooted a lot."

"And the gulls?"

"They cried a lot!"

Such questions and answers may appear trivial, though for us, after our glimpse of a city, they mirrored the essence of our lives. For though a glimpse of a city is a stimulating experience, it also confirms what one already knows, that the great majority of people can only tolerate the pace of their existence by worshiping instant pleasures, and that they have no time, or the patience, to take part in the gentle, subtle aspects of living. When we returned to Minack, the awareness of our luck in having such a home had once again been sharpened.

We had come back, however, to a warm spring, and we do not like warm springs. The sun beat down on the daffodil beds as if it had mistaken March for June, and instead of the daffodils remaining in bud as the market demanded they popped uncontrollably into bloom. All over Cornwall they were popping into bloom.

"Wonderful weather we're having," someone would say to me.

"It's ghastly," I would puzzle them in replying.

Jeannie and I would be up at dawn and out in the meadows picking, catching the blooms before the sun, bent double, hastening up the rows, filling the baskets which waited at either end. Why did we enjoy this simple, automatic task? Why did we feel that something positive was being achieved? An actuary would ridicule us. The computer, he would say, proves that you are wasting your time. Find something else to do.

There was a reward, though, in being out there with the wind coming in from the sea, and gulls waking up, floating into the sky from the rocks, and catching sight of a vixen loping her way back across Fred's Field toward her lair in the cliff, and the space and the silence around us. Sometimes, while Lama lay curled on our bed continuing her sleep, we would be joined by Oliver and Ambrose, and as the sun rose above the Lizard they would play games among the daffodils.

Ambrose, whose first experience of daffodils it was, found it hugely amusing to hide among the green stems, then sneak toward Oliver who was sauntering along a gap between two beds . . . and playfully pounce. There was also another antic which was funny to watch. The two of them would walk together within the rows so that their bodies were hidden, and only the tops of their tails were seen, like the periscopes of two submarines. Then suddenly they would start to play, chasing each other, and the top of their tails would change from being dignified periscopes into looking like flags being waved excitedly, and the sight was amusing enough for us to say whenever they appeared in those early mornings, "The flag wavers have arrived!"

But early-morning picking, however pleasurable, however worthy in intent, has to face reality sooner or later, and for three days in succession we received warnings that we were, as the imaginary actuary had said, wasting our time. The warnings were scrawled on the invoice notes from our Covent Garden salesman . . . "daffs arriving too open," they said. Yet these were the daffs we had

314

picked in the dawn light before the sun had touched them and broken their buds. We had packed them in tight bud. I had driven them to Penzance station confident we were sending them away in ideal market condition, yet they had arrived at Covent Garden too open . . . because daffodil boxes in warm weather generate heat as they travel, crammed one on top of each other in the truck, and our early-morning efforts to beat the sun were therefore valueless.

Indeed so valueless that the morning mail one day brought an invoice with the words, "No sale."

Never in all the years we had been sending flowers to Covent Garden had this happened before.

"No sale," I shrieked in anger to Jeannie and Geoffrey after opening the envelope. And if they didn't shriek back in sound, their looks suggested they were wishing to do so.

We didn't send any daffodils away again after that. We didn't even send the daffodils we had picked that early morning, and which Jeannie had already packed and Geoffrey had tied and labeled. They stood in their boxes on the long bench, a tangible demonstration of wasted effort.

"Never mind," said Jeannie, "they'll give pleasure to the hospital." And later in the day the matron and her staff at the Penzance Hospital had the formidable task of finding vases for dozens of bunches of daffodils.

The flower season was over, and the sun continued to shine as in high summer, and we had time again on our hands.

Jeannie's sister Barbara came to stay with us

315

in May from her home at Coton-in-the-Clay near Derby. She had always referred to Lama as the princess, and when she arrived on this occasion she exclaimed that she had never seen the princess look so pretty. It was easy to agree. The princess was plump, her coat glossy like a ripe blackberry, and her fat tail made a mockery of the object that belonged to Oliver. Her little face, except for the drooping white whiskers, looked as young as a kitten's, and she was often as playful. I would suddenly spy her tapping a paw at a feather which had come from one of the gulls on the roof, or I would watch her indoors chasing a demon under a rug, pushing her head underneath in an effort to catch it. She was still young, it seemed, and there was no sign of the years she had been with us since that day she arrived at the door in a storm. Except that Barbara saw one, though it was a sign which, at the time, I preferred to ignore.

Often, when she settled on my lap after breakfast, lunch or dinner, pinning me down in a corner of the sofa until the time came when she decided to release me, I would make use of the situation by combing her. The comb was kept in the drawer of the small Regency table on the left of the sofa, and I would twist my body into contortions so that I could extract the comb from the drawer without disturbing the princess on my lap.

I would then gently begin my task. First a comb along the ridge of the back, then another between the ears but with such care that she still proceeded to look sleepily at Jeannie in the chair opposite; and next a bolder comb in the thicker fur regions of her side, a move which if successful, reaped a harvest of silky, rich down; and this I would sometimes keep, putting it in a box decorated with seashells, because I thought that one day I would want a tangible memory of her. I had done the same when I used to comb Monty, and his is still there in a small potpourri bowl of Swansea china which stands on top of the bookshelves. Thus I would sit in my corner delicately performing my task until Lama told me she had had enough by crossly attacking the comb. I would immediately stop.

The cross attacks, however, had recently become more frequent. She showed an increasing dislike of my combing the denser parts of her fur, and the reason was easy to understand, for although the surface of her coat appeared to be in perfect condition, underneath it was becoming matted. This was a sign of her age that Barbara pointed out to me

Others pointed it out to me in another way. Visitors who made remarks like:

"Lama's getting on, isn't she?"

"Have you *still* got Lama?"

"She's a good age."

Age, age, age. The British are besotted about age. If a woman walks down a street, slips on a banana peel, falls and breaks her leg, be sure the press will begin the report: "Fifty-five-year-old Mrs. So-and-So . . ." Age had to be tagged on to any news. It's a ritual. It had become a ritual to ask Lama's age . . . and I found myself going back over the years and remembering the same questions being asked about Monty. Nothing had changed. The same dismay at the questions, the same sadness, the same stifled awareness that I was blinding myself to the truth. Yes, I knew that Lama was coming to the end of her time and that she would become a black comma in my memory, but I did

317

not want to be reminded of this by such questions. I could touch her now, pick her up, listen to her purr, and I did not want to be told that these subtle pleasures would one day be only a dream.

Such moments of depression, however, were only a shallow layer on the happiness of that summer. There was, for instance, the amusement and confusion caused by Oliver and Ambrose. We had already become accustomed to those who excitedly exclaimed, "We saw Lama as we were coming up the lane!" . . . when, in fact, they had seen Oliver. But Ambrose had never been called Monty until a friend whom we had not seen for many years was startled by the sight of him on the inside windowsill of the barn.

"I thought Monty was dead!"

"So he is . . . years ago."

"I must have just seen his ghost!"

It has often seemed to me that many people, especially those who are leaders of a country, of a community or of a cause, treat logic as a kind of life belt. They are desperately anxious to believe that they are masters of their own destinies, and that they can control the paths of these destinies by neat planning. Thus logic, backed up by elaborately documented facts and figures, provides the basis of any report on any subject you can name, and the imponderables are ignored because they are too mysterious to contemplate.

The imponderables, in this case, were represented by Oliver and Ambrose. How can anyone, however astute and logical in their thinking, explain the arrival at Minack of two wild, uninvited cats which were the doubles of the only two cats I have ever known?

Sensible people, no doubt, might explain it

away by saying that it was a coincidence and no more. Sensible people are inclined to ignore the existence of those unseen, untouchable, extrasensory forces which push us this way and that during the course of our lives, and this is because the Western world believes itself so civilized that to consider magic as a reality is beneath its dignity. Yet many of us know of incidents that have no rational explanation.

A parson told me the other day of a little girl in his parish of whom he was particularly fond, who was found unconscious by her parents one morning. She had shown no previous symptoms, and when she reached the hospital, doctors were unable to diagnose the cause of her illness. Two days later hope for her life was given up, and the parents asked the parson to hurry to the hospital and give her a blessing. Just before he set off the parson rang up a healer who was a friend of his, and told him of his mission. An hour later he reached the hospital only to be greeted with the news that the child, who had never regained consciousness, was not expected to live more than a few minutes. He hurried to the ward and stood by the girl's bed, then quietly said, "Who is here, Jill? Who is here?" There was stillness for a moment, then the girl stirred, and to the astonishment of everyone murmured, "It's you, Father." From that instant the recovery began, and a month or so later she was riding her pony again in the fields near her home. Was it prayer, the healer or magic which achieved this?

As for my own experience in these mysterious matters, one incident which sticks in my mind concerns the one and only time I have had my hand read by a palmist. I was on a steamer sailing from

Sydney to Hong Kong when one of my fellow passengers, a burly engineer on his way to a job in Hong Kong dockyard, offered to tell me my fortune. So there I was on deck one balmy evening, the steamer sailing through the Aragura Sea, with my hands held out in front of me . . . and the engineer telling me that I would marry a slender, dark-haired girl whose initials were J.E. Five years later I was walking up the aisle of Richmond Church with Jean Everald Nicol.

Anyhow, whatever the explanation for the arrival of Oliver and Ambrose, I the anticat man was now besieged by three cats, and I was endlessly on guard. Lama, although she was no longer frightened by Oliver, understandably disliked his presence, and so we continued to do our best to keep them apart. Thus I was perpetually saying, "No sign of Oliver, Lama can go out." Or, "Keep Lama in. Oliver is around the corner." As for Ambrose, he continued to be elusive, *maddeningly* elusive.

"Come here, Ambrose," I would call, waggling a finger toward him.

Or:

"I have something for you, Ambrose," Jeannie would say, holding a saucer of fish in one hand while hoping to stroke him with the other.

Not a chance.

"Ambrose," I would remark sternly, "pay your rent!"

His markings, month by month, became more beautiful, lines of autumn bracken colors with shapes which reminded me of currents on a quiet sea. True that at times his head, because of his youth, looked scraggy, even his body sometimes looked scraggy, but suddenly for some reason like the change of light, or of mood, he looked his potential. This was going to be a champion cat, just like Monty. Beautiful to look at and highly intelligent though still viewing the human race, and ourselves despite all that we were wanting to offer, with suspicion.

The relationship between him and Lama developed into a quiet understanding so that I would catch sight of them side by side at Monty's Leap, sipping from the trickle of the summer stream, and when they had finished they would walk back together. Of course Ambrose would not dare to take any advantage of her. He recognized that she was the queen. Affection he could offer, but no question of taking liberties.

Oliver, meanwhile, was becoming benign. He was still the outsider, longing to be the insider, and sometimes he took physical steps to achieve his aim. We still had the wire-framed contraption, first used to prevent Monty from jumping out of the bedroom window at night, which we now erected to stop Lama from doing the same. It was an insecurely fixed, clumsy contraption, but firm enough to achieve its purpose. But one night I was awakened from a deep sleep by a terrible battering noise at the window, followed by a crash on the floor, then a thump. Oliver, from the outside, had knocked down the contraption and jumped on the bed.

Jeannie was half awake.

"What's happened? What's happened?"

She spoke in that half-hysterical fashion that half-awake people are inclined to do.

"Keep calm," I hissed, "leave it to me. It's an emergency."

An emergency indeed. Oliver had crawled up to me on my left side, roaring out purrs like the sound of a low-flying, piston-engined aircraft, while on my right side lay Lama.

"Don't wake her," I hissed again; "hold her gently, and I'll deal with Oliver."

"You're panicking."

"Of course I'm panicking . . . the two of them within a foot of each other, and one roaring his head off an inch from my face."

I now seized Oliver firmly in my hands, got out of bed, carried him to the sitting room door, opened it, then opened the porch door into the little garden and dumped him there. I went back to bed.

"A bit cruel, weren't you?"

"Heavens," I answered, "what else could I do?"

Not a movement from Lama. She was still curled on the bed, making the clickety-click noise which was peculiar to her when she was sleeping.

"I just think it was a bit hard on him," said Jeannie sleepily, "he only wants to be loved."

"Oh, Jeannie, you do sometimes say such silly things."

"Shut up, I'm just going off."

I myself didn't go off for an hour or more. I lay awake wondering what Oliver was thinking, and how he was spending the night. Back sharing a straw-filled box with Ambrose, I guessed.

The donkeys viewed Oliver and Ambrose with tolerant amusement. Oliver, they realized, was like Lama, possessing a middle-aged seriousness which forbade any prospect of playing silly games. Nevertheless they would sometimes try. If Oliver was in sight as we led the two of them from the stable meadow up past the cottage, one of them would be sure to advance head down, like a dog following a scent, and try to pull toward him. Oliver, of course, would skedaddle away; and Penny or Fred, whichever it was, would take a bite at the escallonia instead.

Ambrose was a different matter. Ambrose provoked them, especially Fred. Ambrose was like a saucy small boy who taunted his friends to attack him, then ran away before they were able to do so. Ambrose courted danger. Ambrose would find Fred munching grass in the donkey field above the cottage, and proceed to stalk him. This was a dangerous form of Russian roulette because Fred was often in the middle of the field, so that the nearer Ambrose crept the farther he had to run to escape. Perhaps this was Ambrose's deliberate purpose, to experience the sheer thrill of being chased a hundred yards by a donkey. It certainly gave Fred pleasure; it was bliss chasing Ambrose at speed across a field.

Thus there were three cat lives running parallel to each other at Minack that summer. Ambrose, of course, was the most innocent, the years of adventure ahead of him, and the fun, and idiotic predicaments. Oliver, understandably, was bewildered as to what more he had to do to become acceptable . . . choosing to come back in the first place, the cold nights in the Wren House and on branches of gorse when his house was flooded, the efforts to show his affection, the wondrous production by him that Sunday October morning of the double of Monty, his gentle insistence that all he wanted from us was to be loved . . . It wasn't difficult to understand why he was puzzled that we didn't allow him to become a natural part of our life. Yet he had time on his side. He could wait. He could pursue a policy of quietly infiltrating into our lives because he had the edge on Lama. He was younger. He might be made to feel, by our manner toward him, that he was a second-class citizen, but he was prepared to put up with it. He had Ambrose, in any case, as a companion. He wasn't lonely.

Lama, meanwhile, spent more and more of her time in sleep. She would curl herself in her favorite places, on the carpet beside my desk close to the heater, or on the newly washed clothes airing on top of the storage heater in the spare bedroom, or she would settle herself in the dark of the cupboard among my shirts. Not that she showed any serious signs of her age. Her appetite was as good as ever, and she still loved her walks, the walk to the cliff especially.

I remember one hot, early September morning, when Jeannie and I decided to take time off and to go down to the rocks to bathe. We hadn't walked a dozen yards down the path toward Fred's Field when to our surprise Lama rushed past us, then suddenly stopped and looked back at us. This was the old game of chase and stop which we knew so well. A spontaneous gesture of pleasure and excitement.

"I didn't really want her to come," I said.

"Why ever not?"

"I wanted to lie on the rocks and bathe," I said. "I wanted to be on my own without bothering about Lama."

"You old misery."

I accepted that. I was an old misery not to be happy that Lama had chosen to come with us. But I was right about having to bother about her. For the path wending its way down through the daffodil meadows became steeper when it neared the rocks, and at that point Lama would always stop.

She would not walk on the rocks. So when we wanted to bathe, one of us had always to stay with her, or otherwise she would join the gulls' cries with her meows.

Once, at these same cliffs, Lama had saved me from being bitten by an adder. She has always been nonchalant in her attitude toward adders, toward anything wild for that matter, and I have seen her play a dangerous game with an adder, boxing it with her paws as it hissed at her, though keeping her paws just out of reach of the strike.

We had had a picnic on the grass just above the gray rocks which jumble their way down to our little bay. A bottle of Côte du Rhone, homemade bread, Cornish butter and Stilton . . . a banquet, and we thought of those in the Savoy Grill munching their way toward the bill. Lama was with us, and for a while she meandered down to a rock where a sliver of a stream runs, and from which she always liked to drink. Then she came back to where Jeannie and I were lying, and settled herself beside me, looking out toward the sea as we were doing.

There was a desultory, haphazard conversation.

"Funny that Lama has never been frightened by the sea."

"She's known it since she was born."

"How scared Monty was of it!"

"But Monty was a town cat turned countryman. Some town people never get used to the countryside because of the quiet. Monty never got used to the sea."

Silence for a while.

"I see a big tanker on the horizon."

Silence again.

"I never see why the visitors buy sea urchins."

"White's had a pile in their front window."

"They're so ugly . . . but they're good business for the skin divers."

A cormorant was drying its wings on the end rock of our tiny bay, which is known as Gazelle. A great black back gull was close by, terror of the cliffs, magnificent, ready at nesting time to snatch any egg, at growing time any nestling.

More desultory conversation.

"I'll have to buy a new pair of sandals. These are worn out."

Suddenly Lama growled.

A cat's growl is a fearsome affair. It is so unexpected. It is as if a dog, in a moment of great stress, meowed. And Lama's growl was like a rolling crescendo of bass drums.

Then I saw the adder. Black markings on its twisting gray body, tiny head weaving . . . and barely two feet from where I was lying.

Of course I was safe as soon as I saw it. Adders are easily scared away, and when I brought my hand down on the grass with a thump, and shouted, it skidded away into the undergrowth. But it was Lama who had warned me . . . Lama's fearsome growl.

That September morning I let Jeannie go ahead with her swim, while I stayed behind with Lama, lying on the same spot as when she warned me that the adder was about to attack me. She sat on my tummy purring, and I lay there with that sound in my ears and the sound of the sea caressing the rocks, a gull or two soulfully calling, and the poignant trilling of oyster catchers over to my left below Carn Barges. A moment of great happiness, complete, breeding no greedy wish for something better. This was the kind of moment which men and women, in old-fashioned wars, were ready to die for, believing that the simple, basic pleasures offered the key to happiness. A kind of moment which bypassed the sophisticated theories which try to govern our lives today.

Dear Lama, I still can hear her purring.

"Can we see Lama?"

Another spring.

"I'm afraid . . ."

Another summer.

"We've come a long way to take a photograph of Lama."

"I'm sorry but . . ."

Another autumn.

"Is that Lama?"

"No . . . I'll try to explain."

"What *did* happen to her?"

"She died on March third. Just faded away. Nothing that anyone could have done."

"She had a wonderful life."

"Yes."

"So she came to you in daffodil time, and left in daffodil time."

"Yes."

"A strange coincidence."

"As strange as something that happened the evening of the day she died."

"What was that?"

Sometimes I answered this question. Sometimes I changed the subject. It depended upon whether I thought the listener would be in tune with the magical combination of circumstances which took place that evening.

A gale began to blow in from the sea in late afternoon, and by nightfall a storm was raging around the cottage, the same storm it seemed to me as that night when Lama first cried at the door, and suddenly I heard the cry again.

I left my chair and went over to the door, and when I opened it the light shone on Oliver and Ambrose, waiting, side by side in the wind and the rain.

A black cat, and one the color of autumn bracken. As if Lama and Monty had returned to Minack.

DEREK TANGYE

THE AMBROSE ROCK

There must be legions of people who yearn to pack up their jobs and find some patch of land where they can settle down and create their own 'earthly paradise'. Jeannie and Derek Tangye are among the lucky few who have done just that. They have succeeded in turning a dream into a reality at Minack, a flower farm on the wild and beautiful coast of Cornwall. Today, Derek Tangye's heartwarming chronicles of life away from it all are known and loved all over the world. His delightful stories of Minack and the creatures who share his life there not only re-create the magic and beauty of the very special world that he and Jeannie have created, but also impart something of the very spirit of Cornwall.

THE AMBROSE ROCK, Derek's latest book, tells the enchanting story of Ambrose the cat since the loss of Oliver – his partner in crime. Ambrose's exploits at home and away make delightful reading and give you a glimpse of the very special world of Jeannie and Derek Tangye.

AUTOBIOGRAPHY   0 7221 8394 1   £1.50

Also by Derek Tangye and available in Sphere paperback:
LAMA
SOMEWHERE A CAT IS WAITING
A DONKEY IN THE MEADOW
SUN ON THE LINTEL
WHEN THE WINDS BLOW
A CAT AFFAIR
THE WAY TO MINACK
THE WINDING LANE
COTTAGE ON A CLIFF

ROBERT KEE

The World We Left Behind

A CHRONICLE OF THE YEAR

1939

In THE WORLD WE LEFT BEHIND broadcaster Robert Kee vividly recaptures the moods and sensations of 1939 – the news that made the headlines in politics, fashion, entertainment and sport – and the growing anxiety of the British people as the Second World War loomed.

This is a unique portrait of the year as it unfolded, filled with the incident, drama and excitement of one of the most historic twelve months in living memory.

'Authentic . . . absorbing and worth any number of conventional histories.' *The Times*
'All recounted with such brio as can be gobbled up in one day.' *Daily Telegraph*
'Fascinating.' *The New York Times*
'Brilliant.' *Daily Mail*

HISTORY   0 7221 5204 3   **£4.95**

ANN DRYSDALE

FAINT HEART NEVER KISSED A PIG

is the unforgettable tale of adorable Ernest, the burglar-proof porker; Snuff, the blackest sheep you ever saw, who arrived at Hagg House just one hour old, shivering and wet; and Dodo, the indescribably ugly guinea fowl . . .

It is the enchanting tale of one remarkable woman, Ann Drysdale, who, with her three children, left the civilised world of London and a career in journalism, to set up home in a North Yorkshire hill farm.

And how, amidst great hardship and even greater hilarity, the Drysdales and their extended family made out . . .

AUTOBIOGRAPHY   0 7221 3070 8   £1.75

THE 1985 FAMILY WELCOME GUIDE

Jill Foster
Malcolm Hamer

The up-dated and greatly expanded second edition of THE FAMILY WELCOME GUIDE, continuing the search for:

* Hotels which offer the basic facilities of cots, high-chairs, and baby-listening services.

* Pubs which provide separate family rooms (and real ale and reasonably priced food).

* Restaurants which provide high chairs and a little more choice for children than chips with everything.

* Motorways, airports, supermarkets and stores where the needs of young families with children are catered for.

'An essential handbook for anyone planning a family outing.' Parents Magazine.

'You can set off across the country with confidence if you have studied THE FAMILY WELCOME GUIDE.' Katie Boyle, *TV Times.*

'A truly wonderful and original idea.' Mail On Sunday.

REFERENCE   0 7221 4187 4   £3.95

KITTY CAMPION'S

HANDBOOK OF
HERBAL HEALTH

The natural way to a healthier life

Herbalism is the most natural way to get healthy and stay
healthy. This detailed handbook written by a medical
herbalist, tells you everything you need to know about
herbs: how to identify them, collect them, cook with
them and how to prepare traditional herbal remedies for
headaches, high blood pressure, toothache, sunburn and
many other common ailments. There's also advice on
how to make refreshing herbal drinks and details of a
complete herbal cleansing programme that will revitalise
your body.

Covering hundreds of herbs and cures, KITTY
CAMPION'S HANDBOOK OF HERBAL HEALTH
will show you that herbal remedies are as effective today
as they've always been. When you realise the natural
alternatives, you may never have to take an aspirin again.

HEALTH AND MEDICINE   0 7221 2352 3   £2.95

A selection of bestsellers from SPHERE

FICTION

VITAL SIGNS	Barbara Wood	£2.95	☐
THE ZURICH NUMBERS	Bill Granger	£2.75	☐
NOCTURNE FOR THE GENERAL	John Trenhaile	£2.50	☐
HOTEL DE LUXE	Caroline Gray	£2.95	☐

FILM & TV TIE-INS

BOON	Anthony Masters	£2.50	☐
LADY JANE	Anthony Smith	£1.95	☐

NON-FICTION

LIVING WITH DOGS	Sheila Hocken	£3.50	☐
FIT OR FAT TARGET DIET	Covert Bailey	£2.50	☐
MORE LOVE SEX AND ASTROLOGY	Teri King	£2.50	☐
THE CYNIC'S LEXICON	Jonathon Green	£3.95	☐

All Sphere books are available at your local bookshop or newsagent, or can be ordered direct from the publisher. Just tick the titles you want and fill in the form below.

Name _____

Address _____

_____

Write to Sphere Books, Cash Sales Department, P.O. Box 11, Falmouth, Cornwall TR10 9EN

Please enclose a cheque or postal order to the value of the cover price plus:

UK: 55p for the first book, 22p for the second book and 14p for each additional book ordered to a maximum charge of £1.75.

OVERSEAS: £1.00 for the first book plus 25p per copy for each additional book.

BFPO & EIRE: 55p for the first book, 22p for the second book plus 14p per copy for the next 7 books, thereafter 8p per book.

Sphere Books reserve the right to show new retail prices on covers which may differ from those previously advertised in the text or elsewhere, and to increase postal rates in accordance with the PO.